The Stieglitz Informal Reading Inventory

Assessing Reading Behaviors from Emergent to Advanced Levels

THIRD EDITION

Ezra L. Stieglitz

Rhode Island College

ALLYN AND BACON

Boston / London / Toronto / Sydney / Tokyo / Singapore

*To those in my life who have taught me the most
about how literacy is developed—*

My children—Eric, Daniel, and Eve

Series Editor: Aurora Martínez
Series Editorial Assistant: Beth Slater
Marketing Manager: Brad Parkins
Editorial-Production Service: Omegatype Typography, Inc.
Composition and Prepress Buyer: Linda Cox
Manufacturing Buyer: Julie McNeill
Cover Administrator: Kristina Mose-Libon
Electronic Composition: Omegatype Typography, Inc.

Copyright © 2002, 1997 by Allyn and Bacon
A Pearson Education Company
75 Arlington Street
Boston, MA 02116

Internet: www.ablongman.com

ISBN 0-205-33420-2

Printed in the United States of America
10 9 8 7 6 5 4 3 2   06 05 04 03 02

Contents

Preface   vi

Section One   Introduction to The Stieglitz Informal Reading Inventory   1

Components of The Stieglitz Informal Reading Inventory   2

Overall Design of the SIRI   11

Who Can Administer the SIRI?   14

Section Two   Initial Administration and Scoring Procedures   15

*Administering and Scoring the SIRI to Determine Placement
in Reading Material*   15

Sample Analysis of a Sixth-Grade Student   31

Making Sense of Results That Don't Seem to Make Sense   42

Summarizing the Results: Putting It All Together   43

Dictated Story Assessment Strategy   44

Sample Cases   50

Section Three   Diagnostic Options of the SIRI   57

Writing Reflections Interview (WRI)   57

Graded Words in Context Test   58

Graded Words in Isolation Test   61

Practice Passages for the Graded Reading Passages Test   63

Graded Reading Passages Test   64

Strategies for Using Dictated Stories for Assessment   68

The Stieglitz Assessment of Phonemic Awareness (SAPhA)   70

Specific Analysis of Word Recognition Miscues   78

Specific Analysis of Comprehension Errors   83

Summarizing the Results: Using the Synthesis of Information Rubric   84

**Section Four   Student's Test Materials for Initial Administration
and for Diagnostic Options   87**

Student's Test Materials for Initial Administration   89

Graded Words in Context Test: Form A   89
Graded Reading Passages Test: Form A—Expository   98
Graded Words in Context Test: Form B   107
Graded Reading Passages Test: Form B—Narrative   116
Photographs for Dictated Story Assessment Strategy   125

Student's Test Materials for Diagnostic Options   148

Graded Words in Isolation Test: Form A   148
Graded Words in Isolation Test: Form B   152
Practice Passages   156
Graded Reading Passages Test: Form C—Expository   158
Graded Reading Passages Test: Form D—Narrative   167

**Section Five   Examiner's Record Forms and Quick Lists of Instructions
for Initial Administration and for Diagnostic Options   177**

Initial Administration   178

Summary of Student Performance Sheet   179
Reading Reflections Interview Form   180
Quick List of Instructions for Administering the Graded Words
in Context Test   182
Graded Words in Context Test: Form A   183
Quick List of Instructions for Administering the Graded Reading
Passages Test   193
Graded Reading Passages Test: Form A—Expository   195
Graded Words in Context Test: Form B   213
Graded Reading Passages Test: Form B—Narrative   223
Story Retelling Form to Assess Sense of Story Structure
and Comprehension   241
Quick List of Instructions for Administering the Dictated Story
Assessment Strategy   243
Dictated Story Assessment Strategy Record Form   245
SIRI Synthesis of Information Rubric   248

Diagnostic Options   253

Writing Reflections Interview Form   254
Quick List of Instructions for Administering the Graded Words
in Isolation Test   257
Graded Words in Isolation Test: Form A   258
Graded Words in Isolation Test: Form B   263
Practice Passages   268
Graded Reading Passages Test: Form C—Expository   272
Graded Reading Passages Test: Form D—Narrative   290
Summary Sheet of Silent Reading Performance   308
Summary Sheet of Accountable Miscues   309
Summary Sheet for Recording and Analyzing Miscues   310

Summary Sheet for Categories of Comprehension Errors   312
Dictated Story Assessment Strategy Record Form
     for Follow-Up Session   313
The Stieglitz Assessment of Phonemic Awareness Record
     Form (SAPhA)   315

Section Six   **The Development of the SIRI   320**

Constructing the Word List Tests   320

Designing the Dictated Story Assessment Strategy   321

Constructing the Graded Reading Passages Test   321

Estimating Instructional Levels   322

Determining Alternate Form Reliability   323

Examining Reader Familiarity   324

Determining Reader Interest   325

Examining Levels of Comprehension   326

References   327

Preface

*T*he *Stieglitz Informal Reading Inventory: Assessing Reading Behaviors from Emergent to Advanced Levels,* Third Edition, continues to offer a simple and clear approach to reading assessment. The Stieglitz Informal Reading Inventory, known as the SIRI, can be used in a variety of educational settings, such as elementary classrooms utilizing basal or literature-based reading programs, classes for remedial readers, content-area classes at the secondary level, and reading programs for adults. Teachers with limited or no experience with informal reading inventories can easily administer this instrument to place students in reading material. Those with more skill can take advantage of the SIRI's numerous diagnostic options to examine specific reading behaviors in word recognition and comprehension.

The SIRI has the following distinguishing features. First, a Graded Words in Context Test provides data for estimating the starting level in the Graded Reading Passages Test. Second, a Graded Words in Isolation Test supplies information needed to determine students' level of sight vocabulary and decoding ability. Third, a Dictated Story Assessment Strategy offers an opportunity to examine the reading behaviors of emergent and initial readers. This component is unique to the design of an informal reading inventory and can be used with young students, severely disabled older readers, and illiterate adults. Many of the behaviors tested are similar to ones assessed by parts of the SIRI used with fluent readers, such as recognizing words in the context of a story, identifying lists of words in flashed and delayed presentations, and responding to higher- and lower-order questions. This continuity is an integral part of the design of the SIRI. Fourth, comprehension checks for the Graded Reading Passages Test contain critical- and creative-level questions to provide examiners with valuable insights into students' ability to function as reflective thinkers. Finally, procedures are described for determining students' familiarity with and interest in each selection read.

A major goal in the development of the SIRI was to assemble material that younger and older students alike would enjoy reading. To accomplish this, much care and attention was given to the selection of material for the Graded Reading Passages Test. For example, articles on a variety of interesting topics, such as what makes a smelly sticker work and how the game of hide and seek originated, were assembled for expository forms of this test. Also, different types of stories, such as tales and mysteries, were chosen for narrative forms of this test. It is hoped that the content of these selections will positively affect how students respond to this test.

Refinements in this third edition of the SIRI include (1) directions for using the SIRI that are more user-friendly, (2) procedures for interviewing students to discover what they know and how they feel about reading and writing, (3) an instrument that can be used to assess an emergent reader's phonemic awareness skills, (4) new photographs to be used with the Dictated Story Assessment Strategy, and (5) a rubric designed to help the diagnostician synthesize information from the various components of the SIRI and draw conclusions about a student's reading strengths and weaknesses.

Section One provides a general description of the SIRI's components and overall design. Relevant research is cited to justify decisions in developing the inventory. Section Two describes procedures for initial administration and scoring of the SIRI. Use of this inventory for determining placement in reading material and for utilizing the Dictated Story Assessment Strategy is explained with detailed directions and examples. The diagnostic options available in the SIRI are presented in Section Three for the examiner who wishes to go beyond the initial administration and obtain additional information on students' reading behaviors. Here, too, assessment strategies are explained with detailed instructions and examples.

Section Four contains student test materials, and Section Five includes forms for recording the results. To make the SIRI easier to use, forms required for the initial administration are distinguished from those needed while utilizing any of the diagnostic options. Section Six presents information and technical data on the development and validation of the SIRI.

Note

The author encourages comment on the design and contents of the SIRI. Please forward comments to the author via snailmail (Rhode Island College, 600 Mt. Pleasant Avenue, Providence, RI 02908) or e-mail (estieglitz@ric.edu).

Acknowledgments

I am indebted to many people for their assistance during the preparation of this inventory. First, I would like to express my appreciation to the following professionals who helped with the development and field test of the SIRI and provided valuable feedback: Diane Apici, Patricia Berlam, Eileen Biancuzzo, Linda Boisvert, Amanda Brown, E. Aurise Cardin, Donna J. Cole, Christine D'Acchioli, Kathleen Daley, Sandra DeBeck, Catherine Earhart, Celeste Ferguson, Betsy Ferland, Jeanne Galipeau, Alice Gould, Barbara Hanson, Debra Haskell, Ruth S. Jaffa, Virginia Kovolski, Angela Lombardo, Pamela Manninen, Ann McCarthy, Sandra McCarthy, Margaret McEwen, Lauren Pelligrino, Margaret Schick, Judith Schoenfeld, Barbara Scott, Nancy Searle, Audrey Shapiro, Debra Silva, Marcia Siniak, Deborah Sitkin, Varda Stieglitz, Jane Swift, Diane Waters, and Sheila Weinberg. I also appreciate the efforts of graduate students enrolled in Education 485 and 486 (Rhode Island College), who assisted in testing, scoring, and interpreting the SIRI.

I gratefully acknowledge the special assistance provided by the following people: Marie Fontaine and Diana Creed, who wrote some of the stories for the Graded Reading Passages Test; Jack Hanson and Gordon Rowley for providing access to their collections of photographs; and James V. Wyman, vice president and executive director of the *Providence Journal-Bulletin*, for his cooperation in obtaining *Journal-Bulletin* photographs. Special thanks are also due to Dr. Robert E. Carey, director of the Center for Evaluation and Research of Rhode Island College, for his help in analyzing and interpreting the data from the pilot test.

I would also like to thank the reviewers of earlier editions, for their careful reading of the manuscript and many valuable suggestions: Patricia Berlam; E. Aurise Carden, Shea High School; Nancy Clements, Ball State University; Susan Daniels, University of Akron; Alice Gould, Attleboro Public Schools; Dr. Rachel Grant, University of Maryland; Victoria Hare, University of Illinois; Sylvia Hutchinson, University of Georgia; Dr. Beverly J. Klug, Idaho State University; Virginia Kovolski, Brennan Middle School; Sandra McCarthy, John F. Deering Junior High School; Gay Sue Pinnell, Ohio State University; Judith Schoenfeld, Fallon Elementary School;

Marcia Siniak, Curvin-McCabe School; Gary Spray, California State University; and Dr. Janet Towell, California State University at Stanislaus. In addition, I am grateful to the reviewers of the third edition for their thoughtful comments: Alice Gould, Attleboro Public Schools, Massachusetts; and Tracey Lewis, Wilson Elementary School, San Leandro, California. My appreciation is also extended to Aurora Martínez, Beth Slater, and others at Allyn and Bacon who have been of great assistance during the production of this book. The assistance of Katherine Coyle and Sheri Daley of the editorial production team at Omegatype Typography, Inc., is also appreciated.

Next, I would like to acknowledge the Faculty Research Fund of Rhode Island College and the Durrell, Cooper, Crossley Research Scholarship Fund of the New England Reading Association for providing the financial support for field testing this instrument.

Finally, a very special thanks to the members of my family—my wife, Varda, and children, Eric, Daniel, and Eve—for their patience, perseverance, understanding, and encouragement as I worked on this book and from whom countless hours were taken to complete this work.

Introduction to The Stieglitz
Informal Reading Inventory

T eachers often have the task of making decisions about placing students in reading materials. A diagnostic tool that can help teachers accomplish this task is an informal reading inventory (IRI).

Informal reading tests have been available for many years. Their use can be traced back to the 1920s and 1930s (Beldin, 1970). However, the informal reading inventory as we know it today did not evolve until the mid 1930s when Emmett A. Betts used an IRI in the Reading Clinic at Pennsylvania State College (Johns, 1991). Since that time, IRIs have become a popular tool for reading assessment. According to Richek et al. (1996, p. 47), "IRIs provide one of the best tools for observing and analyzing reading performance and for gathering information about how a student uses a wide range of reading strategies." A study conducted by Rogers, Merlin, Brittain, Palmatier, and Terrell (1983) revealed that informal reading inventories were the instruments most frequently used in the clinical component of reading courses at colleges and universities where undergraduate and graduate students worked with children from the community. Recently published textbooks on diagnosis and treatment of reading difficulties continue to devote much attention to the informal reading inventory as a tool for assessment (Collins & Cheek, 1999; Lipson & Wixson, 1997; Walker, 2000).

Traditionally, an IRI is an individually administered test consisting of carefully graded selections from the preprimer level through grade 8 or higher. Accompanying each passage is a set of questions to test comprehension. During the administration of an IRI, the examiner usually has students read aloud passages of increasing difficulty. The examiner then uses the results of students' oral reading performance and responses to comprehension questions to place them in appropriate reading materials. The results can also be used diagnostically to assess specific reading behaviors.

Most IRIs also include a graded word list test. This test consists of lists of words graded in difficulty from preprimer to grade 6 or higher. Students read the words on each list aloud until a predetermined number of words are missed. The results of this test are used to determine the passage on which to begin the oral reading portion of the inventory.

Although few would argue the usefulness of the IRI for diagnosis, there appear to be some problems with the current design of this instrument. Henk believes that most inventories fail to tap several important dimensions of the reading act. According to Henk, "Children are still routinely classified as reading on a certain grade level with limited regard to external factors such as the type of text, its structure, style, and topic, or internal variables such as readers' prior knowledge, interest or purpose" (1987, p. 861). Caldwell states, "Research findings in reading, psychology, and language suggest that the IRI may not be as sensitive an instrument as has been supposed." She concludes, "We may need to revise or adapt the IRI if it is to be a truly useful diagnostic tool" (1985, p. 169).

The Stieglitz Informal Reading Inventory (SIRI) addresses some of these concerns. It was created to provide educators with a modified and expanded version of an informal inventory. The SIRI retains many popular features of an IRI, such as graded passages and words in isolation tests. It also has improved the instrument design by including such components as interview forms to examine a student's thoughts and ideas about reading and writing, a test for recognizing words in context, a dictated story strategy for assessing the reading behaviors of emergent readers, an instrument for assessing phonemic awareness, techniques for assessing the recall of narrative and expository texts, procedures for determining the familiarity and interest level of selections read, and a rubric for synthesizing the results of the SIRI.

Components of The Stieglitz Informal Reading Inventory

The SIRI consists of a Reading Reflections Interview, a Writing Reflections Interview, two forms of a Graded Words in Context Test, two forms of a Graded Words in Isolation Test, a Dictated Story Assessment Strategy, the Stieglitz Assessment of Phonemic Awareness, and four forms of a Graded Reading Passages Test for evaluating reading performance. Student test materials are included in this book, together with forms for recording and summarizing the results. A brief description of each component follows.

Reading Reflections Interview

The SIRI includes various instruments that provide valuable information about a student's reading skills and strategies. However, no review of a student's reading performance is complete without including a procedure for assessing the role of affect in reading. According to Henk and Melnick, "educators and researchers have recognized for some time the importance of knowing as much as possible about the many affective elements that shape readers' engagement" (1995, p. 470). The Reading Reflections Interview is included in the SIRI to help teachers address this important dimension of reading. The interview consists of ten questions. The results provide the diagnostician with valuable information about the learner's knowledge of the reading process, perceptions of reading and his or her reading ability, and interest in reading.

Writing Reflections Interview

The Writing Reflections Interview is a diagnostic option and is included as a companion to the Reading Reflections Interview. This interview consists of thirteen questions. The results provide the diagnostician with valuable information about the learner's knowledge of the writing process, perceptions of writing and his or her writing ability, and interest in writing. The examiner may obtain valuable diagnostic information by comparing the results of the Writing Reflections Interview to the results of the Reading Reflections Interview to determine whether the learner's reflections about these two areas of literacy are similar or different.

Graded Words in Context Test

As previously mentioned, most informal reading inventories include a graded words in isolation component. The results of a word list test can provide valuable information about word recognition skills without the influence of context. In the natural way of reading, however, context is always available, and no word is completely identifiable in the absence of context.

Research seems to support the value of reading words in context. Results of studies by Adams and Huggins (1985), Goodman (1965), Hall and Cunningham (1988), and Nicholson, Lillas, and Rzoska (1988) show improvement in reading accuracy when children read words in story context rather than in isolation. In a study of natural learning of word meanings while reading, Shu, Anderson, and Chang conclude that "Chinese children as well as American children are able to incidentally acquire word meanings from context during normal reading" (1995, p. 88). These authors find that strength of contextual support influences word learning, and state that "the probability of learning words is larger for words surrounded by rich contextual information than for words in less informative contexts" (p. 89). McKenna concludes that "oral errors made on word lists are not good predictors of errors made by the student in context" (1983, p. 676). Therefore, an inventory with a graded words in context component should serve as a better predictor of success on the passages. For this reason, a Graded Words in Context Test is included in the design of the SIRI.

In the Graded Words in Context Test, the target words are presented in boldface within the context of a sentence. The words surrounding a target word are below the grade level of the target word to increase fluency in reading each sentence. Results of the test provide the teacher with a rough estimate of a student's independent reading level. This information is then used to select an entry point into the Graded Reading Passages Test. The aim is, of course, to begin with a passage that the student will find easy to read. Because the Graded Words in Context Test (as well as the Graded Words in Isolation Test) is not a tool for evaluating comprehension, it should not be used as the sole measure for making important decisions about a student's reading performance.

There are two forms of the Graded Words in Context Test, and each contains ten sentence sets. The sentence sets range in level from preprimer through grade 8. The preprimer and primer sets consist of ten sentences each, while the grade 1 through grade 8 sets contain twenty sentences each. The sets of graded words are also presented in list form for the teacher who wishes to test students' recognition of words in isolation. A description of this test follows.

Graded Words in Isolation Test

This test, which is a diagnostic option, is administered to assess how students recognize words without the benefit of contextual clues. The results are used to determine students' level of sight vocabulary and decoding ability. Although the results of the Graded Words in Isolation Test can also help the teacher place students in the Graded Reading Passages Test, the Graded Words in Context Test is probably more suitable for this purpose. Even so, the results of the Graded Words in Isolation Test can give teachers valuable information about how readers attack words.

The Graded Words in Isolation Test consists of two forms, each with ten word lists. The word lists range in level from preprimer through grade 8. The preprimer and primer lists consist of ten words each, and the grade 1 through grade 8 lists contain twenty words each.

Dictated Story Assessment Strategy

It is difficult to test students who read below a first-grade level because they can read so little. Conventional IRIs do have preprimer- and primer-level selections, but such passages are very short, usually quite dull, and provide the examiner with limited information on how well a pupil can read. And what about the student who cannot even read material at the preprimer level?

In an attempt to address these issues, dictated stories were included in the design of the SIRI as a strategy for assessing the reading performance of students whose independent or base level is below grade 1 on the Graded Words in Context Test. Such students probably lack essential behaviors in emergent reading, such as understanding the functions of print and the language print represents. Behaviors of this type form the foundation for subsequent instruction in beginning and later reading.

The dictation process is an integral part of an instructional method known as the language experience approach (LEA). The LEA has been used widely for decades to teach young children to read. Lately, it has also been used with students in the primary grades who have reading problems; with older, severely disabled readers; and with students learning English as a second language. Regardless of the population with which it is used, a major purpose of the LEA is to "build a natural bridge to more formal experiences with print" (Strickland & Morrow, 1990, p. 422).

Activities related to the dictation process prepare emergent readers for formal experiences with print. Students who participate in this process "learn that what they experience and think about may be verbalized, what they say can be written down, and what has been written can be read by others and themselves" (Strickland & Morrow, 1990, p. 422). As they engage in these activities students integrate the language areas of speaking, listening, reading, and writing.

Because the LEA is an ideal technique to use in a reading program, it would seem to have potential also as an informal strategy for yielding diagnostic information about the performance of emergent (and some initial) readers. Agnew (1982) suggests that this potential can be realized if teachers (1) use individually created dictated stories to probe students' understanding of the reading code and (2) utilize the dictation process to determine what students have already learned about how the reading system works. The ideas of Agnew and others (Dixon & Nessel, 1983; McCormick, 1995; Nelson & Linek, 1999; Nessel & Jones, 1981), were used in the design of the assessment strategy for this inventory, which is briefly described below.

The Dictated Story Assessment Strategy utilizes a collection of ten interesting photographs. These photographs become a vehicle for the creation of individually dictated stories. The teacher first directs the student to select a photograph to talk about. That photograph is then used as a stimulus for discussion and for the creation of a story. Finally, the story is written down by the examiner and used to assess the performance of emergent readers.

Stieglitz Assessment of Phonemic Awareness (SAPhA)

The SIRI includes an instrument that can be used to assess an emergent reader's phonemic awareness skills. Phonemic awareness has been defined as the ability to hear and say the separate sounds in words (New Standards Primary Literacy Committee, 1999, p. 54). According to Stahl and Pickle (1996, p. 145), "it is an awareness of sounds in spoken (not written) words."

New Standards Primary Literacy Committee (1999) recommends that, by the end of kindergarten, children be expected to demonstrate the following phonemic awareness skills:

- Recognize pairs of rhyming words and produce rhyming words
- Isolate initial consonants in single-syllable words (e.g., /f/ is the first sound in *fan*) (p. 54)

New Standards Primary Literacy Committee (1999) recommends that, by the end of first grade, students be able to demonstrate more advanced skills, such as

- Separate the sounds by saying each sound aloud (e.g., /t/–/o/–/p/)
- Blend separately spoken phonemes to make a meaningful word (p. 96)

It should be emphasized that phonemic awareness is not the same as phonics. It is not associating written letters with the sounds represented by these letters to decode or to sound out words in print (Yopp & Yopp, 2000, p. 131). Students demonstrate their phonic knowledge when they are asked which letter makes the first sound in *hat* or *ran* or the last sound in *pin* or *lip*.

Yopp (1995) reports that ample evidence shows that skill in phonemic awareness is strongly related to success in reading and spelling acquisition. In a report issued by the National Reading Panel on the most effective teaching methods, the panel found that children must be taught phonemic awareness skills to be good readers (International Reading Association, June/July 2000). However, although the research suggests that the development of phonemic awareness skills should be part of an emergent literacy program, ". . . phonemic awareness should not be overemphasized to the point that other important aspects of a balanced literacy program are left out or abandoned" (International Reading Association, 1998, p. 1). Therefore, instruction in phonemic awareness should be part of a complete reading program that also includes the development of language and thinking skills, decoding, vocabulary, comprehension, positive reading habits and attitudes, and ". . . a sense of the organization of texts such as stories, articles, and reports. All are essential to addressing all the components in the early stages of literacy learning" (International Reading Association, August/September 2000, p. 9).

The Stieglitz Assessment of Phonemic Awareness consists of four tasks. These tasks are to (1) recognize whether pairs of words rhyme, (2) listen to speech sounds and then blend these sounds into words, (3) isolate speech sounds in the beginning, middle, and end positions of words, and (4) segment the sounds of words, each two or three phonemes in length. The tasks range in level from simple to more difficult. The results provide the diagnostician with valuable information about the learner's skill development in phonemic awareness.

Graded Reading Passages Test

The passages used to assess reading performance are a major part of an informal reading inventory. Placement decisions are, to a large degree, based on how well a student performs on this section of an inventory. There was, therefore, a major effort to create a series of graded passages that would be appealing and interesting to students of all grade levels. Passages were carefully selected from a variety of sources. Many of the selections were written specifically for this test. A few passages were taken from original sources such as children's magazines. Some were based on adaptations of existing material found in collections of tales and in newspapers. Each passage was checked for difficulty, using either the *Spache Readability Formula* (Spache, 1974) or the *Fry Readability Graph* (Fry, 1977). The Spache was used for selections from grade 1 through grade 3, and the Fry was used for passages from grade 4 through grade 9.

The SIRI clearly distinguishes between expository and narrative prose, providing an opportunity to examine the coping behaviors of students with both types of text. The primary purpose of expository text is to inform or explain. This form of discourse plays an important role in communicating knowledge in materials such as textbooks, newspapers, and magazines. Narrative text is a form of discourse that is used to tell a story, and it is most often found in novels and short stories. Two forms (A and C) of the Graded Reading Passages Test are based on expository text, and two forms (B and D) are based on narrative prose. The reading level for each set of passages ranges from grade 1 through grade 9.

Selections of the descriptive type are included in the narrative forms of the passages test. Descriptive discourse provides the reader with a picture in words. The verbal picture painted by the author depicts a character, an event, or a setting. This form of prose is often found in stories, and it seems logical to include selections of this type in the narrative passages test. Because descriptive passages lack the story line usually found in narrative prose, some readers may find this type of discourse difficult or less interesting. For this reason, it was decided to concentrate most of the descriptive selections at the upper levels of the Graded Reading Passages Test.

Every attempt has been made to assemble a wide range of materials for assessing reading performance. Tables 1.1 and 1.2 present information on the four sets of passages selected for the SIRI. It should be noted that the type of discourse at each level is the same in parallel forms of the expository and narrative passages. For example, the articles found in the two forms of the grade 5 expository passages are based on social studies content (biographies) and the stories written for the grade 3 narrative selections are both tales. This parallel feature allows teachers to use an alternate form to administer the same type of passage at a particular level if there is a need for retesting.

To aid the teacher, letter codes and icons are used to label each of the graded reading passages in the Examiner's Record Forms section (Section Five). The letter code on the examiner's copy designates the type of prose used in the selection (*E* for

TABLE 1.1   *Information on Expository Passages*

GRADE LEVEL*		CONTENT AREA	WORD COUNT	
Form A	*Form C*		*Form A*	*Form C*
1.8	1.7	Science (passage 1)	81	87
2.5	2.3	Social Studies (passage 2)	104	105
3.6	3.6	Science (passage 3)	141	150
4	4	Science (passage 4)	167	157
5	5	Social Studies (passage 5)	189	198
6	6	Science (passage 6)	202	227
7	7	Social Studies (passage 7)	209	237
8	8	Consumer Education (passage 8)	239	279
9	9	Science (passage 9)	279	310

*The *Spache Readability Formula* was used to determine the readability levels of passages 1 through 3, and the *Fry Readability Graph* was used to determine the readability levels of passages 4 through 9.

TABLE 1.2   *Information on Narrative Passages*

GRADE LEVEL*		SELECTION TYPE	WORD COUNT	
Form B	*Form D*		*Form B*	*Form D*
1.6	1.7	Descriptive (passage 1)	79	88
2.5	2.2	Tale (passage 2)	134	148
3.7	3.3	Tale (passage 3)	145	142
4	4	Tale (passage 4)	171	174
5	5	Humor (passage 5)	204	226
6	6	Mystery (passage 6)	222	234
7	7	Descriptive (passage 7)	201	213
8	8	Humor (passage 8)	267	256
9	9	Descriptive (passage 9)	253	264

*The *Spache Readability Formula* was used to determine the readability levels of passages 1 through 3, and the *Fry Readability Graph* was used to determine the readability levels of passages 4 through 9.

expository and N for narrative), and the icon labels the content category. For example, the icon used to identify a science passage is a microscope. Table 1.3 shows the icons that are used in the various passages. With this feature, the diagnostician can, at a glance, determine the prose type and content category of each selection on the examiner's record form.

Most IRIs use performance in word recognition and comprehension on the graded passages test to estimate a student's reading level. An analysis of word recognition errors, or miscues, made during the oral reading of IRI selections provides the examiner with important information about a student's reading behavior. *Miscue* is defined as ". . . a deviation from text during oral reading . . ." (Harris & Hodges, 1995, p. 155). For example, a miscue occurs when a student says *puppet* for *puppy* in the sentence *Look at the puppy run up the hill!*

TABLE 1.3 *Information on Passage Types and Icons*

PASSAGE TYPE	CONTENT AREA	ICON	PASSAGE TYPE	CONTENT AREA	ICON
Expository	Science		*Narrative*	Descriptive	
	Social Studies			Tale	
	Consumer Education			Humor	
				Mystery	

There are numerous examples of systems for analyzing and interpreting reading miscues. The procedure suggested by Harris and Sipay (1990) is a good example of a system for scoring oral reading miscues. The authors make a distinction between major and minor miscues. Their system focuses attention on the quality rather than the quantity of miscues made by a student. The oral reading marking system for the SIRI is an adaptation of the Harris and Sipay procedure described below.

1. Count as one error: (a) each response that deviates from the printed text and disrupts the intended meaning; (b) each word pronounced for the child after a 5-second hesitation.
2. Count as one-half error: each response that deviates from the printed text but does not disrupt the intended meaning.
3. Count as a total of one error, regardless of the number of times the behavior occurs: (a) repeated substitutions, such as "a" for "the" . . . ; (b) repetitions; (c) repeated errors on the same word, regardless of the error made.
4. Do not count as an error: (a) responses that conform to cultural, regional, or social dialects; (b) self-corrections made within 5 seconds; (c) hesitations; (d) ignoring or misinterpreting punctuation marks. (1990, pp. 227–228)

Additional information on this marking system is presented in Section Two.

A set of six questions for use in assessing comprehension accompanies each graded reading passage in the SIRI. Although the comprehension check for each passage of an IRI should include literal-level questions, attention should also be given to assessing students' understanding of the passages at the higher comprehension levels. Unfortunately, many IRIs go only as high as the interpretive level in checking a reader's comprehension of the material (Pikulski, 1990, p. 516). In the SIRI, a critical- or creative-level item is included in the comprehension check for each passage. Next, the terms related to these comprehension levels will be discussed.

At the literal level, readers understand what the author is saying. They are able to read the lines and paraphrase material presented explicitly in the text. Students exhibit a literal understanding of the content when they can answer factual questions. For example, the following question, based on the story "Little Red Riding

Hood," is written on a literal level: Who did Little Red Riding Hood meet on the way to her grandmother's house?

Readers who comprehend a passage at the interpretive level are able to understand what the author means. They demonstrate skill in "reading between the lines" by answering textually implicit questions such as the following one from "Little Red Riding Hood": Why could Little Red Riding Hood be described as naive?

Understanding discourse at the critical and creative levels involves reading beyond that which is presented. Readers who comprehend at these levels use ideas from prior experiences in their response to the text. At the critical level, students are able to evaluate or judge what is read based on criteria they have formulated. They can answer questions such as: Why didn't you like the character of the wolf in the story of "Little Red Riding Hood"? At the creative level, readers apply what they already know to generate ideas that are unique and far-reaching. The teacher who says, "Gee, I never thought of that. That's a great answer!" is probably responding to a student's creative-level answer. An example of a creative-level question is: What can the reader learn from the story of "Little Red Riding Hood"?

The SIRI's comprehension check for passages 1 through 6 consists of four literal, one interpretive, and one critical- or creative-level question. For passages 7 through 9, the mix is three literal, two interpretive, and one critical- or creative-level question.

All of the literal- and interpretive-level questions of the Graded Reading Passages Test are designed to be passage dependent. This means that the reader must understand the passage to answer the questions successfully. Some of the critical- and creative-level questions are more open-ended and thus less passage dependent. These questions are included to "encourage students to use their knowledge, background, and experience in conjunction with the information presented in the passage to engage in what some reading authorities identify as higher-level thinking" (Johns, 1997, p. 65). Because these questions are less passage dependent, they are scored, but the results are not used to determine each student's reading level. The fact that these results do not have quantitative value in the scoring of the SIRI should not detract from their value or minimize their importance. They are included because such questions can provide examiners with valuable insights into students' ability to function as reflective thinkers. Reflective thinkers can read beyond that which is presented. They are capable of judging, analyzing, and synthesizing information.

To increase the level of passage dependency, an attempt was made to create expository selections with familiar topics but unfamiliar content. For example, the topic of one expository selection entitled "Hide and Seek" (Form A) is familiar to most students, but the content of the selection (the origin of the game) is probably not. Most of the narrative passages will be unfamiliar to students since they were written especially for this test.

Vocabulary questions are not included in the SIRI's comprehension check because such items are of limited value on an IRI. In a study on the value of vocabulary questions on informal reading inventories it was "found that the vast majority of vocabulary questions did not function properly. Many questions lacked validity because . . . the meanings of the target words as used in the selections tended to be familiar to the students and, therefore, could not be used to test students' contextual analysis ability" (Duffelmeyer, Robinson, & Squier, 1989, p. 147). The examiner may wish to use the SIRI's Graded Words in Context Test to assess vocabulary. An explanation of how the Graded Words in Context Test can provide such information is presented in Section Three.

The SIRI offers the examiner the opportunity to use probed recall, free recall (also known as retelling), or a combination of the two techniques to check the comprehension of each passage. Using the probed recall procedure, the teacher asks the questions that accompany each selection. With free recall, the student is directed simply to talk about the content of the passage. The retelling option is used to assess a student's skill in organizing information and making inferences about it ". . .

by constructing a personal rendition of the text" (Gillet & Temple, 1994, p. 231). Two relatively simple and straightforward procedures for utilizing free recall for comprehension assessment are described in Section Two.

The results of the Graded Reading Passages Test are used to analyze each student's reading performance. The examiner uses the data to determine each student's independent, instructional, and frustration levels. Quantitative and qualitative indicators are used to estimate these levels. Following is a definition of each level and the criteria used to determine it.

The *independent level* is the level at which material is read with little difficulty and with the absence of instruction. Selections read for enjoyment, personal recreation, and information should be written on this level. Teachers should assign material on this level for classwork or homework when assistance is not provided. All material such as tradebooks and magazines that is presented to students should be easy for them to read.

At the independent level, the reader is expected to recognize words in passages 99 percent of the time or better and to answer questions in the comprehension check or give complete retellings with 90 percent accuracy or better. Reading is fluent, expressive, and rhythmical, with few deviations from print (Johnson, Kress, & Pikulski, 1987, p. 21).

The *instructional level* is the level at which material is read with understanding as a result of instruction. At this level, a teacher's assistance and guidance are required due to the nature of the material and the background of the student. With appropriate instruction, the student should have little difficulty understanding the material. Of all the reading levels discussed here, the instructional level is probably the most important to determine. Reading group assignments should be based on each student's instructional level, as determined by the results of an informal reading inventory.

At the instructional level, the reader is expected to recognize words in passages 95 percent of the time or better and to answer questions in the comprehension check or give complete retellings with 75 percent accuracy or better. As in the previous level, reading is fluent, expressive, and rhythmical with few deviations from print. Miscues made do not affect meaning and deviations from print are usually self-corrected.

The *frustration level* is the level at which the student is unable to benefit from the reading material, even with instruction. When this level is reached, it is obvious that the material is too difficult for comprehension. This circumstance may be due to inadequate skills in word recognition, poor background knowledge for understanding the content, or a combination of the two. Students should not be assigned material written at this level.

The frustration level is reached when word recognition is below 90 percent and comprehension is less than 50 percent. Behavioral indicators that clearly show that the material is too difficult include laborious and nonfluent reading, deviations from the text that affect meaning, and lack of skill in organizing the content. Also, the reader may show signs of disinterest, fatigue, and anxiety and refuse to continue.

A potential problem in interpretation arises for the teacher when the reader scores between 90 percent and 95 percent in word recognition, 50 percent and 75 percent in comprehension, or within this range for both word recognition and comprehension. The teacher may be unsure about how to use these data to determine a student's instructional and frustration levels. To make it less confusing when this situation occurs, a fourth level has been added to the three already discussed. This is the *questionable level* (Ekwall & Shanker, 1988, pp. 403–406). When students score within the questionable area, the teacher must decide whether the student's overall performance is closer to the instructional or frustration end of the continuum. The teacher, of course, must use his or her best judgment in making this decision. In order to make this determination, the teacher may need to consider both quantitative and qualitative indicators. An illustration of the various levels of word recognition and comprehension is found in Figure 1.1.

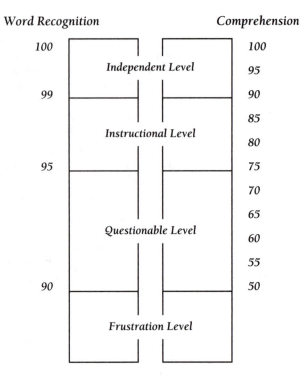

Word Recognition   Comprehension

FIGURE 1.1

Percentage of errors used to determine levels of word recognition and comprehension

Source: Eldon E. Ekwall and James L. Shanker, *Diagnosis and remediation of the disabled reader,* 3rd ed. Copyright © 1988 by Allyn and Bacon. Reprinted by permission.

The effect of prior knowledge on the reading of passages is a factor that needs to be considered when evaluating a student's performance. What the reader already knows about a topic can significantly influence the results. For example, a sixth-grade selection may be easier than a fifth-grade selection if the reader has good background for the topic. For this reason, a procedure to determine reader familiarity with the content of each reading selection is built into the design of the SIRI. This information is gathered *after* rather than *before* (the procedure followed by some IRI authors) a selection has been read because students are in a better position to provide such information after they have been first exposed to the content.

For example, the student who is asked before reading the expository selection on smelly stickers, "How much did you know about how smelly stickers work before reading this article?" may self-perceive her level of prior knowledge as high because she loves to play with smelly stickers. She may not realize that the article is about a topic with which she is probably unfamiliar—the technical aspects of what makes smelly stickers work. Therefore, the student is in a better position to make this judgment *after* having read this article rather than *before*.

Another important factor to consider while evaluating a pupil's performance is the level of student interest in the passage. McKenna believes that there is a strong relationship between interest in a topic and reading comprehension. He states, "Low interest in a given passage . . . can cause underestimation of a student's ability because of a deflated score" (1983, p. 671). At the same time, it appears that when material is highly interesting to students, comprehension is improved. Often, when low-achieving students are presented with material that is highly interesting to them, they are able to understand it even though the selection is written at their frustration level. In response to the interest-level relationship, the SIRI includes a procedure to determine the level of reader interest in each passage.

Forms for Recording and Summarizing the Results

An important feature of the SIRI is the inclusion of a variety of forms to help the examiner record and summarize the results. They can be found in Section Five of this book. Forms are provided to record the results of both the initial procedures and the diagnostic options. To distinguish the two, on some of the forms, spaces for entering initial procedure results are clear, whereas areas for recording diagnostic option results are shaded (e.g., see Summary of Student Performance Sheet, page 179). Other forms used for recording the results of diagnostic options are located in the Diagnostic Options portion of Section Five (e.g., see Summary Sheet of Accountable Miscues, page 309).

Some of these forms provide the diagnostician with a detailed record of a student's performance on any of the SIRI subtests. An example is the form used to record and score the Graded Words in Context Test (see pages 183–192). Other forms help the examiner to review and summarize test results. Examples are the Summary of Student Performance Sheet on page 179 and the Summary Sheet of Silent Reading Performance on page 308. The SIRI Synthesis of Information Rubric on pages 248–252 is the last form to be filled out because it helps the teacher to discover patterns in behaviors, synthesize information from the various subtests administered, and prepare a final summary of the results.

There is space on most forms for the diagnostician to present quantitative as well as qualitative information about a student's performance on the SIRI. Directions for using each form, along with sample record sheets, are presented in Sections Two and Three. Permission is granted by the publisher to reproduce any of the forms included in this book. In preparation for testing students, the examiner should make sure that enough copies of the appropriate forms have been duplicated and are available.

Instructions for Administering the Components of the SIRI

Directions for administering the components of the SIRI are explained in detail in Sections Two and Three. An abbreviated and parallel list of instructions, referred to as *quick lists,* accompany some of the examiner's record forms found in Section Five. These quick lists are included so that the examiner does not have to return to the detailed directions. Quick lists are available for the following components of the SIRI: Graded Words in Context Test, Graded Reading Passages Test, Graded Words in Isolation Test, and the Dictated Story Assessment Strategy. These quick lists could be copied and laminated for easy referral when administering the SIRI.

Directions for using the Reading Reflections Interview, the Writing Reflections Interview, and the Stieglitz Assessment of Phonemic Awareness appear on the examiner's record form for each procedure. Directions for using diagnostic options that are quite easy to administer and score, that is, finding a listening comprehension level, are found only in Section Three. After repeated practice in using the SIRI, the diagnostician should be able to administer the various components of the SIRI without having to refer to the directions.

Overall Design of the SIRI

The SIRI is designed to meet the differing assessment needs of teachers and their students. It is a flexible tool that can be used by diagnosticians to obtain general or specific information about a student's reading performance. Teachers may use as few or as many of the test parts and strategies as they wish. If teachers need to determine students' placement in reading material, the SIRI can function as a survey instrument. The flowchart in Figure 1.2 provides an overview of the sequence of steps for using the SIRI to place students in reading material. These initial procedures are followed when the examiner needs general information about students' perception of reading, levels of reading performance, prior knowledge, and interest in reading narrative or expository text. To illustrate, consider the situation of Ms. Madison, a reading specialist in a junior high school remedial program. It is the beginning of the school year, and she needs to place fifty students in reading classes as soon as possible. To accomplish this

FIGURE 1.2

Flowchart of initial procedures to determine placement in reading material and examine emergent reading behaviors

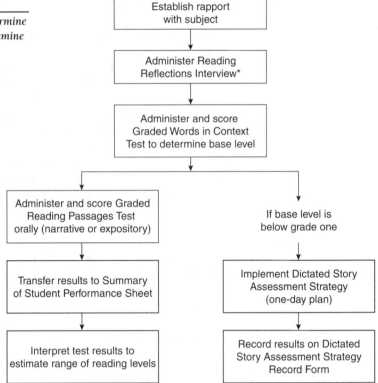

*This can be administered at a later time if the examiner wishes to quickly determine a student's reading levels.

task, Ms. Madison follows the procedures for initial administration, outlined in Figure 1.2, as she examines each student individually. The bottom line is that Ms. Madison needs a measure of her students' reading performance. Ms. Madison does not have time at this point in the semester to use any of the diagnostic options included in the SIRI. Therefore, she decides to follow the initial procedures for administration to obtain this basic information.

(The directions for administering the SIRI for initial assessment are presented in Section Two. The time required for this initial administration of the SIRI is approximately 45 minutes. However, test time can be decreased if the teacher only administers the Graded Words in Context and Graded Reading Passages Tests to determine a student's reading levels. The Reading Reflections Interview could then be administered at a later date. The inexperienced examiner will probably need more time to administer this test, and the time required will, of course, vary from student to student.)

Although the results collected from the initial administration of the SIRI can be used for placement decisions, at times more information is required. Return to the case of Ms. Madison. A few days after her students have been placed, Ms. Madison finds that she needs more information about their reading strengths and weaknesses in order to plan a program of instruction. She needs answers to such questions as:

What strategies are used by the reader to identify unfamiliar words?

Can the reader understand material at the higher as well as lower levels of comprehension?

How well does the reader process material from two types of prose (narrative versus expository)?

Ms. Madison decides to utilize several of the diagnostic options presented in Figure 1.3. The flowchart in Figure 1.3 not only provides an overview of the procedures for

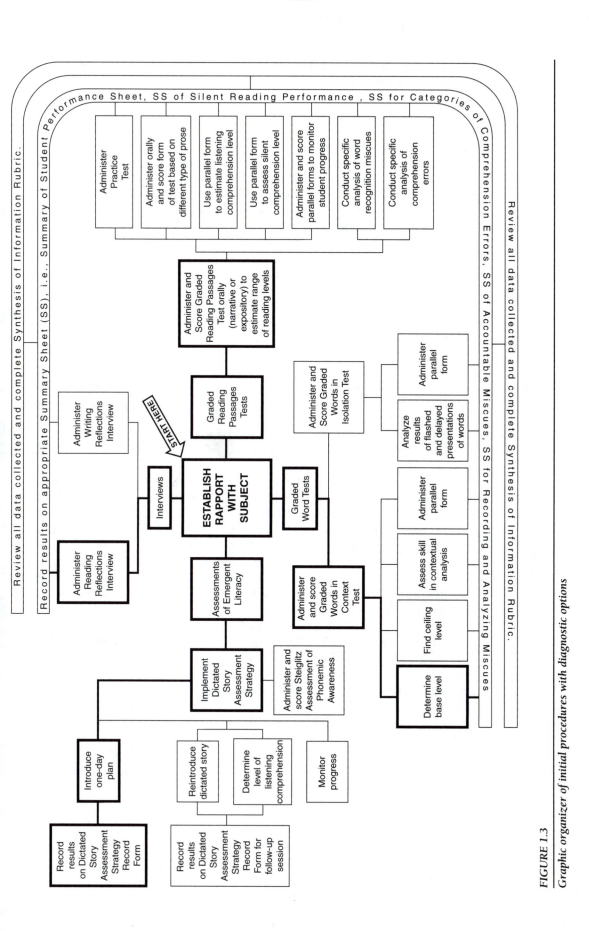

FIGURE 1.3

Graphic organizer of initial procedures with diagnostic options

13

initial administration but also the addition of numerous diagnostic options. (Directions for using each of these diagnostic alternatives are presented in Section Three.)

Who Can Administer the SIRI?

The SIRI can be used by any educator who wishes to evaluate students' reading performance. Examiners might include college students at the preservice level who are in a teacher preparation program, college students enrolled in a graduate-level reading program, elementary or secondary classroom teachers, adult basic education teachers, reading specialists, special education teachers, and school psychologists.

Some of these professionals may choose to use the SIRI to estimate students' reading levels; others may decide to engage in a more thorough analysis of their students' strengths and weaknesses. The decision regarding how many parts of the SIRI to administer should be based on the diagnostic expertise of the examiner and the time available.

Students who are in a preservice teacher education program and professionals who have limited experience in reading assessment should be exposed only to the components of the SIRI described in Section Two. In all likelihood, such individuals lack the experience and knowledge necessary to use many of the more technical components of the SIRI presented in Section Three. The diagnostic options described in that section are best used by professionals with more experience in assessment, such as teachers enrolled in a graduate-level reading program or reading specialists working in clinical settings.

Time constraints are also a factor in determining how much of the SIRI to administer. Classroom teachers who are responsible for many students often do not have the time to utilize the various diagnostic options offered by the SIRI. Such teachers may only want to use the procedures for initial administration to place students in reading material (e.g., basal readers, tradebooks, content area textbooks) or to learn more about students' emergent reading behaviors. They may decide to administer the SIRI to every student or to a select few. On the other hand, reading specialists and special education personnel who usually work with smaller groups of students may choose to use more of the features of the SIRI to answer questions about students' specific strengths and weaknesses in reading. The results of this more complete assessment can then be used by these diagnosticians to formulate specific instructional plans for their students.

In summary, the SIRI is an informal reading assessment instrument that can help educators place students in reading materials and determine their strengths and weaknesses in word recognition and comprehension. Although the SIRI is based on the classic design of an informal reading inventory developed many years ago, it has new and improved features, such as a graded words in context test and a strategy for assessing the needs of emergent readers. The SIRI also contains many diagnostic alternatives. Specific instructions for using the SIRI are presented in Sections Two and Three.

Initial Administration
and Scoring Procedures

The first section of this book provided an introduction to The Stieglitz Informal Reading Inventory (SIRI). This section contains specific instructions for administering the SIRI to determine placement in reading material and to examine emergent reading behaviors. In preparation for testing, the teacher should

- become familiar with the procedures for administering, scoring, and interpreting the results of the SIRI;
- find a quiet place free of distractions to administer this test;
- gather all of the test materials, including copies of examiner's record forms, needed to administer the SIRI;
- have a tape recorder available to record the testing session;
- allow adequate time for testing.

Administering and Scoring the SIRI to Determine Placement in Reading Material

The steps for administering the SIRI to determine placement in reading material are as follows:

1. Establish rapport with the subject.
3. Administer the Reading Reflections Interview. (This can be administered at a later time if the examiner wishes to quickly determine a student's reading levels.)
2. Administer and score the Graded Words in Context Test to determine a base level.
3. Administer and score the Graded Reading Passages Test.
4. Record and interpret test results to estimate a range of reading levels.

A detailed discussion of these steps is presented next, followed by a sample record of a student's performance.

Step 1: Establish Rapport with the Subject

The examiner should establish a relationship with the student before administering the SIRI. This is especially important when the student is unfamiliar with the diagnostician. Initially, involve the individual in light conversation. Discussions about experiences in school and life at home can help the student feel more comfortable. If used judiciously, the time devoted to establishing rapport can provide valuable diagnostic information. Once rapport has been established, turn to your copy of the Summary of Student Performance Sheet found on page 179 in this book. Ask questions needed to fill out the top portion of this form. If the student is unable to answer some of these questions, check with another professional, such as a classroom teacher or a guidance counselor, for this information.

Step 2: Administer the Reading Reflections Interview

The Reading Reflections Interview (RRI) is an introspective procedure for gathering information about the affective elements that shape the learner's interaction with text. The RRI provides the reader with an opportunity to reflect on his or her reading experiences. The responses to the questions often bring to light information not revealed by traditional diagnostic techniques.

The RRI consists of ten open-ended questions that explore the student's knowledge of the reading process, perceptions of reading and his or her reading ability, and interest in reading. This interview is based, in part, on a reading comprehension interview technique developed by Wixson, Bosky, Yochum, and Alvermann (1984). The reading process questions explore the student's understanding of the goals and purposes of reading; the perception questions explore the student's knowledge of different reading task requirements, both in terms of the task demands and the teacher's criteria for evaluation; and the interest in reading questions reveal information about a reader's likes and dislikes.

The form for recording the results of this interview (pages 180–181) includes directions for administering the interview, provides the questions to be asked, and contains a section for summarizing the results. There is no student test material because all the items are read by the examiner. A sample interview administered to a third-grade student named Ricky is found on pages 17–18.

Note: As a supplement to the RRI, the teacher may wish to administer the Elementary Reading Attitude Survey (commonly referred to as Garfield the Cat survey). This instrument is included in an article by McKenna and Kear (1990) and referred to in a copyright update by the same authors (1995/1996). This survey provides quantitative estimates of important aspects of children's attitudes toward reading. It can be given to an entire class in a matter of minutes.

Step 3: Administer and Score the Graded Words in Context Test to Determine a Base Level

The purpose of this test is to examine how well a student can pronounce words in the context of a sentence. (Student test material appears on pages 89–97 and 107–115; examiner's record form appears on pages 183–192 and 213–222; and the quick list of instructions appears on page 182.) The results are used to determine the student's entry into the Graded Reading Passages Test. The Graded Words in Context Test consists of ten sentence sets, ranging in difficulty from the preprimer level through grade 8. Each set contains twenty sentences, except for the preprimer- and primer-level sets, which contain ten sentences each. A target word is highlighted in boldface type within each sentence. Consider the following example from the grade 2, form A, set: "The top of this **mountain** is very high." The target words in each set are graded. For example, every target word in the second sentence set is on a second-grade level. As an aid to fluency, the words surrounding a target word are all on a lower level (except for the first set, where every word is on a preprimer level).

The SIRI uses the following identification system to prevent students from knowing the grade level of each sentence set, which is indicated on the student's copy of the test for organizational purposes:

PP	Preprimer	**FO**	Grade Four
PR	Primer	**FI**	Grade Five
ON	Grade One	**SI**	Grade Six
TW	Grade Two	**SE**	Grade Seven
TH	Grade Three	**EI**	Grade Eight

It is strongly recommended that a tape recorder be used during the administration of the Graded Words in Context Test (as well as the Graded Reading Passages

SAMPLE RESULTS OF A READING
REFLECTIONS INTERVIEW

Reading Reflections Interview Form

Student's Name: __Ricky_____ Sex: __M__ Age: __8__ years __6__ months

School: __Truman_____ School System: __Uxbridge_____ Grade Placement: __3__

Interviewer: __Lisa Ferrelli_____ Date of Interview: __October 13_____

INTERVIEWER INSTRUCTIONS: During the interview, feel free to probe to elicit information about the student's knowledge of the reading process, perceptions of reading and his or her reading ability, and interest in reading. General probe questions such as, Can you tell me more about that? or, Anything else? may be used and, when asked, should be recorded on this form.

Throughout the interview, look for patterns of responses. This can serve as the basis for answering the summary questions listed at the end of this form.

STUDENT DIRECTIONS: Read the following directions to the student.
"I will be asking you some questions to find out what you think and feel about reading. There are no right or wrong answers. Just do the best you can to answer each question. As you are answering these questions, I will be taking some notes. This is to help me remember what you have said. Let's begin with this question."

Knowledge of Reading

1. What is reading? __It is with words that you read. Could be with lots of stories in it. You can use your finger to help you read.__

2. Why do people read? __Reading helps you learn. It helps you to know better. It helps people know the words.__

3. Can you read if you don't have a book? (Additional prompt: What else can a person read besides a book?)

   __No.__

Perceptions of Reading and Reading Ability

4. How did you learn to read? __By reading math. I don't know how that happened. By people telling me what the word is. By trying to sound the words out.__

5. Are you a good reader? How do you know? __Yes, I read a lot. I do math a lot. I practice a lot. I read 20 minutes every day.__

6. How does a teacher decide which students are good readers?

   __By how they speak and what words they know.__

7. What does a person have to learn to be a good reader?

Saying the words

Interest in Reading

8. Are there some things you *like* about reading? Please explain.

I like to put my finger under words to find out who's talking. I like to read math

books and practice books.

9. Are there some things you *don't like* about reading? Please explain.

No!

10. Finish this sentence: If I could choose anything to read, I would like to read about . . . (Prompt student to add to this sentence by saying: "Can you think of anything else you would like to read about?")

I would like to read reptile books and things about animals.

(Interviewer: "Can you think of anything *else* you would like to read about?")

I would like to read math books.

SUMMARY

What does the student know about the nature of reading?

Ricky seems to understand the main purpose of reading, that is, "Reading helps you learn." However, Ricky's answers reveal a somewhat narrow view of reading. He states that reading is about words and learning how to read words. He believes that pointing to words helps one read. Ricky's responses seem to reflect a view of reading that emphasizes bottom-up processing (decoding emphasis).

What are the student's perceptions of reading and his or her reading ability?

Though he states that he enjoys reading, Ricky's answers support the idea that reading is more about knowing words than about knowing what is read and why it is read. Again, his answers reflect a bottom-up view of reading.

What are the student's reading interests?

Ricky enjoys reading about animals and about topics in math.
It's not clear what topics in math Ricky enjoys reading about.

Additional comments:

Ricky seems to like reading. However, during the interview, Ricky did not say much about reading for understanding. He seemed to place more stress on the lower order units of reading, i.e., knowing the words.

Based on an interview administered by Lisa Ferrelli.

Test that follows). No matter how experienced the diagnostician is, maintaining an accurate record of a student's performance during testing can be difficult because of behaviors and responses that may be overlooked in the activity of the test situation. When a tape recorder is used, the examiner does not have to be overly concerned with the accuracy of the records kept during testing, and therefore can devote more attention to observing the student perform.

It is important to keep in mind that the presence of a tape recorder can be upsetting to some students. To lessen anxiety, give the student an opportunity to play with the recorder and hear how he or she sounds on tape. This procedure can also serve as a check to make sure that the tape recorder is working properly before the test is given.

As you begin, have a student's copy of the Graded Words in Context Test and a copy of the appropriate form to record the student's responses. (*Note:* When testing older readers, it may be necessary to reduce the type size of the lower-level sentence sets and passages because such individuals may be insulted by the oversized type. This can be done by using a photocopy machine with a reduction feature or by retyping the appropriate selections.) As a rule of thumb, begin with the sentence set that is two grade levels below the student's actual grade placement or two grade levels below a student's grade equivalent score on a recently administered norm-referenced test. Adjust this entry level upward or downward based on knowledge of the student's reading performance. Keep in mind that the objective of this test is to find the highest sentence set at which the student is able to read every target word correctly. The scoring is based on how well the student is able to pronounce *only* the target words in each sentence set.

Give the following directions to the student:

> "I have some sentences that I want you to read to me. Some of these sentences will be easy for you to read, and others may be more difficult. Try hard to read all the words in each sentence. If there are words you don't know, try to figure them out. Do the best you can. As you are reading these sentences, I will be taking some notes. This is to help me remember what you have read. Do you have any questions? Let's begin with this sentence."

Open the test booklet to the appropriate page in the Student's Test Materials, and place the booklet in front of the student. Then point to the first sentence of the appropriate set, and have the student begin reading to you. When a target word is pronounced correctly, place a + on the line to the left of the sentence on the record form. If the target word is missed, place a – on the line to the left of the sentence. The examiner should pronounce all nontarget words that the student has difficulty with (after a 5-second hesitation). However, when a 5-second hesitation occurs with a target word, do not assist the student. Tell the pupil to move on to the next sentence. (Better readers will not dwell on an unknown word. They will skip it, read to the end of the sentence, and then return to the unfamiliar word for a second try. Make a notation on the examiner's record form if this strategy is used.)

Use the following coding system for recording miscues with target words only.

Nonword substitution	Record mispronounced word above target word (e.g., **ints** for **insects**, **chemics** for **chemicals**).
Whole word substitution	Record substituted word above word in text (e.g., **brothers** for **bothers**).
Reversal	Record reversed word above word in text (e.g., **stop** for **pots**).
Does not attempt to pronounce target word	Place a **DK** over the target word.

Self-correction of target word   If a student misses and then self-corrects (a nonaccountable error) a target word, place a ⓒ over the target word.

An example of how responses are recorded is presented below:

13. eventual __+__ The team never lost hope of **eventual** victory.

poison

14. poisonous __−__ Stay away from **poisonous** snakes.

DK

15. nuisance __−__ The sound of a dripping faucet can be a **nuisance**.

worthlist ⓒ

16. worthless __+__ The fake coin he bought was found to be **worthless**.

The target words are the only ones considered in the scoring. However, for a more complete record of a student's performance, miscues of nontarget words should also be recorded. An explanation of this diagnostic option is presented in Section Three.

After two target words are missed in a sentence set, *stop*. Discontinue administering the set at this level, and begin with the next lower sentence set. Continue until every target word in a sentence set is pronounced correctly. If every target word in the first sentence set is attempted and pronounced correctly, move on to the next higher set and continue until two target words are missed. Remember that the purpose of administering this test is to obtain a base level. The base level is the highest sentence set in which the student is able to pronounce every target word correctly. The base level will be used to determine the grade level of passage to begin with on the Graded Reading Passages Test. Of course, the aim is to begin with a passage on the student's independent reading level.

Record the percent of correct target word responses on the line provided at the bottom of each sentence set (e.g., **95** percent) on the examiner's record form. When two target words are missed and testing is discontinued before the set is completed, write **inc.** (incomplete) on this line.

Proceed to Step 4 if the student's base or estimated independent level is grade 1 or higher. If the base level is below grade 1, it does not make sense to continue with the passages test because the lowest-level selection is written on a first-grade reading level. In such cases, skip Step 4 and use the Dictated Story Assessment Strategy, described later in this section.

In some situations, the teacher may deem it worthwhile to use the Dictated Story Assessment Strategy with students who earn a base level of grade 1 on the Graded Words in Context Test. For example, if a student does well on the grade 1 sentence set but does poorly on the grade 2 set, use of the Dictated Story Assessment Strategy could provide the diagnostician with valuable information about that student's emergent and initial reading behaviors. Of course, teachers should use their best judgment in making decisions of this type.

Step 4: Administer and Score the Graded Reading Passages Test

The purpose of the Graded Reading Passages Test is to estimate students' reading levels when reading expository or narrative text. (Student test material appears on pages 98–106, 107–115, 158–166, and 167–175; examiner's record form appears on pages 195–212, 223–240, 272–289, and 290–307; and the quick list of instructions appears on pages 193–194.) This test consists of a set of graded passages for oral reading. The selections range in level from grade 1 through grade 9. The SIRI uses the following coding system to identify the grade level of each passage on the student's copy of the test.

PP	Preprimer		**TW**	Grade Two
PR	Primer		**TH**	Grade Three
ON	Grade One		**FO**	Grade Four

FI   Grade Five   EI   Grade Eight
SI   Grade Six   NI   Grade Nine
SE   Grade Seven

Selection of Text

Time constraints may not allow the teacher to administer both narrative and expository forms of the Graded Reading Passages Test, and the examiner must decide which prose type to use in the initial administration of the SIRI. At the primary level, where story reading is usually emphasized, the teacher may decide to administer the narrative selections. In a middle-, junior-high, or high-school setting, where reading in the content areas is emphasized, the examiner may prefer to use the expository selections. Although some teachers have found the expository passages to be more difficult, the results of the SIRI pilot test revealed little difference in the reading levels obtained when both types of passages were administered to the same population of students. (Information on the field test is provided in Section Six.) Therefore, examiners can use a form based on either prose type to determine students' general reading levels. However, the structure of the two types of text is different, and both expository and narrative forms of the SIRI should be given, whenever possible, to determine how well students interact with text based on each prose style.

Once the decision on prose type is made, turn to Section Five and reproduce copies of the appropriate two-page record forms in the examiner's material for recording results. Then decide which selection will be used to begin the testing. In the case of a student whose base level on the Graded Words in Context Test is grade 3, start with the third-grade selection on the passages test.

Give the following directions to the student:

"I am going to have you read some material to me out loud. Some of these passages will be easy for you to read, and others may be more difficult. Try hard to pronounce as many of the words as possible. Also, try to remember what you are reading. When you have finished, I will take the booklet away and ask you some questions." [Free Recall option: "When you are finished, I will take the booklet away and ask you to tell me what you remember about the passage."] "I will again be taking notes. This is to help me remember what you have read. Do you understand? Let's begin with this passage."

Open the test booklet to the appropriate page, and place the booklet in front of the student. Refer to the duplicated copy of the examiner's record form for the selected passage on the Graded Reading Passages Test. Read the introductory statement at the top of the page to the student. Have the pupil read the passage out loud, beginning with the title. Use the examiner's form to record information on the student's performance in word recognition and comprehension according to the following directions.

Word Recognition

As the student is reading the material aloud, use the Marking System for Oral Reading Miscues presented in Table 2.1 to record miscues in word recognition on the examiner's record form. Encourage the student to pronounce as many words as possible, but do not provide too much assistance when the pupil has difficulty. In other words, when the reader makes a miscue, it is all right to say "Do the best you can." However, *do not* say "Read to the end of the sentence, and then try to pronounce this word again."

Roughly score performance in word recognition as the student progresses through the passages. A more accurate scoring of miscues takes place after testing, when a tape recording of the session is played back. According to the SIRI miscue marking system, some errors are counted as full miscues and others are counted as

TABLE 2.1   *Marking System for Oral Reading Miscues*

TYPE OF MISCUE	VALUE OF MISCUE	DESCRIPTION	MARKING SYSTEM
Nonword Substitution	Full (1)	The printed word is substituted by a nonword or word part that disrupts the intended meaning.	*pape* Pat opened a paper bag. *gen–* Generations of children have been fascinated with toys.
Whole Word Substitution	Full	The printed word is substituted by a real word that disrupts the intended meaning.	*ounce* There was once some children who were always fighting.
	Half ($\frac{1}{2}$)	The printed word is substituted by a real word that does not disrupt the intended meaning.	The tightly packed center of the *wet* kernel is moist.
Word Pronounced by the Examiner	Full	The examiner pronounces the word after a 5-second hesitation.	Good dental care is essential to the preservation of our teeth.
Omission	Full	A whole word or a group of words is omitted and it disrupts the intended meaning.	Bill and Kim could (not) wait to build something with the snow. Toy animals were (also popular) among the ancient Greeks.
	Half	A whole word or a group of words is omitted and it does not disrupt the intended meaning.	You get a hangnail when (the) skin around your nail gets a little dry. A wasp needs paper (in order) to build a nest.
Insertion	Full	An extra word is added to the text and it disrupts the meaning.	*not* The lollipop was ∧ strawberry.
	Half	An extra word is added to the text and it does not disrupt the meaning.	*even* Without light, we could not ∧ see.
Reversal	Full	A word is reversed or the order of words is reversed in a sentence.	At sixteen, she ran in the Olympics *now* and won a bronze medal. So far, they can't put the smell *sticker on a hamburger* of a hamburger on a sticker.
Repetition	Full	Three or more words are repeated.	Many products are sold in supermarkets and drugstores.
Repetition	Not counted as a miscue	Two words or less are repeated.	Let's catch all the leaves we can.
Self-Correction	Not counted as a miscue	A miscue is self-corrected without assistance.	There was a fellow who had a *strong* © strange way of doing business.
Dialect Variations	Not counted as a miscue	A pupil reads orally in accordance with his or her dialect. (Many New Englanders do not pronounce the /r/ in words such as *car* and *park*.)	*ca–* Ⓓ It's time to buy a new car.

Source: Adapted from Stieglitz, E. L. (1980). Initial assessment for individualization. In Diane Lapp (Ed.), *Making reading possible through effective classroom management* (pp. 106–107). Newark, DE: International Reading Association. Reprinted with permission of Ezra L. Stieglitz and the International Reading Association.

half miscues. Record a full miscue when the miscue disrupts the intended meaning of the passage. Record a half miscue when it does not disrupt the intended meaning of the passage. When there is doubt about the value of a miscue, count it as a full miscue. Examples of the two values of miscues are given in Table 2.1.

Record the number of full and half miscues and the total miscue count in the spaces provided under Accountable Miscues on the passage record form. Then transfer this information to the Levels of Word Recognition and Comprehension scale on the same form. Let **x** mark the spot on the word recognition side of this scale to show the miscue count and equivalent reading level for each passage read by the student. Figure 2.1 provides a sample passage from the test with handwritten notations.

Comprehension

When the student has finished reading a passage, remove the manual and begin the comprehension check. Decide whether to use probed recall, free recall, or a combination of the two procedures to check comprehension of each selection.

The conventional approach to assessing comprehension is probed recall. After the student has read the article, remove the text and ask the questions listed on the record form. The following coding system identifies each question type.

L   Literal-Level Question
I   Interpretive-Level Question
C   Critical- or Creative-Level Question

The scoring is based on how well a student can answer *only* the literal- and interpretive-level questions. Critical- and creative-level questions are included in the Comprehension Check, but they are not considered in the scoring because they are not always passage dependent. (Note the broken scoring lines next to these questions.) Questions of this type are more open-ended and are designed to provide qualitative information on students' reflective thinking abilities. Because of their nature, higher-level questions can elicit a range of "acceptable" responses. For example, when they were asked, "Why do you think smelly stickers are made for people to buy?" students participating in the SIRI pilot testing responded with, "People want to smell something really nice," "Because you can't make them yourself," and "They're nice to have." Student answers to a similar question from the narrative selection "The Story of an Old Attic" (Form B) provide another example. When they were asked, "Could this story have happened?" students responded with, "Yes, because cats' eyes can glow in the dark and this makes them look like ghosts" and "Yes, because some houses have attics and cats can go into these attics." Answers such as these provide the examiner with valuable information about students' ability to apply ideas from their own experiences to the text in order to perceive associations and relationships.

Another approach to comprehension assessment is free recall. If this strategy is used, ask, "What can you tell me about the passage you have just read?" Record in the free recall column on the record form questions from the probed recall that are addressed during the free recall, or retelling, of the article. Probe for information not given in full during the free recall by asking the remaining questions listed on the record form. A technique for measuring the free recall of narrative text is described in detail below.

Students' responses to questions are entered on the passage record form. If a question is answered correctly, place a + on the line in the probed recall column to the right of the printed question (or in the free recall column if this procedure is used). If a question is missed, place a – on the line to the right.

The record form provides examples of suitable responses in parentheses following each Comprehension Check question. These answers are included only as a guide to the examiner. The student may give other answers that are deserving of full

FIGURE 2.1

Sample recording of word recognition miscues on the Graded Reading Passages Test (Form A)

  Teeth to Spare (6)

INTRODUCTION: Please read this article to learn more about an animal who doesn't need to visit a dentist.

Teeth to Spare

Good dental care is *essential* to the ~~essential ①~~
preservation of our teeth. Once a permanent ~~prevention ①~~

tooth is lost . . . that's it! Only a false tooth

can fill the gap.

    Sharks don't need to be concerned

about their teeth as we do because they are

given an endless supply. A shark always has

a full mouth of teeth. When a tooth is lost, it

is replaced by another one. The tiger shark, ①

as an example, is said to grow twenty-four

thousand teeth over a ten-year period.

    Teeth are attached to the shark's jaws

in several rows. Usually, only the outermost

rows of ∧teeth are functional. Some species of *the* ①⁄₂

sharks have as many as forty rows of teeth.

Each row is slightly larger than the last, with *bigger* ①⁄₂

the outermost rows being the largest. ⟨New⟩ ①

teeth originate in an area behind the jaws *organic* ①

and move outward as they form and harden.

As ⟨the⟩ teeth in the front begin to wear down ①⁄₂ *this* ①⁄₂ ①

or are lost when a shark attacks its prey, they

are replaced by those behind. Since new

teeth form continually, there is a conveyer *consiently* ①

belt system of tooth replacement. The shark,

therefore, always has a set of razor-sharp

teeth to use at will.

Accountable Miscues

Full Miscues:	**7**	×	1	= **7**
Half Miscues:	**4**	×	$\frac{1}{2}$	= **2**
			TOTAL	**9**

LEVELS OF WORD RECOGNITION AND COMPREHENSION

Word Recognition MISCUES		*Comprehension* ERRORS
0		0
1,2,3	Independent Level	
		½
4,5		
6,7	Instructional Level	
8,9 **X**		1
10,11		
12,13		1½
14,15	Questionable Level	
16,17		2
18,19		
20		2½
	Frustration Level	

Based on an example provided by Susan Russell.

credit. To keep an accurate record of a student's performance, enter all responses on the record form, whether correct or incorrect. If a student does not respond to a question or does not know the answer, enter **DK** (don't know) on the line to the right of the question and move on to the next one. Students may receive full or partial credit ($\frac{1}{2}$ point) for a response. For example, if the question is, What are the names of two countries mentioned in the article? and the student identifies the name of only one country, partial credit is given. In such cases, enter $\frac{1}{2}$ on the line to the right of the question. Examiners must call upon their best judgment to determine whether a response is deserving of full or partial credit or whether further probing is required. For example, if a student were asked the question, "What would probably happen to the shark if it had only one set of permanent teeth?" and that pupil responded with "It would lose all its teeth," the examiner should then ask, "What might happen to the shark if it lost all its teeth?"

Quickly score the comprehension segment of the passage test by totaling the number of literal and interpretive comprehension errors, and enter the number on the Total Comprehension Errors line on the record form. Figure 2.2 presents a sample comprehension check with scoring notations. Then transfer this information to the Levels of Word Recognition and Comprehension scale. Let **x** mark the spot on the comprehension side of this scale to show the error count and equivalent reading level for the passage read.

Look at the results of the first selection read. If the word recognition and comprehension data clearly show that the student read this passage on an independent reading level (independent level is attained in both word recognition and comprehension), then move on to the next highest selection. However, if the results indicate that this passage is not on the student's independent level, then introduce the next lowest passage.

Have the student read as many selections as are necessary to gather enough information to delineate the range of reading levels: independent, instructional, and frustration. If, on a given passage, a student experiences great difficulty in word recognition, the examiner may decide to discontinue administering that portion of the test.

Procedure for Assessing the Free Recall of Narrative Text

The procedure for utilizing retelling to assess a student's sense of story structure and comprehension is based on a technique described by Morrow (1988). (Story Retelling Form to Assess Sense of Story Structure and Comprehension is provided on pages 241–242.) This procedure can be used with narrative passages from the SIRI that are tales, mysteries, or stories with humor. Because the purpose of this strategy is to assess a student's sense of story structure, this technique will not work as well with passages from the SIRI that are purely descriptive (passages 1, 7, and 9 in Forms B and D). The procedure described below can be used to assess oral, listening, and silent comprehension of narrative prose.

To begin, the diagnostician must first identify the story elements that should be addressed during a reader's retelling of a story. Included are the following:

Setting
This includes the time and location of the story.

Character
This is comprised of the main and other characters in the story.

Initiating Event
This causes the main character to react, form a goal, or face a problem.

Plot Episodes
This is the order of how things happen in a story. During these episodes, the main character attempts to attain a goal or to solve a problem.

FIGURE 2.2

Sample recording of comprehension check on the Graded Reading Passages Test (Form B)

COMPREHENSION CHECK			LEVELS OF WORD RECOGNITION AND COMPREHENSION	

The Crow and the Pitcher (3)

	Probed Recall	*Free Recall*	*Word Recognition* MISCUES		*Comprehension* ERRORS

L 1. What was the crow looking for?   +   ____

(water)

L 2. What did the crow find at the beginning of the story?   +   ____

(a water pitcher)

L 3. How much water did the crow find in the pitcher?   +   ____

(She found only a little.)
(She didn't find much water.)

I 4. What did the crow do to solve the problem of getting the water at the bottom of the pitcher?   –   ____

(any logical description of how the pebbles were used)   **She put her beak in.**

L 5. What did the crow do at the end of the story?   +   ____

(She quenched her thirst.)
(She was able to quench her thirst and save her life.)   **She threw her beak into it and drank the water.**

C 6. What is the lesson we can learn from this story?   =   ____

(Accept any logical response, such as "It pays to be persistent.")   **Open your container**

Total Comprehension Errors   __1__
(L & I)

Word Recognition MISCUES:

0
1,2   Independent Level
3
4,5
6   Instructional Level
7
8,9
10
11,12   Questionable Level
13
14,15
16   Frustration Level

Comprehension ERRORS:

0
½
1 ✗ (at Instructional Level)
1½
2
2½

Resolution
The character attains a goal or solves a problem (or, as can occur in some stories, the goal is unattained or the problem is unsolved) and the story ends.

Theme
This is the central idea or moral that the author wishes to convey to the reader.

For example, an analysis of the story "The Boy and the Fox" (Form B) reveals the following story structure:

Setting
One day a boy saw a fox sleeping on top of a rock.

Character
The boy is the main character and the fox is another character.

Initiating Event
The boy thought about killing the fox.

Plot Episodes
First Episode: The boy was anticipating all the ways he could profit if he killed the fox.

Examples of this are (1) the boy thought about how the skin of the dead fox could be used to buy and plant bean seeds, (2) the boy thought about how the money from the beans he sold could be used to buy a field, (3) the boy thought about how he could plant bean seeds in his own field, (4) the boy thought about how people will see his beautiful beans and admire them, and (5) the boy thought about how he will need to tell people to keep away from his beans.

Second Episode: The boy shouted so loudly that the fox woke up and ran away.

Resolution
The boy was left with nothing.

Theme
"Don't count your chickens before they hatch" (or the equivalent).

Next, the examiner selects a narrative passage and gives the following directions to the student:

"I am going to have you read [or listen to] a story. Try to remember what you are reading [or listening to]. After you have read [or listened to] this story, I am going to take the book away and ask you to retell this story in your own words." [Another way of phrasing this is, "Be ready to tell this story to a friend who has never heard this story before."]

Morrow (1988) suggests that the examiner use the following prompts only when necessary:

If the child has difficulty beginning the story retelling, suggest beginning with "Once upon a time . . ." or "Once there was . . . ."

If the child stops retelling before the end of the story, encourage continuation by asking, "What comes next?" or "Then what happened?"

If the child stops retelling and cannot continue with the prompts offered, ask a question about the story that is relevant at that point in the story at which the child has paused. For example, "What was Jenny's problem in the story?" (p. 130)

If a student does not state the theme of a story, ask questions such as, What is this story all about? or, What lesson can be learned from this story?

Record a student's retelling for playbacks, as needed, by the diagnostician. To analyze the retelling, make a comparison between the story elements identified by the examiner and the story elements identified by the student during retelling of the passage. Use the degree of match between the two sets to determine the student's comprehension level. To assist the examiner, a Story Retelling Form to Assess Sense of Story Structure and Comprehension is provided on pages 241–242.

Figure 2.3 presents a sample transcription of a third-grade student's retelling of "The Boy and the Fox" and an analysis of the results. Eve's retelling of "The Boy and the Fox" showed that she could comprehend this material at the instructional level. Here is how the examiner scored the results of the retelling.

Eve earned a perfect score for the items listed under *setting* and *character*. Although her example of the *initiating event* was different from the one stated in the sample story structure analysis on page 27, the examiner decided to give her full credit for this response: ". . . a boy who wanted to make some money. . . ." Eve was given credit for the first plot episode because the teacher felt she understood the gist of the events in this part of the story. Her retelling also included information about the second plot episode. Eve showed some understanding of the story's resolution. She mentioned that the boy didn't attain his goal of killing the fox because he ". . . was not very smart. . . ." However, she failed to explain how the story ended. Eve's retelling showed that she only had a partial understanding of story sequence. She did not say anything about the fox sleeping on top of a rock at the beginning of the story and, as stated before, did not include information about how the story ended. Finally, Eve's response to the teacher's prompt question at the end of the session showed that she had only a partial understanding of the story's theme. In summation, Eve's sense of story structure and understanding of the text were fairly good.

The main advantage of the retelling strategy is that assessment and instruction can be linked easily together. The results of a retelling session such as the one with Eve can provide the teacher with valuable information about a student's mastery of narrative prose. The teacher can use such information to plan instructional activities that will improve a student's sense of story structure and text comprehension.

Prior Knowledge and Level of Interest

A Prior Knowledge scale is used to determine the familiarity level of each passage. Note the difference in this procedure for expository versus narrative text. After the student finishes reading an *expository* selection, show the pupil the Prior Knowledge scale. First, explain the purpose of this scale. Then, read the question and have the student determine a self-perceived level of prior knowledge. If the student gives prior knowledge a high rating (4 or 5), ask questions such as, "When did you learn so much about _____?" or "Where did you get this information?" and "Do you know anything else about _____?" Record responses on the record form, as in the following example.

Old Toys (7)

How much did you know about the favorite toys of children of long ago before reading this article?

I read books about ancient China and Greece. I learned about toys that children played with back then.

I knew:

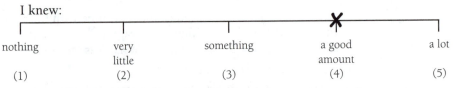

nothing	very little	something	a good amount	a lot
(1)	(2)	(3)	(4)	(5)

After the student finishes reading a *narrative* selection, ask, "Have you ever read this story before?" Record the student's answer on the form. If the pupil responds "Yes," then ask questions such as, "When did you read this story? Do you remember the book it was in?" Again, record responses on the form.

FIGURE 2.3

Sample transcript with analysis of results

SAMPLE TRANSCRIPT OF A RETOLD STORY—
"THE BOY AND THE FOX"

Teacher: What can you tell me about the story you have just read?

Student: There was once a boy who wanted to make some money to buy bean seeds to plant beans in his field. When they grew he wanted to sell them to make some more money to buy the field across the way. So now the boy thought until he thought of a plan to kill the fox and sell his skin to make the money to buy the bean seeds to grow the bean seeds and sell the beans to buy the field across the way. But suddenly the fox woke up because the boy was not very smart because instead of thinking to himself he was thinking out loud.

Teacher: What did you learn from this story?

Student: I think you should never talk out loud to yourself when you have a good idea.

SAMPLE ANALYSIS OF TRANSCRIPT

Story Retelling Form to Assess Sense of Story Structure and Comprehension

Student's Name: __Eve_____ Sex: __F__ Age: __8__ years __11__ months

School: __P.S. 145_____ School System: __New York_____ Grade Placement: __3__

Examiner: __Philip Cannon_____ Date of Administration: __1/16_____

Title of Story: __The Boy and the Fox_____ Form: __B_____

Based on (Check one): _____ Oral Comprehension   __✔__ Silent Comprehension

_____ Listening Comprehension

DIRECTIONS: Score each item according to the directions given below. Add the results in the <u>second</u> column to obtain the Student's Score. Compare the Student's Score to the Highest Possible Score to determine the student's comprehension level for this passage.

If an item does not apply, enter "NA" and do not consider it in the scoring.

Setting

a. Begins story with an introduction (Score "1" if included in retelling)   __1__

b. Includes statement about time or place (1)   __1__

Character

a. Names main character (1) (Credit can be given if student says "girl," "boy," or "dog" in place of character's name.)   __1__

b. Number of other characters named (Credit plurals as "2," e.g., "friends" in place of the names of four characters.)   __1__

c. Actual number of other characters   __1__

d. Score for "other characters" (b/c)   __1__

(continued)

FIGURE 2.3

Continued

Initiating Event

Refer's to main character's primary goal or problem to be solved (1)   _____1_____

Plot Episodes

(Credit can be given if student understands *gist* of the plot.)

a.   Number of episodes recalled   _____2_____

b.   Number of episodes in story   _____2_____

c.   Score for "plot episodes" (a/b)   _____1_____

Resolution

a.   Names problem solution/goal attainment (1)   _____1_____

b.   Ends story (1)   _____0_____

Sequence

Retells story in structural order: setting, initiating event, plot episodes, resolution (Score "2" for proper order, "1" for partial, "0" for no sequence)   _____1_____

Theme

States central idea or moral of story (1)   _____.5_____

Highest Possible Score: _____11_____   **Student's Score:** _____8.5_____

Retelling Comprehension Score: _____77.3_____

(Student's Score/Highest Possible Score)

Level of Comprehension: Instructional

Independent Level   90–100%
Instructional Level   75–89%
Questionable Level   50–74%
Frustration Level   Below 50%

Any prompting required? If yes, describe below.

Prompting was needed to have the student identify the theme of the story. Otherwise, the student did not need any assistance from the teacher.

Additional Comments:

Source: Adapted from Morrow, Lesley Mandel (1988). Retelling stories as a diagnostic tool. In *Reexamining reading diagnosis: New trends and procedures*, S. M. Glazer, L. W. Searfoss, and L. M. Gentile (Eds.). Newark, DE: International Reading Association, pp. 143–144. Reprinted with permission of Lesley M. Morrow and the International Reading Association. All rights reserved.

A 5-point scale similar to the one used to assess prior knowledge with expository prose is used to determine a student's level of interest or expository and narrative passages. Here, too, it may be necessary to explain the purpose of this scale. Point to the Level of Interest scale, read the question, and have the student determine a self-perceived level of interest. Occasionally probe with such questions as, "Why did you enjoy this story/article?" or "Why did you dislike this story/article?" Record the student's response on the scale.

Step 5: Record and Interpret Test Results to Estimate a Range of Reading Levels

After the Graded Words in Context and the Graded Reading Passages Tests have been administered, the examiner needs to transfer the information to a photocopy of the Summary of Student Performance Sheet on page 179.

Begin with the data from the Graded Words in Context Test. Record the results in the appropriate spaces on this form. Next, record the results of the Graded Reading Passages Test. Transfer the information recorded on the Levels of Word Recognition and Comprehension scale to the Summary of Student Performance Sheet. Then, transfer the Prior Knowledge and Level of Interest data to the Summary Sheet. This procedure is illustrated in the sample analysis of a sixth-grade student (see pages 33–41).

When a score falls within the questionable zone, the examiner must eventually decide which of the two levels is more appropriate—instructional or frustration. When making this decision, the examiner may first need to review a student's performance on previous and subsequent passages.

Use the results recorded on the Summary of Student Performance Sheet to estimate a student's independent, instructional, and frustration reading levels. If the levels for Word Recognition and Comprehension are inconsistent, as a rule of thumb, select the lower of the two when making this estimate. For example, when a student reading a grade 7 passage performs at the independent level for word recognition but on the instructional level for comprehension, select instructional level as the placement for seventh-grade level material. The instructional level can be listed as one grade level or as a range of no more than two grade levels. Thus, if a student performs at the instructional level with third- and fourth-grade passages, the instructional level would be recorded as **3–4**.

Sample Analysis of a Sixth-Grade Student

A sample set of the Graded Words in Context and Graded Reading Passages Tests administered to a sixth-grader named Irina is found on pages 33–41.

It is the first month of the school year and Irina's teacher, Ms. Santagata, is organizing a literature-based reading program for her students. In preparation for this program, Ms. Santagata has assembled a wide variety of materials for the classroom library, such as tradebooks, magazines, and pamphlets. A major feature of this program is that students are given the opportunity to freely select material from this library to read in class. In order to select material her students will enjoy, Ms. Santagata obtains information on her students' reading interests by administering an interest inventory. The results show that Irina enjoys reading about topics in social studies and science. Therefore, Ms. Santagata decides to administer an expository form of the SIRI to her for quick placement in reading material for this program. Here is Ms. Santagata's summary and analysis of the test results.

Irina was directed to begin reading sentences from the grade 2 set of the Graded Words in Context Test. She performed well, pronouncing every target word correctly. On the grade 3 set, Irina made one whole word substitution and achieved a score of 95 percent. Testing was stopped with the sixth word on the grade 4 set when Irina missed a second target word. From these results, Irina's base level was estimated to be at grade 2. This was the level at which she was to begin reading selections from the Graded Reading Passages Test.

The results of the Graded Reading Passages Test were used to estimate Irina's range of reading levels on expository material. The completed summary sheet shows an independent level of grade 2, an instructional level of grade 3, and a frustration level of grade 4. The results showed that Irina had little or no familiarity with the content of passages read, and her interest in the selections was "good."

Irina was quite fluent in her reading of the grade 2 selection, making only one major miscue. She self-corrected three times during the reading of this passage. The number of miscues increased as she read selections of increasing difficulty. As she progressed through the passages, more of Irina's miscues disrupted the intended meaning of the text. For example, most of the miscues Irina made during her reading of the grade 4 passage disrupted the meaning of the text.

Irina's comprehension of the material was very good. She had a perfect score on the grade 2 Comprehension Check and missed only one item (interpretive level) on the grade 3 check. Of the three critical/creative questions asked, Irina received full credit for her answers to the grades 2 and 3 questions and half credit for the grade 4 higher-level question.

On the grade 4 passage, Irina scored in the questionable zone in word recognition. The decision regarding whether her overall performance was closer to the instructional or frustration end of the continuum was based on her performance on the Comprehension Check. Because of her poor performance in comprehension (a total of three comprehension errors), it was decided to rank her at the frustration level with fourth-grade material. Irina's performance in word recognition and comprehension on the grade 4 passage shows that material written on a fourth-grade level would probably be too difficult for her.

The results of this initial administration of the SIRI show that Irina is capable of reading third-grade material with some teacher assistance. She can read material written below a third-grade level with little difficulty. Generally, Irina should not be given material written above a third-grade level. The results show that Irina's instructional level is about 3 years below her actual grade placement. Suitable reading material will need to be located for Irina's interest and maturity levels (high-interest, low-vocabulary) if she is to participate successfully in a literature-based reading program.

The next nine pages show you a sample summary of Irina's performance, with accompanying record sheets.

SAMPLE SUMMARY OF STUDENT PERFORMANCE WITH ACCOMPANYING RECORD SHEETS

Summary of Student Performance Sheet

Student's Name: __Irina__ Sex: __F__ Age: __12__ years __2__ months

School: __Brennan__ School System: __Attleboro__ Grade Placement: __6__

Examiner: __D. Santagata__ Dates of Administration: __9/14__

Graded Words in Context Form: __A__ Oral Reading Form(s): __A__

Listening Comprehension Form(s): _____

Graded Words in Isolation Form: _____ Silent Reading Form(s): _____

GRADED WORDS TESTS

GRADE LEVEL	PERCENT	CORRECT
	Context	Isolation
PP		
P		
1		
2	100	
3	95	
4	inc.	
5		
6		
7		
8		

ESTIMATED READING LEVELS

	GRADE LEVELS	
	Expository	Narrative
Independent	2	
Instructional*	3	
Frustration	4	
Listening		

*List as one grade level or range of two grade levels (e.g., 5–6).

▢ Shaded areas are used to record results of diagnostic options.

GRADED READING PASSAGES TEST

EXPOSITORY

Grade Level	Word Recognition	Oral Comp.	List. Comp. (%)	Prior Knowledge (1–5)	Interest (1–5)
1					
2	IND	IND		2	4
3	INST	INST		1	3
4	QUEST/FRUST	FRUST		1	3
5					
6					
7					
8					
9					

NARRATIVE

Grade Level	Word Recognition	Oral Comp.	List. Comp. (%)	Prior Knowledge (Y–N)	Interest (1–5)
1					
2					
3					
4					
5					
6					
7					
8					
9					

Based on a case provided by Deborah Santagata.

Grade 2

1. low	+ _____	The water in the lake is very **low**.
2. deer	+ _____	Will the little **deer** find her mother?
3. few	+ _____	A **few** children hid under the table.
4. afraid	+ _____	Some children are **afraid** of the dark.
5. rest	+ _____	He took a **rest** in his bed after dinner.
6. mile	+ _____	The school is a **mile** from her house.
7. such	+ _____	The boy said, "You have **such** a nice smile."
8. I'd	+ _____	**I'd** like to see my friend next week.
9. carry	+ _____	She has many books to **carry** to school.
10. puppy	+ _____	Look at the **puppy** run up the hill!
11. owl	+ _____	The **owl** is a bird with two big eyes.
12. seven	+ _____	There were **seven** fish in the lake.
13. quick	+ _____	The **quick** rabbit ran faster than the mouse.
14. mountain	+ _____	The top of this **mountain** is very high.
15. visit	+ _____	Grandma will **visit** us next week.
16. follow	+ _____	When will your sister **follow** us to school?
17. dragon	+ _____	I heard a story about a bad **dragon**.
18. anyone	+ _____	Is there **anyone** in this room who has a snake?
19. farmer	+ _____	I know a **farmer** who has many animals.
20. evening	+ _____	He reads to his children every **evening**.
	100 _____	%

Grade 3

1. crop	+ _____	The farmer had a nice **crop** of corn.
2. force	+ _____	Give it to me at once, or I will **force** you to!
3. motor	+ _____	A car cannot run without a **motor**.
4. usual	+ _____	He was late to school as **usual**.
5. yesterday	+ _____	We went to the zoo **yesterday**.
6. bother	+ _____	She will like you more if you don't **bother** her.
7. enjoy	+ _____	You will really **enjoy** this magic show.
8. history	+ _____	We will learn about the **history** of our country.
9. nibble	+ _____	A rabbit likes to **nibble** on a carrot.
10. scratch	+ _____	If you are not careful, this cat will **scratch** you.
11. parent	+ _____	Which **parent** will visit the school today?
12. television	+ _____	Some children watch too much **television**.

13.	whisker	+	The man found a gray **whisker** growing on his chin.
14.	treat	+	I do my best to **treat** my pets well.
15.	accident	+	I spilled paint on your pants by **accident**.
16.	dare	+	I **dare** you to take that frog to school.
17.	understand	+	Did you **understand** the answer to that question?
18.	notebook	+	I write everything down in my **notebook**.
19.	amaze	−	*surprise* Your magic tricks will **amaze** everyone.
20.	familiar	+	The man in the green shirt looks so **familiar**.
		95 %	

Grade 4

1.	plot	−	*plat* Did you understand the **plot** of this story?
2.	rhyme	+	"Name" and "game" are two words that **rhyme**.
3.	uproar	+	There was an **uproar** when the lion escaped from his cage.
4.	bold	+	The **bold** girl protected her friend from danger.
5.	fashion	+	It is in **fashion** to wear this kind of shoe.
6.	property	−	*DK* Do you know how much **property** he owns on this street?
7.	aware		I was too sleepy to be **aware** of how cold it was.
8.	cookbook		I bought a **cookbook** with 9 recipes for making fish.
9.	hoarse		A bad cold often makes a person sound **hoarse**.
10.	represent		He has a friend who will **represent** him in court.
11.	slope		It is hard to climb a mountain with a steep **slope**.
12.	excellent		She earned a high or **excellent** grade on this test.
13.	telegraph		A **telegraph** is used to send a message to someone.
14.	oyster		This pearl came from an **oyster**.
15.	fortunate		She was **fortunate** to have won the contest.
16.	subject		Reading is my favorite **subject** in school.
17.	taxi		This **taxi** will take you to the airport.
18.	downhill		It is lots of fun to ride a sled **downhill**.
19.	increase		If you eat too much, your weight will **increase**.
20.	thunderstorm		Children are usually frightened by a **thunderstorm**.
		inc. %	

Hide and Seek (2)

INTRODUCTION: Have you ever played the game of "hide and seek"? Please read this article to learn about the first people to do hide and seek.

Note: If necessary, provide background information about how the game is played.

Hide and Seek

Many children like to play "hide and seek."

Hide and seek did not begin as a game. It

started many years ago in a far away land.

   Hid©   great©
Hide and seek was something grown-ups

did each year when winter was over. People
   tried①
were tired of the cold and the long nights.

They wanted to know if spring was on

the way.

   Grown-ups would leave their village

and go into the woods. They tried to find or

"seek out" birds and flowers. It was
   remember©
important to return with a bird or flower. If

one did, this was a sign that spring had

really started.

Accountable Miscues

Full Miscues: __1__   × 1 =   __1__

Half Miscues: __0__   × $\frac{1}{2}$ =   __0__

                       TOTAL __1__

COMPREHENSION CHECK

	Probed Recall	Free Recall

L 1. When did hide and seek start?   **+**   ____

   (many years ago)   **a long time ago**

L 2. Many years ago, who did hide and seek?   **+**   ____

   (grown-ups)

L 3. During what time of the year did grown-ups do hide and seek?   **+**   ____

   (after winter)

   (at the beginning of spring)

   (springtime)

L 4. Name two things people looked for when they did hide and seek.   **+**   ____

   (birds and flowers)

I 5. Hide and seek was something grown-ups did each year. Why was it so important for them to do hide and seek?   **+**   ____

   (It was used to find out when spring had really started.)

   (It was an important custom.)

C 6. Hide and seek is different today. Why is this so?   **_±_**   ___

   (It is no longer a ritual or custom.)   **Because today it is a game that kids play. Back then it wasn't.**

   (We have better ways of determining the start of spring.)

   (Because a long time ago it wasn't a game, but today it is a game.)

Total Comprehension Errors   __0__

                                (L & I)

PRIOR KNOWLEDGE

How much did you know about how hide and seek started before reading this article?

I knew:

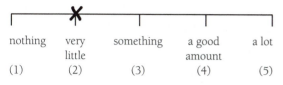

nothing	very little	something	a good amount	a lot
(1)	(2)	(3)	(4)	(5)

LEVEL OF INTEREST

How much did you like reading this article?

This article was:

horrible	fair	good	very good	terrific
(1)	(2)	(3)	(4)	(5)

LEVELS OF WORD RECOGNITION AND COMPREHENSION

Word Recognition   *Comprehension*
MISCUES   ERRORS

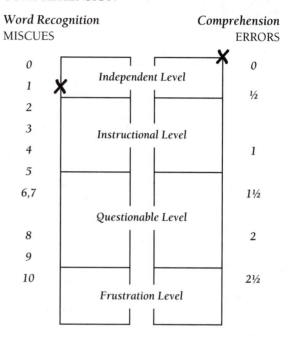

Hangnails (3)

INTRODUCTION: Please read this article to learn something about hangnails.

Hangnails

What is a hangnail? First of all, a hangnail
DK ①
is not really a nail. It is a tough, little piece

of skin that hangs loosely at the side of

your fingernail.

You get a hangnail when the skin

around your nail gets a little dry. Then a

piece of skin might start peeling off. Soon
the ①/₂
the piece of skin starts rubbing against your
nails ①   are ①
other fingers or against objects that you

touch. The rubbing bothers the hangnail
or ©
and makes the skin red and sore.

What do you do with a hangnail? Don't
Don't ©
pick it. Don't bite it off. That will only

make it worse. Instead, cut it off with

scissors or nail clippers.

You can avoid getting hangnails by
¹/₂
taking (good) care of your hands and nails.

After washing your hands, dry them well.

Use lotion to keep dry skin smooth.

Source: Reprinted from "What Is a Hangnail?" in *3-2-1 Contact Magazine*, April 1988, p. 5. Copyright © Sesame Workshop, 1988.

Accountable Miscues

Full Miscues:	__3__	× 1	=	__3__
Half Miscues:	__2__	× ½	=	__1__
			TOTAL	__4__

COMPREHENSION CHECK

	Probed Recall	Free Recall

L 1. What is a hangnail?   **+**   ____

(A hangnail is a tough, little piece of skin that hangs loosely at the side of your fingernail.)

L 2. You get a hangnail when the skin around your nail gets to be what?   **+**   ____

(dry)

L 3. What shouldn't you do to a hangnail?   **+**   ____

(pick it) (bite it off)

L 4. How should a hangnail be removed?   **+**   ____

(with scissors or nail clippers)

I 5. Why can a hangnail hurt?   **DK**   ____

(Because the skin is red and sore from rubbing against something.)

C 6. Why should a young child ask an adult to remove a hangnail?   **±**   ____

(Young children may not know how to use scissors or nail clippers properly.)

(for safety reasons)

Children could get hurt with scissors.

Total Comprehension Errors   __1__
                                 (L & I)

PRIOR KNOWLEDGE

How much did you know about hangnails before reading this article?

I knew:

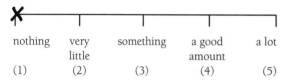

nothing	very little	something	a good amount	a lot
(1)	(2)	(3)	(4)	(5)

LEVEL OF INTEREST

How much did you like reading this article?

This article was:

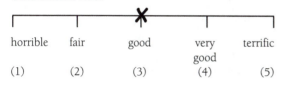

horrible	fair	good	very good	terrific
(1)	(2)	(3)	(4)	(5)

LEVELS OF WORD RECOGNITION AND COMPREHENSION

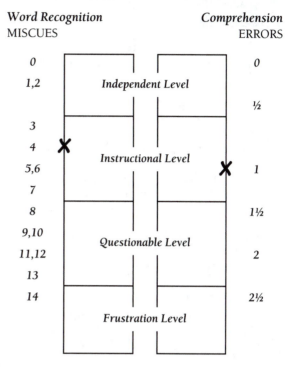

Word Recognition
MISCUES

0
1,2
3
4
5,6
7
8
9,10
11,12
13
14

Independent Level

Instructional Level

Questionable Level

Frustration Level

Comprehension
ERRORS

0
½
1
1½
2
2½

Smelly Stickers (4)

INTRODUCTION: Please read this article to learn how scratch and sniff or smelly stickers work.

Smelly Stickers

How do smelly stickers work? Almost any

smell you can think of, from pizza to
peanuts(½)   **compared**(1)
peanut butter, can be captured and put on a

scratch and sniff sticker. But there's more to

them than meets the nose!

Take a look at a sticker. All you see is a

picture of something. But hundreds of
DK(1)   **contents**(1)
thousands of super-small containers are
this(½)
glued to that sticker. Inside each container is
DK(1)
a little bit of fragrance. The smell may come
picked(1)
from the object pictured or it may have been

made in a laboratory with chemicals.

When you scratch the sticker, you break
release(½)
open some of the containers. That releases
do not(½)
the smell. But don't scratch too hard. You

only need to open a few to catch the scent
(½)
and your sticker will last (a lot) longer.
capped(1) **fair**(1)
Some smells can't be captured. So far,
be(1)
they can't put the smell of a hamburger on
won't(½)
a sticker. But wouldn't you rather smell the
it(1)
real thing . . . just before you bite∧into a

double cheeseburger?

Source: Reprinted from "How Do Smelly Stickers Work?," in *3-2-1 Contact Magazine,* March 1988, p. 33. Copyright © Sesame Workshop, 1988.

Accountable Miscues

Full Miscues: __9__ × 1 = __9__

Half Miscues: __6__ × $\frac{1}{2}$ = __3__

                              TOTAL __12__

COMPREHENSION CHECK

		Probed Recall	Free Recall
L 1.	Name a smell mentioned in the story that can be put on a smelly sticker.	+	____
	((pizza))		
	(peanut butter)		
L 2.	Name a smell that has not been put on a smelly sticker.	+	____
	(hamburger)		
	((cheeseburger))		
L 3.	There are hundreds of thousands of what glued to a smelly sticker?	DK	____
	(containers)		
L 4.	What happens when you scratch a smelly sticker?	—	____
	(You break open some of the containers. This releases a smell.)	**It smells.** (No response after examiner probed with "Why?")	
I 5.	Janet has a smelly sticker. Her smelly sticker lost its smell much faster than Bill's. Why?	DK	____
	(Janet scratched her smelly sticker too hard.)		
C 6.	Why do you think smelly stickers are made for people to buy?	$\frac{1}{2}$	____
	(for fun) (entertainment)	**To make kids feel better**	
	Note: If pupil's answer is "to smell," probe with: "But why do people buy them?"		

Total Comprehension Errors   __3__
                                       (L & I)

PRIOR KNOWLEDGE

How much did you know about smelly stickers before reading this article?

I knew:

nothing	very little	something	a good amount	a lot
(1)	(2)	(3)	(4)	(5)

LEVEL OF INTEREST

How much did you like reading this article?

This article was:

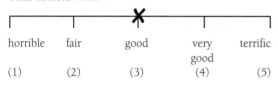

horrible	fair	good	very good	terrific
(1)	(2)	(3)	(4)	(5)

LEVELS OF WORD RECOGNITION AND COMPREHENSION

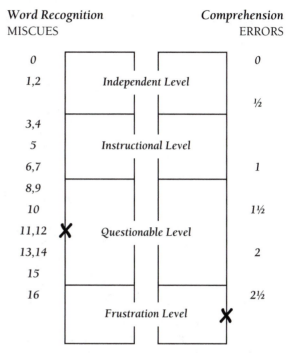

Word Recognition
MISCUES

Comprehension
ERRORS

0	*Independent Level*	0
1,2		½
3,4	*Instructional Level*	
5		
6,7		1
8,9		
10	*Questionable Level*	1½
11,12 ✗		
13,14		2
15		
16	*Frustration Level*	2½ ✗

Making Sense of Results That Don't Seem to Make Sense

Occasionally, there may be some difficulty in estimating reading levels because of inconsistencies in the data. In the first example, presented in Figure 2.4, it does not seem logical that a student could progress from worse to better on the Graded Reading Passages Test. However, such an outcome is possible if a student misunderstands the directions and does not concentrate on the meaning of the first passage read orally or if a student is very anxious during the testing session. In such situations, it is best to give the student the benefit of the doubt. In the case shown in Figure 2.4, the examiner considered the student's independent level to be grade 5.

The results in the second example, presented in Figure 2.5, also do not seem to make sense. However, when one notices the high prior knowledge given by the student for the sixth-grade passage, it appears obvious that this student's performance improved rather than declined because of her rich background of knowledge in the content of this selection. In this case, it is probably best *not* to give the student the benefit of the doubt because much of the material presented at this level would probably be too difficult for her to read.

Generally, in cases where the results are irregular or inconsistent, examiners should review the data from every section of the SIRI, as well as data collected from other sources, and use their best judgment in deciding on students' reading levels. In a few cases, an examiner may decide that the results are invalid and retest the student with another form of the SIRI. Invalid results may be due to (1) the student's anxiety, disinterest, or preoccupation with other matters, or (2) to the inexperience of the examiner in using a diagnostic tool. (*Note:* If a student appears to be overanxious, it may be wise to use the practice passage option described in Section Three.)

Cases of inconsistent or irregular results demonstrate that no IRI will produce perfect results each time it is used. Even though much attention has been given in the preparation of this instrument to setting the levels of the passages, "a student's ability to comprehend is not fixed or constant; rather, comprehension will vary across texts, tasks, and settings (prior knowledge and interest are two powerful factors that contribute to variability on reading tasks)" (Brozo, 1990, p. 523). Therefore, when there are inconsistencies in the data, teachers must use their best judgment in determining each student's independent, instructional, and frustration levels. After all,

FIGURE 2.4

Sample recording of student who misunderstood directions

	GRADED READING PASSAGES TEST				
	Narrative				
Grade Level	Word Recognition	Oral Comp.	List. Comp. (%)	Prior Knowledge Y–N	Interest 1–5
1					
2					
3					
4	IND	FRUST		N	4
5	IND	IND		N	4
6	IND	INST		N	5
7	INST	INST		N	3
8	FRUST	FRUST		N	3
9					

FIGURE 2.5

Sample recording of student with high prior knowledge score for a passage

GRADED READING PASSAGES TEST					
Expository					
Grade Level	Word Recognition	Oral Comp.	List. Comp. (%)	Prior Knowledge 1–5	Interest 1–5
1					
2					
3	IND	IND		1	4
4	INST	IND		2	3
5	QUEST/INST	QUEST/INST		1	4
6	QUEST/FRUST	IND		5	5
7	FRUST	FRUST		1	2
8					
9					

"the accurate use of IRI's requires judgment and interpretation, not the mechanical calculation or application of scores" (Johnson, Kress, & Pikulski, 1987, p. 13).

Summarizing the Results: Putting It All Together

The SIRI can provide the diagnostician with a wealth of information about a student's reading behaviors. The results can be used to identify areas of strength and pinpoint reading behaviors that require special attention.

It is advantageous for the teacher to have a complete picture of the student's reading performance before he or she develops a plan of action. This requires the diagnostician to draw conclusions about a learner's performance based on patterns found in the results of the SIRI. The SIRI Synthesis of Information Rubric found on pages 248–252 is provided to help the examiner "put it all together." Directions for using this rubric are provided on the form itself and in Section Three on pages 84–86. This rubric contains criteria to evaluate the student's performance in five major areas of reading measured by the SIRI and differentiates among different levels of performance within those criteria. The six major areas are

- Knowledge and perceptions of reading
- Reading interests
- Reflections on writing
- Oral fluency
- Word recognition
- Comprehension

The rubric also includes a category for describing student behaviors exhibited during testing.

More or fewer items on this rubric may be rated based on the number of SIRI components utilized by the examiner. Obviously, the teacher who administers the SIRI just to determine a student's placement in reading material will have less information about a learner's reading behaviors than the teacher who utilizes many of the diagnostic options described in Section Three and will, as a result, only be able to rate the student on some of the items included on the SIRI Synthesis of Information Rubric. For example, information gathered from the administration of the Graded

Words in Isolation Test (a diagnostic option) is needed to rate the student on the Word Recognition item Sight Vocabulary in Isolation.

As indicated above, decisions made about a student's performance should, whenever possible, be based on patterns rather than isolated behaviors. The teacher should review the results of more than one component of the SIRI as well as information gathered from classroom assessments when making a judgment about a student's performance on a specific skill or task. Three examples follow.

First, a student's responses to items 8, 9, and 10 on the Reading Reflections Interview and rating of the level of interest in each article or story read can be used by the examiner when completing the Reading Interests section of the SIRI Synthesis of Information Rubric. Second, the results of a student's performance on both the Graded Words in Context and the Graded Reading Passages Tests can be used to rate the student on the Word Recognition item Context Clues. Third, because the SIRI does not include a formal test to measure oral reading fluency, the diagnostician must use information gathered from the administration of the Graded Words in Context and the Graded Reading Passages tests to rate the student in this important area of reading.

In addition, the teacher may wish to utilize the results of a running record of a student's oral reading of classroom material (i.e., excerpt of a novel or magazine article). According to Richards (2000), reading fluency involves three components. These are reading pace or rate, the automaticity of word recognition, and reading with expression (the element of prosody). Each of these components is included as an item in the Oral Reading Fluency category of the rubric.

The examiner should consider a student's overall performance when completing the SIRI Synthesis of Information Rubric. For example, the oral reading fluency ratings for a third-grade student whose reading instructional level is estimated at the fifth grade may still be quite high even if she was unable to read material accurately, quickly, and in phrased units written at a sixth-grade level (determined to be her frustration level). At the same time, however, the oral reading fluency ratings for a student in sixth grade may be quite low even if he was able to read second-grade material accurately, quickly, and in phrased units but exhibited very little fluency with material written above that grade level.

The information recorded on the SIRI Synthesis of Information Rubric (as well as the Summary of Student Performance Sheet) can be placed in a learner's literacy portfolio. The results recorded at the beginning of the school year can be compared to the results obtained at the midpoint or end of the year as a result of administering different forms of the instruments (i.e., Form A of the Graded Reading Passages Test versus Form C of the same test) to determine whether progress has been made. The results for a student could also be compared from year to year.

The SIRI Synthesis of Information Rubric may be of less value for students functioning on an emergent literacy level. For these students, the teacher should utilize techniques such as the Dictated Story Assessment Strategy described below and record the results on the record form prepared for this strategy. (Refer to pages 245–247.)

Dictated Story Assessment Strategy

The purpose of this strategy is to obtain information on an emergent reader's performance with text. This part of the SIRI is used with students whose base level on the Graded Words in Context Test is below grade 1. The following materials are needed to implement this procedure:

- Pad of paper
- Sheet of carbon paper
- Set of photographs to stimulate discussion (pages 127, 129, 131, 133, 135, 137, 139, 141, 143, and 145)

- Photocopy of questions for photographs (pages 128, 130, 132, 134, 136, 138, 140, 142, 144, and 146)
- Dictated Story Assessment Strategy Record Form (pages 245–247)

The steps for administering the SIRI to examine emergent reading behaviors are the following:

1. Select a photograph for discussion.
2. Use the photograph to stimulate discussion.
3. Record the story dictated by the student.
4. Have the student read his or her dictated story.
5. Check the student's recognition of words in isolation.
6. Have the student copy his or her story.
7. Record the results on the Dictated Story Assessment Strategy Record Form.
8. Measure print and word awareness (if necessary).

A plan for administering this strategy is presented below, followed by a discussion of two sample cases. This one-day plan is designed for completion during the initial testing session. A quick list of instructions for using the Dictated Story Assessment Strategy is found on pages 243–244.

Step 1: Select a Photograph for Discussion

This book contains a collection of ten interesting photographs that will appeal to students of different ages and interests. Teachers may use these photographs to stimulate discussion for the eventual creation of a dictated story.

First, select three or four photographs that may be of interest to the student. Display these photographs in front of the student one at a time. Next, ask the student to choose a photograph to talk about. After a photograph is selected, give the student a minute or two to study it. If none of the photographs is of interest to the student, display other photographs from the collection or have the student select a photograph from another source such as a magazine, newspaper, or book. If discussion cannot be stimulated through a photograph or illustration, use an interesting activity, such as making whipped cream or experimenting with magnets, to capture the attention of the student. Regardless of the medium used, the main objective is to have the student dictate a story that can be used to diagnose strengths and weaknesses in reading.

Step 2: Use the Photograph to Stimulate Discussion

The dialog between teacher and student is based on the subject of the photograph and is used to prepare students for the next step—the creation of a dictated story.

Begin with the following questions: "Why did you choose this photograph?" Some students may respond with little prompting from the teacher. As a follow-up to these questions, it may only be necessary to say, "Please tell me more." Other students may require more direction from the teacher. A suggested list of additional questions to prompt or guide the discussion about each photograph is provided on the reverse side of each photograph. Since students will be viewing the photographs in Section Four of this book while this strategy is being administered, it is suggested that examiners have their own photocopy of these questions to which they may refer. Teachers must decide which questions to ask and should not feel restricted to ask only questions from the lists.

Samples of lower- and higher-level questions appear on these lists. For example, in the photograph of the mangy camel, the question "What do you see in this photograph?" is at a literal-level (observing details), "Why is there a fence in this photograph?" is an interpretive-level question, and "Would you like to visit this camel? Why?" is a creative-level question.

Step 3: Record the Story Dictated by the Student

The teacher should end the discussion when he or she feels the student is prepared to dictate a story about the photograph. Keep the photograph in front of the student. At the appropriate moment say:

> "Now, I want you to remember what we just talked about and tell me a story about this photograph. As you talk, I will write down your thoughts and ideas. If you wish, you may look at the photograph. Please begin."

When taking dictation, use a sheet of carbon paper so that there are two copies of the story. The original will serve as the student's copy and the examiner may use the carbon to maintain a record of the student's performance. Write in a larger size of print when recording the stories of younger children.

If desired, a computer may be used in place of paper and pencil to record a student's thoughts. To administer the Dictated Story Assessment Strategy with a computer, the teacher will need access to a computer system (computer, monitor, printer) and a word processing program. When the strategy is administered this way, have the student dictate the story in front of the monitor. The use of word processing software permits a student's thoughts to be entered into the computer and displayed immediately on the monitor's screen. When the dictation is completed, print two copies of the story (and do not forget to save the story on a disk). Again, one copy will be used by the student, the other by the examiner.

During the dictation process, note how much prompting is required to get the student to produce ideas. Say each word aloud as the story is being written. Allow the student to make changes in the text as the dictation progresses. However, to maintain an accurate record of the dictation, the teacher should not make changes in the student's story. For example, if the student says, "The camel have one hump," record this incorrect usage as dictated.

The student should be encouraged to dictate no less than three nor more than six sentences. Assessment is more manageable if the dictated story is not too long. However, be careful not to stifle students who are very verbal.

At the completion of the dictation ask, "What would be a good title for your story?" Although this question may be asked at the outset, it is preferable to have the entire story dictated before the title is requested. At that point in the activity students are better prepared to generate an appropriate title for the story. Of course, teachers should use their best judgment in determining the appropriate moment to ask the title question. Write the title, and below it enter a credit line (e.g., by Daniel Cohen) to give the student a sense of ownership of the story. The title question may need to be rephrased for some students such as younger children and language-different learners. An alternative question is, Can you think of a good name for this story?

Step 4: Have the Student Read the Dictated Story

First, follow the standard procedures for administering a language experience activity. Beginning with the title, read the story back to the student, pointing to or running your hand under each word as it is read. Then, read the story again, but this time with the student. Now, determine how much of the story the student can read back without teacher assistance. Place a copy of the story in front of the student. Point to the title and ask the student to begin reading. Stop the oral reading when the student seems frustrated. If this happens, try to have the student read back only selected parts of the story (e.g., sentences or parts of sentences). If there is still a problem, ask, "Are there any words in your story that you can pronounce for me? Please read them," or point to a specific word in the text, such as a student's name, and ask, "Can you pronounce this word for me?" Maintain a record of the student's performance on the second copy of the story. Place a check mark above each word pronounced correctly, and use the Marking System for Oral Reading Miscues (presented in Table 2.1) to record miscues in word recognition. In the following example, Nicholas dictated a story based on Photograph 6. He read this story fluently, pronouncing most of the words correctly.

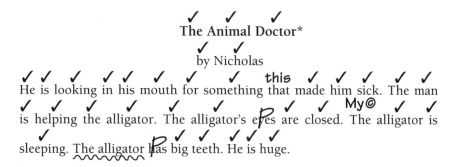

The Animal Doctor*

by Nicholas

He is looking in his mouth for something that made him sick. The man is helping the alligator. The alligator's eyes are closed. The alligator is sleeping. The alligator has big teeth. He is huge.

If a student is unable to read any portion of the story, or is able to read only selected parts, or attempts to read the entire story but makes miscues that account for more than 10 percent of the words in the text (an indication of frustration level on the Graded Reading Passages Test), it may be fruitless to continue on to Step 5 of the assessment. (Refer to items in Part II of the Dictated Story Assessment Strategy Record Form found on page 246).

For example, Peter dictated a forty-four-word story to his teacher. This word count included the story title and the credit line. In his oral reading, Peter read the entire story. However, his teacher recorded four full miscues and two half miscues. Thus, Peter's total miscue count was five and his miscue percentage was computed to be 11.3 (rounded off to the nearest tenth). This figure was obtained by dividing the miscue count (5) by the total number of words in the dictated story (44). Based on Peter's miscue percentage, his teacher decided to skip the steps for assessing word recognition and follow the procedures for measuring print and word awareness. (Refer to Part IV of the Dictated Story Assessment Strategy Record Form found on page 247.) The directions for using this part of the Dictated Story Assessment Strategy are presented in Step 8. Because Peter's miscue percentage was just below the 10 percent minimum, another teacher could just as easily have decided to give Peter the benefit of the doubt and check his performance in words in isolation and comprehension of content. In cases of this type, the decision to skip to Part IV should be based on the best judgment of the teacher. Obviously, the decision regarding which part of the strategy to administer next is much easier to make if a student is able to pronounce correctly only 50 percent of the words in the dictated story.

Step 5: Check the Student's Recognition of Words in Isolation

Use this part of the session to check a student's ability to recognize story words in isolation.

Begin by selecting five to seven words from the story to present in scrambled order. List these words vertically on a sheet of paper, using carbon paper so that both teacher and student may keep a copy. Do not let the student see the list. Begin with words that will probably be easier for the student to recognize, and spread the more difficult words as evenly as possible throughout the list (Dixon & Nessel, 1983, p. 34). Write in the student's name and date of testing on the examiner's copy. Also on this sheet, label two columns for recording the results, the first for flashed

---

*This example of a dictated story was provided by Beth Machado.

presentation and the second for delayed presentation. A sample record of Nicholas's performance (examiner's copy) follows:*

Student's Name: _____ **Nicholas** _____   Date: _____ **Oct. 15** _____

	Flashed	*Delayed*
man	+	
him	+	
alligator	+	
sick	slept	+
looking	look	+
big	+	
mouth	DK	moth

Percent of Correct Responses: _____ **57.1** _____ %

These words are to be shown in both flashed and delayed presentations. During the flashed presentation, expose each word less than a second to assess recognition on sight. It is useful to have a slotted card to reveal each word or an index card to slide under each word as it is being exposed. Place a + next to each word recognized on sight in the first column of the teacher's record sheet. Keep all notations on this sheet out of the student's view. If the word is not pronounced correctly, record the miscue according to the coding system described earlier in Section Two for the Graded Words in Context Test (see pages 19–20). When the student hesitates, have him or her move on to the next word. Write **DK** (don't know) on the appropriate line in the first column. Corrected miscues are counted as acceptable responses. At the bottom of the Flashed column, calculate the percent of correct responses by dividing the number of words pronounced correctly by the number of words on the list. So, in the above example, seven words were presented in the flashed presentation, of which four were pronounced correctly. The percentage of correct responses is, therefore, 57.1 (rounded off to the nearest tenth).

Missed words are then shown again, but this time the presentation is delayed to examine skills in decoding. Record the results of this assessment on the corresponding teacher's copy of the word list in the Delayed column. Place a + next to each word recognized. If the student takes too much time on a word (about 10 seconds or when it is apparent the word is unknown), write **DK** on the appropriate line in the second column and have the student move on to the next word on the list. Use the coding system mentioned above for recording all miscues.

Step 6: Have the Student Copy the Dictated Story

Give the student an opportunity to make a copy of the story. Provide the pupil with a sheet of lined paper and a pencil. Place a copy of the story in front of the student and direct him or her to reproduce the teacher-prepared version. If this task is too difficult, encourage the student to copy down a portion of the story, such as the title, a sentence, or a few words. Carefully observe the student's attempt to produce a copy of the story.

---

*This example of the Recognition of Words in Isolation procedure was provided by Beth Machado.

Step 7: Record the Results on the Dictated Story Assessment Strategy Form

Summarize the results of this procedure by filling out the Dictated Story Assessment Strategy Record Form. A sample record of a student's performance is shown in the Appendix on pages 53–55. Attach any test materials to this form, such as teacher- and student-produced copies of the dictated story and the results of the Recognition of Words in Isolation procedure.

Step 8: Measure Print and Word Awareness (If Necessary)

The following diagnostic procedure is used with students who have difficulty reading their story on their own without teacher assistance. The technique assesses an emergent reader's basic awareness of print and words. The strategy described here is based on a method for the informal diagnosis of a student's awareness of the technical aspects of print and words (Agnew, 1982). The following directions match the steps outlined in Part IV of the Dictated Story Assessment Strategy Record Form on page 247. Record the results on this form. Directions to the student appear in quotes.

Identifying Boundaries of Written Words

"Show me a word from the story."

Have the student point to any word from the story and cup his or her hands around the word to indicate knowledge of where a word begins and ends. (An alternate procedure is to have the student point to the beginning of the word with one finger of one hand and the end of the word with a finger of the other hand.) Do not ask the student to pronounce the word. Repeat this task with two or three other words.

Matching Words
Write a word from the story on a pad of paper. See if the student can find the matching word in the story. Repeat this task with several other words.

Matching Sentences
Write a sentence from the story on a pad of paper. See if the student can find the matching sentence in the story. Repeat this task with several other sentences.

Building a Word from a Model
Select a target word such as *help* from the story. Highlight this target word in the story or rewrite this word on a sheet of paper. Prepare tile-sized pieces of paper, and place each letter of the target word on a separate piece of paper. Mix up the order of the letters and display them. Point to the target word from the story, and ask the student to build the target word using the separate letters. As the student is completing this task, ask for the names of the letters being used. Repeat this activity with two or three different target words from the story.

Supplying a Spoken Word That Begins with the Same Phoneme as a Given Printed Word
Point to and identify a word in the dictated story that begins with a single consonant. Ask the student if he or she can think of a word that begins with the same sound heard at the beginning of the word identified. Repeat the task with three or four other words. Each word should begin with a different initial consonant sound.

Understanding Terms
Understanding words such as *beginning, end,* and *same* is essential if the student is to comprehend directions given by the teacher. Repeat each task as often as

necessary to assess a student's knowledge of these terms. These strategies are especially useful with students who have limited English proficiency.

Beginning and End
"Where is the beginning of the story?"
"Point to the beginning of the story."
"Where is the end of the story?"
"Point to the end of the story."
"This word is _____." (Point to the word in the story and pronounce it.)
"Where is the beginning of this word?" "Where is the end of this word?"

Same
"This word is _____." (Point to the word in the story and name it. Write down the sentence that contains the word on a separate sheet of paper.) "Now look at this sentence. Point to the same word."

Different
"This word is _____." (Point to the word in the story and name it. Write two words from the story on a separate sheet of paper. One is the target word, and the other is a different word from the story.) "Here are two words from the story. One of them is different from _____." (Repeat the word that was just identified in the story.) "Point to the word that is different from _____." (Name the target word.)

First
"Here is the last word in the story." (Identify this word in the story.) "Point to the first word in the story."

Last
"Here is the first letter in the word _____." (Point to this word in the story as it is named.) "Point to the last letter in the word _____." (Repeat the word just identified.)

Line
"Run your finger under a line in the story." (Also observe to assess skill in left-to-right directional orientation.)

Top
"Point to the top of the page."

Bottom
"Point to the bottom of the page."

Recognizing Letters of the Alphabet
"Point to any letters you can name in the story." (Have the student recognize as many letters as necessary. Note the student's knowledge of uppercase and lowercase letters on the record form.)

Sample Cases

Here are the dictated stories and data analyses of two students who experienced the Dictated Story Assessment Strategy.

The first student, Theresa, is a 6-year-old student in first grade. The examiner discontinued administering the Graded Words in Context Test after Theresa missed the first two target words on the primer-level sentence set. She did not miss any words on the preprimer-level sentence set. As a result of her performance on this test, the examiner decided to administer the Dictated Story Assessment Strategy. A record of her participation in this strategy appears on pages 53–55 in the Appendix at the end of this section.

When she was given three photographs to select from, Theresa chose to talk about the picture of the mangy camel. After some discussion, Theresa was able to dictate the following four-sentence story with a little prompting from the teacher.

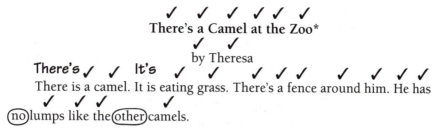

There's a Camel at the Zoo*

by Theresa

There is a camel. It is eating grass. There's a fence around him. He has no lumps like the other camels.

An analysis of the story and a review of the assessment session that followed revealed that the story Theresa created made some sense. She presented accurate information about the photograph. However, the four sentences she dictated did not represent a complete thought. Also, she didn't show much originality in the expression of her ideas.

Theresa was able to read sentences from her dictated story after the examiner read the story back to her. She made miscues that accounted for more than 10 percent of the words in the text (13.8 percent). The types of miscues she made did not, for the most part, alter the meaning of the text (except when she omitted the word *no* in "He has no lumps like the other camels."). Theresa showed some hesitation in generating a title for her story. After a few minutes, she decided to title it "There's a Camel at the Zoo."

Because Theresa's miscue percentage was below the minimum of 90 percent, the examiner decided to administer the Measuring Print and Word Awareness part of this strategy. The results showed that Theresa has an excellent awareness of the technical aspects of print and has already developed many of the emergent reading skills prerequisite to instruction in beginning reading. The examiner recommended that Theresa have more opportunities to dictate stories and practice reading them. These activities would help Theresa to expand her sight vocabulary, master strategies in decoding words, and develop fluency in reading. It was also recommended that Theresa read commercially produced preprimer-level materials.

The second student is also a 6-year-old first-grader. Her name is Crystal. The examiner discontinued administering the Graded Words in Context Test after Crystal missed two target words from the grade 1 sentence set. She did not miss any target words on the preprimer set and missed only one word on the primer-level sentence set. Based on these results, the examiner decided to have Crystal experience the Dictated Story Assessment Strategy. (The summary of Crystal's performance is based, in part, on information recorded on the dictated story record form, which is not included in this book.)

Crystal also selected the photograph of the mangy camel and had no difficulty dictating the following story about this animal.

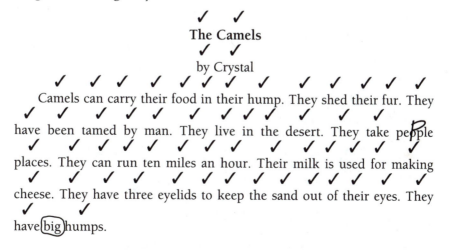

The Camels

by Crystal

Camels can carry their food in their hump. They shed their fur. They have been tamed by man. They live in the desert. They take people places. They can run ten miles an hour. Their milk is used for making cheese. They have three eyelids to keep the sand out of their eyes. They have big humps.

---

*This example of a dictated story was provided by Dana Silva.

She was very verbal and enjoyed sharing her knowledge with the diagnostician. Crystal's dictated story went beyond the information provided in the photograph. The details in her story showed that she had good prior knowledge of the habitat of this animal. Crystal used a variety of words to express her ideas. She was able to give a title that was appropriate to the story but not to the photograph.

Crystal could read back most of the story after the teacher read it to her aloud. She was quite fluent and did not make any miscues disruptive to the meaning of the text. When seven words from the story were presented to her in isolation, Crystal was able to recognize three of these words on sight and the remaining four in a delayed exposure. Finally, Crystal found the copying task to be laborious and, as a result, quit after copying the title and the first two sentences of her story.

The results showed that Crystal is highly verbal and prepared for instruction in beginning reading. It would appear that she, too, would benefit from the language experience approach to reading instruction. Crystal should also be given the opportunity to read material written on the preprimer or primer level.

The examiner recommended further assessment of Crystal through some of the diagnostic options described in Section Three. These might include (1) reintroducing the camel story the next day to determine how much was retained from the previous day's dictation and (2) reading selections from the Graded Reading Passages Test aloud to determine Crystal's listening comprehension level.

For students who read on or below a grade 1 level, the SIRI ends with the completion of this strategy, unless the teacher wishes to utilize any of the diagnostic options for the Dictated Story Assessment Strategy described in Section Three.

APPENDIX

Dictated Story Assessment Strategy Record Form

Student's Name: __Theresa_____ Sex: __F__ Age: __6__ years __5__ months

School: __Martin Luther King, Jr.__ School System: __Providence_____ Grade Placement: __1__

Examiner: __Dana M. Silva_____ Date of Administration: __11/30_____

Source of Stimulus: __Photograph_____ Topic of Dictated Story: __Mangy Camel____
(i.e., photograph, object, activity, etc.)

		FOR THE MOST PART	TO A CERTAIN DEGREE	NOT AT ALL	NOT APPLICABLE OR OBSERVABLE
		(Place check on line in appropriate column.)			

I.   QUALITY OF DICTATED STORY

		FOR THE MOST PART	TO A CERTAIN DEGREE	NOT AT ALL	NOT APPLICABLE OR OBSERVABLE
A.	Does the student present ideas with little prompting from the teacher?	✓			
B.	Does the story make sense?		✓		
C.	Are the ideas/events presented in a logical sequence?			✓	
D.	Does the student speak in complete sentences?	✓			
E.	Does the student use proper grammatical structures?	✓			
	(*Note:* Make notation below if English is a second language or if the student is using a dialect of American English.)				
F.	Are ideas expressed with a variety of words?		✓		
G.	Does the student express ideas that show uniqueness and originality?		✓		
H.	Is the student able to give an appropriate title for the story?		✓		

Comments:

Theresa's story consisted of four sentences about the camel. The sentences did not relate to one another.

II.   LANGUAGE FACILITY

    A.   Story Read by Student After Teacher Has Read Story Aloud

        Check ONE that applies:

      _____✓_____   1.   The student read back most of the story.

      _____   2.   The student read back only selected parts of the story (i.e., sentences, parts of sentences).

      _____   3.   The student read back only a few words and/or short phrases.

      _____   4.   The student was unable to read back any part of the story.

	FOR THE MOST PART	TO A CERTAIN DEGREE	NOT AT ALL	NOT APPLICABLE OR OBSERVABLE
	(Place check on line in appropriate column.)			

    B.   Word Recognition

	FOR THE MOST PART	TO A CERTAIN DEGREE	NOT AT ALL	NOT APPLICABLE OR OBSERVABLE
1. Was the recognition of words automatic (fluent) throughout the reading?	✓			
2. Were miscues NOT disruptive to the meaning of the text?		✓		
3. Can the student recognize words from the story presented in isolation with flashed exposure?		✓		
4. Can the student recognize words from the story presented in isolation with delayed exposure?	✓			

Comments:

III.   WRITING/COPYING SKILLS

	FOR THE MOST PART	TO A CERTAIN DEGREE	NOT AT ALL	NOT APPLICABLE OR OBSERVABLE
Is the student able to copy the story accurately?	✓			

Comments:

IV. PRINT AND WORD AWARENESS

Consider administering this part if

1. The student is unable to read back any part of the story.

2. The student can read back only a few words and/or phrases.

3. The student makes miscues that account for more than 10 percent of the words in the text.

	FOR THE MOST PART	TO A CERTAIN DEGREE	NOT AT ALL	NOT APPLICABLE OR OBSERVABLE
	(Place check on line in appropriate column.)			

A. Is the student able to

		FOR THE MOST PART	TO A CERTAIN DEGREE	NOT AT ALL	NOT APPLICABLE OR OBSERVABLE
1.	Identify the boundaries of written words?	✓			
2.	Match words?	✓			
3.	Match sentences?	✓			
4.	Build a word from a model?	✓			
5.	Supply a spoken word that begins with the same phoneme as a given printed word?	✓			

B. Does the student understand terms such as

		FOR THE MOST PART	TO A CERTAIN DEGREE	NOT AT ALL	NOT APPLICABLE OR OBSERVABLE
1.	Beginning?	✓			
2.	End?	✓			
3.	Same?	✓			
4.	Different?	✓			
5.	First?	✓			
6.	Last?	✓			
7.	Line?	✓			
8.	Top?	✓			
9.	Bottom?	✓			

C. Can the student name letters?

(Circle the letters identified.)

A ⓐ	G g	L l	Q q	V v
B b	Ⓗⓗ	M m	R r	W w
ⒸⒸ	I i	N n	S ⓢ	X x
D d	J j	O ⓞ	ⓉⓉ	Y y
E e	K k	P p	U u	Ⓩ z
F f				

Comments: **Theresa was able to identify every letter that the examiner pointed to in her story.**

Based on a case submitted by Dana Silva.

Source: Part IV adapted from Agnew, A.T. (1982). Using children's dictated stories to assess code consciousness. In *The Reading Teacher, 35,* 450–454. Copyright by the International Reading Association. All rights reserved.

Diagnostic Options of the SIRI

A lthough the results collected from the initial administration of the SIRI can be used for placement decisions, sometimes more information is required. When this is so, the SIRI can provide examiners with several diagnostic options. It is the responsibility of the examiner to decide which, if any, of these diagnostic alternatives to employ. The procedures for utilizing each diagnostic option are presented in this section. Refer to the graphic organizer in Figure 1.3 (see page 13) for an overview of the options available.

Writing Reflections Interview (WRI)

The Writing Reflections Interview (WRI) is an introspective procedure for gathering information about the affective elements that shape the learner's interaction with text. The WRI provides the reader with an opportunity to reflect on his or her writing experiences. The responses to the questions often bring to light information not revealed by traditional diagnostic techniques.

The WRI consists of thirteen open-ended questions that explore the student's knowledge of the writing process, perceptions of writing and his or her writing ability, and interest in writing. The writing process questions explore the student's understanding of the goals and purposes of writing, the perceptions questions explore the student's knowledge of different writing task requirements, both in terms of the task demands and the teacher's criteria for evaluation, and the interest in reading questions reveal information about a writer's likes and dislikes.

The form for recording the results of this interview (pages 254–256) includes directions for administering the interview, provides the questions to be asked, and contains a section for summarizing the results. There is no student test material because all the items are read by the examiner. Because reading and writing share similar processes (Tompkins, 2001), the diagnostician should review the results of the Reading and Writing Reflections Interviews to determine whether a student's understandings of and reactions to these areas of literacy are similar or different. As an example, let's compare two students' responses to parallel questions from the WRI and RRI.

Example 1: Andrew, Grade 4

Knowledge of Reading

1. What is reading?

   Reading is being able to pronounce words correctly.

Knowledge of Writing

  1. What is writing?

Writing is knowing how to spell and use good grammar.

Example 2: Cynthia, Grade 4

Knowledge of Reading

  1. What is reading?

Reading is getting meaning and learning from text.

Knowledge of Writing

  1. What is writing?

Writing is being able to share your ideas with others.

These examples show that Andrew has a rather narrow view of literacy because his responses stress the mechanical aspects of reading and writing, and Cynthia has a better understanding of the nature of reading and writing because her responses stress the meaning aspects of these processes.

Note: As a supplement to the WRI, the teacher may wish to administer the Writing Attitude Survey (commonly referred to as the Garfield the Cat survey). This instrument is included in an article by Kear, Coffman, McKenna, and Ambrosio (2000). This survey provides quantitative estimates of important aspects of children's attitudes toward writing. It can be administered individually or to an entire class in a few minutes.

Graded Words in Context Test

A function of the Graded Words in Context Test is to help the teacher identify the passage with which to begin the oral reading portion of the inventory. However, this test can also be used to (1) determine a range of levels, from base to ceiling; (2) assess skill in contextual analysis; and (3) measure progress made by using a parallel form of this test.

Base and Ceiling Levels

It was stated in the previous section that when the Graded Words in Context Test is used to find a base level, the examiner discontinues testing when the student misses two target words at a particular level. Additional information can be gathered if the teacher continues testing beyond the base level in order to find the ceiling level. The steps required to obtain this information are discussed below.

Directions

After the base level has been determined, continue testing by having the student read target words in sentence sets of increasing difficulty until five target words in a sentence set are missed (a score of 75 percent when there are twenty sentences in the set). The results is the student's ceiling level. This rule of 75 percent applies to sentence set levels one through eight where there are twenty sentences in each set. The criterion for ceiling level for the preprimer and primer sets is two target words missed (a score of 80 percent) because there are only ten items in each of these lower-level sets.

As the task becomes more difficult, observe how well students are able to utilize strategies needed to recognize unfamiliar words. For example, when a difficult word is encountered, does the student read to the end of the sentence and then return to the unfamiliar word to attempt it again, stop and try to sound it out, or just skip the word and continue reading?

Use the system for recording responses explained on pages 19–20 in Section Two, where only miscues of target words are recorded. However, for a more complete record of a student's performance, note miscues of both target and nontarget words.

For this diagnostic option, use the Marking System for Oral Reading Miscues presented in Table 2.1 on page 22. An example of how the results are recorded is shown in Figure 3.1.

In this illustration, Jessica's teacher went beyond the standard method for administering the Graded Words in Context Test and continued testing to obtain a ceiling level. Jessica reached this point on the grade 5 sentence set when she missed five target words. A review of the data shows that Jessica made good use of context to self-correct deviations from meaning. The examiner noted that when Jessica encountered an unfamiliar word and made a miscue, she read to the end of the sentence, realized she had erred, and returned to the target word to self-correct her miscue (items 6, 11, 16, and 19). For item 11, Jessica skipped the target word, read to the end of the sentence, and returned to pronounce this omitted word correctly.

Skill in Contextual Analysis

The Graded Words in Context Test can also be used to assess a student's use of context to figure out the meanings of unfamiliar words. The following procedure is used to implement this strategy.

Directions

Identify a sentence set that has words unfamiliar (in meaning) to the student. This could include words that were correctly decoded but not understood. Select a sentence with a potentially unfamiliar target word in a good contextual setting. An example is the following sentence: It pays to be **cautious** when driving a car on an icy road.

Write this word on a sheet of paper for the student to see. Point to it and ask,

"Can you tell me what the word *cautious* means?"

If the reader knows the meaning of this word out of context, present another target word the same way. However, if the student does not know the meaning of this word, reveal the word in context, read the sentence aloud from the student's copy (pointing to each word), and ask,

"Now can you tell me what the word *cautious* might mean?"

If the student can provide a good definition of the word in context, ask,

"How did you figure out what this word means?"

Probe to determine whether the reader understands how context can be used to unlock the meaning of an unknown word.

If the reader is unable to provide a good definition, then continue testing with additional sentences until a judgment can be made about the student's ability to use context. (Because sentences are read aloud by the teacher, sets at or above the ceiling level can be used to assess this skill.)

FIGURE 3.1

Example of Jessica's ceiling level performance on the Graded Words in Context Test (Form A)

Grade 5

1.	conquer	+	The terrible king tried to **conquer** the world.
2.	injure	+	If you are not careful, this saw will **injure** you.
3.	plantation	−	Many crops can (be) grown on a large **plantation**. *(grow, planatation)*
4.	wrist	+	He wore a gold watch on his **wrist**.
5.	gratitude	−	I am filled with **gratitude** for the favor you did. *(graduate)*
6.	attract	+	Sweets can **attract** flies at a picnic.* *(eat ©)*
7.	delightful	+	One day we had a **delightful** ride in the country.
8.	furnish	+	Can you **furnish** this room with only two chairs?
9.	emerald	+	An **emerald** is (a) bright green stone or jewel.
10.	manufacturer	+	The **manufacturer** of this car also makes trucks.
11.	shrewd	+	She was (shrewd) to buy a house ten years ago.* *(©)*
12.	treatment	+	This pill is a good **treatment** for that illness.
13.	obvious	−	It is **obvious** that two and two make four. *(obovious)*
14.	satisfactory	+	He was happy to earn a **satisfactory** grade in spelling.
15.	assignment	+	Your **assignment** for tomorrow is to read Chapter 5.
16.	brightness	+	The **brightness** of the sun can damage your eyes.* *(brights ©)*
17.	dreary	−	A cloudy, rainy day is a **dreary** day. *(deary)*
18.	universe	+	Our earth is but a small part of (the) **universe**. *(rether)*
19.	somersault	+	We are learning (to) **somersault** in gym class.* *(supper ©)*
20.	prehistoric	−	The dinosaur is an example of (a) **prehistoric** animal. *(periostic)*
		75 %	

*Jessica read to the end of the sentence and returned to the target word to correct her pronunciation.

Based on an example provided by Jill Giarrusso.

Use the results to discover strategies used by readers to recognize unfamiliar words in context. Through this procedure, the examiner can learn the degree to which semantic, syntactic, and graphophonic cues are utilized by readers when difficult words are encountered. *Semantic cues* involve using the surrounding text (individual words and combinations of words) to predict the meaning of unfamiliar words. *Syntactic cues* involve understanding the grammatical relationships within sentence patterns to help construct meaning. *Graphophonic cues* involve utilizing the print itself (recognition of letters and the sounds they represent) to decode words in the text.

Parallel Forms of the Test

There are two forms of the Graded Words in Context Test included in this book. Both forms are used in conjunction with the Graded Reading Passages Test to determine placement in reading material. Form A should be used in the initial testing of students, usually at the beginning of the school year. Form B can be used a few or many months later to measure progress in reading. Form B can also be used to retest students when there is doubt about the validity of the results. This second administration may be necessary to verify or disconfirm the results of the first administration. The diagnostic options described above can be used with both forms of this test.

Graded Words in Isolation Test

The Graded Words in Isolation Test is administered to reveal how students recognize words in isolation. (Student test material appears on pages 148–151 and 152–155; examiner's record form appears on pages 258–262 and 263–267; and the quick list of instructions appears on page 257.) It is not meant to substitute for the Graded Words in Context Test as an instrument for placing students in the Graded Reading Passages. Instead, the Graded Words in Isolation Test is used when the teacher wants to examine students' level of sight vocabulary and decoding ability.

In the administration of this instrument, words are first exposed in flashed presentation to determine the number that the student can identify on sight. Automaticity is important in word recognition because, according to van den Bosch, van Bon, and Schreuder (1995, p. 111), ". . . a failure to decode words rapidly lies at the heart of reading difficulty." Words not identified on sight are then exposed in a delayed presentation to determine the number the student can recognize by applying rules for decoding.

As with the Graded Words in Context Test, there are two forms of this test available—one for initial testing and another for verifying the results of the initial administration or for monitoring the progress of students later in the school year. The words selected for each form are the same as those found in comparable forms of the Graded Words in Context Test (i.e., Form A of the Graded Words in Isolation Test and Form A of the Graded Words in Context Test, and Form B of both tests). The difference is, of course, in the mode of presentation. As a result of administering both tests, teachers can compare strategies used by students to identify words in context versus words in isolation.

Directions

First, decide whether to use a form of the Graded Words in Isolation Test that matches or does not match the Graded Words in Context Test already administered. Either type of administration can reveal important information about how a student recognizes words. Of course, when matching forms are used, the teacher must take into account the practice effect of the Graded Words in Context Test. To minimize this effect, allow at least 1 or 2 weeks between the two administrations.

Have a student's copy of the test and an examiner's copy of the corresponding form to record student responses. Use the student's base level score on the Graded Words in Context Test to determine the level on which to begin the Graded Words in Isolation Test. For example, if a student attained a base level of grade 3 on the Graded Words in Context Test, begin with the grade 3 list on the Graded Words in Isolation Test. Follow the identification system outlined in Section Two for the Graded Words in Context Test to determine the grade level of each list on the student's copy. Based on the above example, select the list with the code for grade 3 (TH). A sample record of a student's performance on Form B of this test is presented in Figure 3.2.

FIGURE 3.2

Sample recording of Graded Words in Isolation Test (Form B)

Grade 3

		Flashed	Delayed
1.	chop	+	
2.	expect	+	
3.	knife	+	
4.	visitor	+	
5.	lettuce	+	
6.	insist	+	
7.	fry	+	
8.	serious	+	
9.	husband	+	
10.	sugar	+	
11.	complain	+	
12.	refrigerator	+	
13.	alarm	+	
14.	tongue	+	
15.	kettle	+	
16.	princess	+	
17.	difference	+	
18.	obey	+	
19.	useful	+	
20.	immediate	+	

100 %

Grade 4

		Flashed	Delayed
1.	cane	+	
2.	wisdom	+	
3.	duty	+	
4.	publish	+	
5.	argue	+	
6.	cautious	+	
7.	mosquito	+	
8.	habit	+	
9.	bitter	+	
10.	original	+	
11.	uniform	+	
12.	jealous	DK	jails
13.	valuable	+	
14.	honest	+	
15.	nation	+	
16.	patience	+	
17.	flake	+	
18.	raincoat	+	
19.	entertain	+	
20.	suggestion	+	

95 %

Grade 5

		Flashed	Delayed
1.	shack	shake	+
2.	baggage	+	
3.	error	+	
4.	cabinet	+	
5.	legal	+	
6.	weird	+	
7.	series	+	
8.	fumble	+	
9.	accurate	DK	+
10.	machinery	+	
11.	operation	+	
12.	dismiss	+	
13.	eventual	evental	evental
14.	poisonous	DK	+
15.	nuisance	newseeance	newseeance
16.	worthless	+	
17.	landmark	+	
18.	organize	+	
19.	investigate	investage	+
20.	conclusion	conkersant	+

65 %

Give the following directions to the student:

"I want you to read some lists of words for me. Some of these words will be easy, and others may be more difficult. Try hard to read as many words as possible. I will be taking notes as you read the words on each list. This is to help me remember what you have read. Do you have any questions? Let's begin with this word."

Open the test booklet to the appropriate page, place the booklet in front of the student, and select the appropriate list. Then point to the first word at the top of the page and have the student pronounce this word quickly (exposure time is less than a second). If this word is pronounced correctly, place a + next to the word in the Flashed column on the record sheet. All notations made on this form should be kept from the student's view. If the word is not pronounced correctly, record the miscue according to the coding system described on pages 19–20 for the Graded Words in Context Test. When the student hesitates, have him or her move on to the next word. Write **DK** (don't know) on the appropriate line in the first column. Corrected miscues are counted as acceptable responses. Move down the list of words at a steady pace. It is useful to have a slotted card to reveal each word or an index card to slide under each word as it is being exposed.

When all words on a list have been exposed, return to the words that were missed and present them again, but this time with delayed exposure. Place a + in the second column next to each word recognized. If the student takes too much time with a word (about 10 seconds or when it becomes apparent that the word is unknown) or says that he or she does not know a word, write in **DK**. Record miscues by using the same coding system as before.

At the bottom of the form, record the percent of words pronounced correctly in the flashed presentation test. Each correct response is worth 5 points on lists for grade 1 through grade 8. Each correct response is worth 10 points on preprimer- and primer-level lists.

Continue to administer this test until the base and ceiling levels are reached. Use only the results of the flashed presentations to determine these levels. The base level is the highest list at which the student is able to read every word correctly. The ceiling level is the list on which the student misses five or more words (a score of 75 percent or less) on a list. The results of the Graded Words in Isolation Test can be compared to the results of the Graded Words in Context Test to see how well students are able to identify words in different modes of presentation: flashed in isolation, untimed in isolation, and presented in context.

Practice Passages for the Graded Reading Passages Test

The examiner has the option of administering one of two practice passages for the Graded Reading Passages Test. (Student test material appears on pages 156–157; examiner's record form appears on pages 268–271; and the quick list of instructions appears on pages 193–194.) The first selection is intended for those students who are reading on a first- or second-grade level, and the second passage is written for those students who are reading on a third-grade level or higher.

Directions
First, decide which students will be administered the practice, or warm-up, passages. Students with a high level of test anxiety or students unaccustomed to the format of this test might benefit from experiencing a warm-up passage since these practice passages are meant to prepare such students for the Graded Reading Passages Test.

Use the results of the Graded Words in Context Test to determine which practice passage to administer. If the student has a grade 1 or grade 2 base level on the

Graded Words in Context Test, select the first passage. If the student's base level is grade 3 or higher, select the second passage.

The directions for administering a practice passage are, for the most part, the same as for the Graded Reading Passages Test (see pages 20–31). Because this is a practice passage, maintaining a record of the student's performance is optional.

Graded Reading Passages Test

The results of the Graded Reading Passages Test are used to determine placement in reading material. Once this information is obtained, the teacher has numerous diagnostic options. These include (1) administration of an alternate form of this test based on a different type of prose, (2) use of alternative passages to estimate a student's listening comprehension level, (3) use of an alternate form to assess silent reading ability, and (4) use of different forms of this test to monitor student progress during the school year, (5) analysis of specific word recognition miscues, and (6) analysis of specific comprehension errors.

Administration Based on a Different Type of Prose

Students process expository and narrative materials differently because these two types of text are structured differently. When teachers wish to compare and contrast students' performance with these two prose styles, expository and narrative forms of the Graded Reading Passages Test can be administered in separate test sessions. To minimize the effects of learning and to make sure that the results are comparable, the passage of time between the two administrations should not exceed a week.

Directions

The initial administration of the Graded Reading Passages Test yielded information on a student's independent reading level, and the examiner begins testing with the alternate-form passage that corresponds to this level. For example, if the estimated independent level was found to be grade 5 on an expository form of the test, commence with the grade 5 selection on a narrative form of the test.

Repeat the procedures described in Section Two (Step 3: Administer and Score the Graded Reading Passages Test) and transfer the data to the examiner's copy of the Summary of Student Performance Sheet (page 179). When reviewing the results, look for differences and similarities in the estimated reading levels. Also compare the level of interest scores to see whether a student prefers reading one type of prose over the other.

Finding a Listening Comprehension Level

During the administration of this diagnostic option, selections from the Graded Reading Passages Test are read aloud and comprehension is checked to determine the highest level of material students can satisfactorily understand when it is read to them.

The listening level is reached when a student comprehends 70 percent to 75 percent of the material (Ekwall, 1986, p. 5). Because the Comprehension Check in the passages test is based on the scoring of five questions (20 points each and partial credit may be given), the lower percentage of 70 is used to determine the listening level. The listening comprehension level can serve as an indicator of the student's current capacity for reading achievement. The premise is that if no limiting factors are present, such as problems with word recognition, the student can read and understand material written on this level. Information of this type is useful when comparisons are made between a student's instructional level and listening comprehension level. For example, a third-grade student in a remedial reading class with an instructional level of grade 1 and a listening comprehension level of grade 3 probably has the potential to make significant progress in a well-designed program.

However, the examiner may not always be able to use a listening comprehension test to estimate reading potential, especially with populations of students such as English as a second language learners and students in junior or senior high school. English as a second language students may, for example, comprehend better when they have the opportunity to read the material silently rather than have it read to them. They just may not be good listeners of English text. Moreover, many readers in junior or senior high school seem to "perform better in reading than in listening." This is because efficient readers at this level "can use reading more effectively than listening—slowing down at difficult points, reading faster at easy points, and rereading as necessary" (Johnson, Kress, & Pikulski, 1987, p. 54). With such populations of students, it may be inadvisable to use the results of a listening comprehension test to estimate reading potential. Nonetheless, using graded passages to assess listening comprehension is still a good procedure to employ, if only to get an idea of a student's aural understanding and memory.

Directions

Select passages from an alternate form with the same prose type. For example, if a student reached the frustration level on the grade 5 narrative passage and there is a need to find a listening comprehension level, select passages from the alternate narrative form and begin testing with the grade 5 passage.

Give the student the following directions:

> "I am going to read to you. Listen carefully because after I have finished reading, I am going to ask you a few questions about the material. Do you understand? Let's begin."

Enter the percentage of correct responses to the comprehension questions for each passage attempted on the examiner's copy of the Summary of Student Performance Sheet found on page 179. Record these percentages in the column labeled Listening Comprehension. Then, use the criterion information presented in this section to determine the student's listening level. Enter this grade-level information in the Estimated Reading Levels table.

A similar procedure for estimating the listening comprehension levels of *emergent* and *initial* readers is discussed on pages 69–70.

Finding a Silent Reading Comprehension Level

Additional information about a student's reading behaviors can be gathered by assessing silent reading ability. As in the oral administration of the Graded Reading Passages Test, the results from the silent administration can also be used to estimate a student's reading levels. The results of the oral and silent administrations can then be compared to determine whether comprehension is better in either mode. The silent reading option can also be utilized to learn about a student's silent reading behavior (e.g., maintains attention to the task and reads the text at an appropriate rate).

Directions

Select a Graded Reading Passages Test form that the student has not read orally, preferably one based on the same prose type. Use the results of the oral reading test to determine the passage with which to begin. The initial passage read silently should be on the student's independent level. For example, if the student scores at the independent level on the grade 4 passage of the oral reading test, begin with an equivalent-level passage on the silent reading test.

Say to the student:

"I am going to have you read some material to yourself. Some of these passages will be easy for you to read, and others may be more difficult. Do the best you can. I want to see how well you can read without my help. Try to remember what you are reading. When you are finished, I will take the booklet away and ask you some questions." [Free Recall option: "When you are finished, I will take the booklet away and ask you to tell me what you remember about the passage."] "Do you understand?" [Examiner reads introductory statement and places test booklet in front of student.] "Begin reading here. Please look at me when you have finished."

Use a stopwatch or a clock with a second hand to determine the number of seconds it takes for the student to read each passage. Observe the student during the silent reading, and note behavioral characteristics such as finger pointing, lip movements, and inattentiveness.

When the student is finished, note the time taken to read the passage (in seconds), remove the booklet from view, and use the examiner's record form to check passage comprehension with probed recall, free recall, or a combination of the two. Follow the procedures for assessing comprehension described in Section Two (pages 23–28).

Be sure to transfer the results of the Comprehension Check for each passage attempted to the Levels of Word Recognition and Comprehension scale. Let **x** mark the spot on the comprehension side of this scale to show the error count and the corresponding reading level. Continue with more difficult (and in some cases, easier) selections until there is enough information to determine the range of silent reading levels: independent, instructional, and frustration. Here, too, the examiner should follow the procedures to assess a student's self-perceived interest in and familiarity with the content of each selection. Enter the results in the Prior Knowledge and Level of Interest section of the passage record form.

Transfer all information to the Summary Sheet of Silent Reading Performance on page 308. Then compare the sets of data from the oral and silent administrations of the passages test. Review these results to determine whether the reading levels are comparable or dissimilar. For example, the results may be different for students who are self-conscious or feel extremely anxious when reading aloud. Such students may feel more relaxed when reading silently; therefore, they are apt to perform better when the passages are administered silently instead of orally. In cases of this type, the results of the silent administration may provide a more accurate assessment of a student's comprehension performance.

Obtain information on reading rate by using a stopwatch or a clock with a second hand to determine the number of seconds needed to read each selection. The following equation is a formula for calculating the rate in words per minute (WPM) read.

$$\text{WPM} = \frac{\text{Number of words read} \times 60}{\text{Number of seconds spent reading selection}}$$

The word count information for each passage is listed in Tables 1.1 and 1.2 (refer to page 6). For example, suppose it took Ruth, a student in fifth grade, 115 seconds to read the grade 3 expository passage on hangnails. Also assume that the material is at her instructional level. According to the data presented in Table 1.1, there are 141 words in this article. Using the formula for calculating rate in words per minute, the teacher would first multiply 141 by 60 and divide the total by 115. The result of these calculations shows that Ruth's word-per-minute rate is 73.6. This information is entered in the appropriate place on the Summary Sheet of Silent

Reading Performance. The examiner can determine whether this rate is appropriate for a fifth-grader by comparing the student's rate to a set of norms for reading rate at different grade placements. The data on reading rate presented below are based on a study reported in Harris and Sipay (1990). According to Harris and Sipay, "these norms are based on students who scored 70% or better in comprehension when reading material of average difficulty for the grade" (p. 333).

GRADE	RATE WITH COMPREHENSION (words per minute)	GRADE	RATE WITH COMPREHENSION (words per minute)
1	80	8	204
2	115	9	214
3	138	10	224
4	158	11	237
5	173	12	250
6	185	College	280
7	195		

When Ruth's actual rate is compared to the expected rate for a fifth-grader, it is obvious that she is reading at a speed well below the norm. Ruth's low rate may be due to such factors as an overreliance on decoding skills, lack of interest in the content, or simply never having been taught to read faster.

Monitoring Student Progress

The examiner can use different forms of this test to monitor student progress during the school year. Three examples of testing schedules are presented below.

SCHEDULE #1		SCHEDULE #2		SCHEDULE #3	
Month	Form	Month	Form	Month	Form
September	A (Expository)	September	A (Expository)	September	A (Expository)
			B (Narrative)	November	B (Narrative)
May	C (Expository)	May	C (Expository)	February	C (Expository)
			D (Narrative)	May	D (Narrative)

Using the first schedule, the examiner administers two forms of the same prose type (either narrative or expository), one at the beginning and the other at the end of the school year. The results of the two administrations are compared to see whether progress has been made. The second testing schedule is similar, except this time both narrative and expository forms of the test are administered, first at the beginning and then again at the end of the school year. In the last schedule, four forms of the Graded Reading Passages Test are used to monitor student progress at different times in the school year—the beginning, two mid-intervals, and the end. The SIRI is flexible enough so that examiners can use any of the schedules described above or follow schedules of their own design. The results of multiple administrations of the SIRI can be especially useful to teachers for reporting progress to students and their parents.

Strategies for Using Dictated Stories for Assessment

A 1-day plan for using a dictated story to assess reading performance was presented in Section Two. Three options for using this diagnostic technique beyond the first day are described below. These are (1) to reintroduce the dictated story on another day, (2) to determine a listening comprehension level, and (3) to periodically monitor student progress.

Reintroduce the Dictated Story

The first option is to reintroduce the dictated story the following day (or soon after the first session) to determine how much was retained from the previous day's administration.

Directions

Have a copy of the original story and a photocopy to record information on the student's performance. If a word processor was used during the dictation process, then simply print two copies of the story.

Ask the student to read the dictated story aloud. This time, determine how much of the story the student can read without teacher assistance. (This is a departure from the standard procedure for implementing a language experience activity. Normally, the teacher reads the dictated story back to the student first. This change in strategy gives the examiner an opportunity to evaluate how much was retained from the previous session.)

Stop the oral reading if the student has difficulty. Then try to have him or her read back only selected parts of the story (i.e., sentences or parts of sentences). If there is still a problem, ask, "Are there any words in your story that you can pronounce for me? Please read them" or point to a specific word in the text and ask, "Can you pronounce this word for me?" Maintain a record of the student's performance on the photocopy.

When a student is unable to read back most of the story, read the story to the pupil, pointing to each word as it is read. Then read the story again, but this time with the student. Finally, determine how much of the story the student can read back without teacher assistance. If the student has difficulty, ask the pupil to read back only selected parts of the story. If there is still a problem, ask, "Are there any words in the story that you can pronounce for me? Please read them."

Again, maintain a record of the student's performance on the photocopy of the story. This time, write above the markings recorded for the first reading of the story, as in the example presented below.

Session #2
Session #1

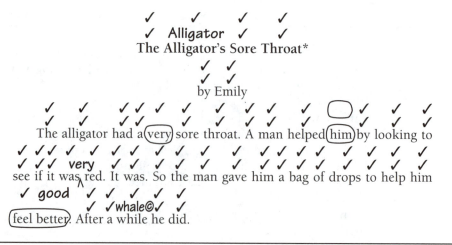

*This example of a dictated story was provided by Stacy Wilder.

In the first session, five to seven words from the story were used to check the student's ability to recognize words in isolation. This same list of words can be used again to assess the student's words in isolation skill, or the examiner can opt to expand this list by adding five to seven new words. As before, the teacher should prepare two copies of this scrambled list. The procedures for administering and recording the results of this test are the same as for the first day (see Section Two, Step 5).

Summarize the results by filling out the Dictated Story Assessment Strategy Record Form for Follow-Up Session on pages 313–314. Attach any test materials to this form, such as the examiner's copies of the dictated story and the Graded Words in Isolation Test. Record the student's name and date of testing on each attachment. Be sure to answer the question, Are there differences in the student's performance during this session when compared to the first session? For example, the examiner should note whether a student was able to read more of the story or was able to pronounce more words in isolation on sight during the second session.

Determine Listening Comprehension Level

The procedure for finding a listening comprehension level described on pages 64–65 can also be used for estimating the listening comprehension levels of emergent and initial readers. The objective is basically the same—to determine students' potential to understand text written beyond their frustration level.

Directions

First, decide on the type of passages to read—narrative or expository. Once this decision is made, select the appropriate form of the Graded Reading Passages Test.

Read passages of increasing difficulty aloud until the student's comprehension falls below 70 percent. The highest level at which a student can understand at least 70 percent of the selection is the pupil's listening comprehension level.

Check comprehension with probed recall, free recall, or a combination of the two. The directions for administering and scoring are similar to the procedures described in Section Two for the Graded Reading Passages Test (see pages 23, 25–28). Also assess a student's interest in and familiarity with the material. Follow the steps described in Section Two (pages 28 and 31) to obtain Prior Knowledge and Level of Interest information for each passage read aloud to the subject.

Refer to the examiner's copy of the passage record form for the grade 1 selection (or a higher-level passage if it is felt the student can comprehend more difficult material), and read aloud the introductory statement from the top of the page. Then read the story or article to the student.

If the student's comprehension score on the grade 1 selection is above 70 percent, continue reading more difficult passages aloud until the student is unable to achieve a score of at least 70 percent. The highest selection at which the student attains a score of at least 70 percent is considered to be the pupil's listening comprehension level.

Enter information on the student's listening comprehension level on the Dictated Story Assessment Strategy Record Form for Follow-Up Session (see the procedure for finding a listening comprehension level, pages 64–65). After each passage is read, assess the student's interest and familiarity with the material. Follow the steps discussed in Section Two (pages 28 and 31) to obtain this information, and enter the data on the summary form.

The effort to determine a listening comprehension level is especially worthwhile when the student is severely disabled. In the example presented below, Carlos is an eighth-grade student with a grade 2 instructional reading level. His teacher decides to determine his listening comprehension level. The results reveal that the seventh-grade passage is the highest level at which Carlos can understand expository text with a comprehension score of 70 percent or above. Based on these data,

Carlos certainly seems to have the potential to make significant progress in an effective remedial program.

ASSESSMENT OF LISTENING COMPREHENSION			
Grade Level	Listening Comp. (%)	Prior Knowledge Y–N or 1–5	Interest 1–5
5	100	1	5
6	85	2	4
7	75	1	4
8	65	1	3

Student's Listening Comprehension Level: _____7_____

Monitor Progress

As a final option for using the Dictated Story Assessment Strategy beyond the first day, the teacher can use other photographs from the collection in this book to periodically monitor student progress in mastering emergent reading processes. Of course, in addition to the photographs in this book, the examiner may wish to use photographs from other sources or use interesting classroom activities (e.g., making popcorn, building a model airplane) to stimulate discussion for the creation of dictated stories. Refer to Section Two for discussion of the Dictated Story Assessment Strategy.

Make photocopies of the Dictated Story Assessment Strategy Record Form (pages 245–247), and use it to summarize the results of each session. Records of students' performances can be maintained in portfolios. Portfolios are designed to emphasize a student's strengths and to provide evidence of reading growth. They can include results of teacher-made tests, samples of writing, attitude and interest surveys, teacher observations, and samples of materials students are reading. A comparison of dictated story episodes completed during the school year usually reveals dramatic evidence of progress.

The Stieglitz Assessment of Phonemic Awareness (SAPhA)

It was stated in Section One that phonemic awareness plays an important role in the successful acquisition of reading and spelling. The SAPhA is an easy to administer instrument that provides the diagnostician with valuable information about a learner's level of phonemic awareness development. (Examiner's record form appears on pages 315–319.)

In their article on this topic, Griffith and Olson (1992) present strategies teachers can use to assess a learner's phonemic awareness. The design of the SAPhA described below is based on information presented in this article.

Four phonemic awareness tasks are assessed by the SAPhA: (1) to recognize whether pairs of words rhyme, (2) to listen to speech sounds and then blend these sounds into words, (3) to isolate speech sounds in the beginning, middle, and end positions of words, and (4) to segment the sounds of words, each two or three phonemes in length. The tasks range in level from simple to more difficult. Performance data for kindergarten children performing similar tasks as reported in a study by Yopp (1988) can be used as a basis of comparison when analyzing the performance of each student.

The Rhyming Words task is the simplest of the four. The task consists of twenty pairs of common monosyllabic words. Half of the word pairs rhyme and half do not. Each word pair is pronounced by the examiner and the student is asked whether they rhyme.

The Blending Speech Sounds into Words task is rated as simple. The task consists of thirty monosyllabic words. The first ten have two phonemes (e.g., /i/–/f/); the other twenty words have three or four phonemes. Ten of these longer words are divided before the vowel (e.g., /l/–/et/), and the others are segmented completely (e.g., /t/–/ee/–/th/). The examiner pronounces each word in a "secret language," and the student is asked to determine what the word is.

The Isolating Speech Sounds task is a higher-level phonemic awareness activity. This task consists of fifteen three-phoneme monosyllabic words. Sounds are targeted at the beginning (**s**un), middle (b**e**d), and end (ja**r**) of words. There are five examples of words targeted at each position. The examiner says the target word and the position of the sound and asks the student to say that sound.

The Complete Segmentation of Phonemes task is more difficult. This task consists of twenty-two monosyllabic words, each two or three phonemes in length. The examiner pronounces a word and the student is required to segment this word into its component phonemes. For example, if the examiner says the word *it*, the student should respond with the sounds /i/–/t/.

The SAPhA can be administered to students functioning on an emergent literacy level (learners who are nonreaders or who can only read a few words). These might be students in kindergarten or first grade, or older students found to have moderate to severe reading difficulties. Students who perform poorly on the Dictated Story Assessment Strategy may be good candidates for phonemic awareness testing.

Directions for Using the SAPhA

Directions for administering each of the four phonemic awareness tasks described above are provided on the examiner's record form (purpose of task, level of task, examiner instructions, and student directions). There is no student test material because all the items are read aloud by the examiner. The results of a student's performance on each task are recorded on this form. A cover sheet is provided to compile the results. This cover sheet furnishes the mean score of kindergarten children performing each task as determined by Yopp (1988). This data should be referred to when the examiner reviews the results. For example, children who earn similar scores as the comparison group are probably demonstrating phonemic awareness at or near the kindergarten level. Students who earn lower scores are likely to be at a prekindergarten level and students who earn higher scores are likely to be above a kindergarten level in regard to their attainment of phonemic awareness skills.

There is a place on the cover sheet for the teacher to estimate a student's overall level of reading acquisition. These levels are based on information found in Leslie and Jett-Simpson (1997). The levels and descriptors are presented as follows. Note that phonemic awareness is only one of a number of factors that contribute to growth in reading acquisition. Students who are beyond the *beginning reader* level (approximately second grade level and higher) should be rated as *above beginning reader* on the SAPhA form for recording the results. Generally, these students have attained most of the phonemic awareness skills, are capable of reading a variety of text, and demonstrate a higher level of fluency. Therefore, the teacher should check *above beginning level* if the student exhibits behaviors more advanced than those described here for beginning readers.

LEVEL	DESCRIPTORS
Emergent Readers	Some skill in phonemic awareness
	Develop understanding of print conventions, that is, learn directionality, where to start reading on a page, how printed words represent spoken words
	Do pretend reading
	Begin to write and name letters
	Focus on pictures
Transitional Readers	More skill in phonemic awareness
	Begin to recognize some sight words
	Use pictures and some initial consonants to figure out words
	Do early forms of writing
	Begin to use some cues to self-correct
Beginning Readers	Advanced use of phonemic awareness
	Expand sight word vocabulary
	Focus on letter–sound cues
	Focus on meaning cues
	Increase use of cues to self-correct
	Increase use of standard spelling

The determination of a student's level of reading acquisition should be based on data collected from more than one source, that is, performance on the SAPhA, performance on the Dictated Story Assessment Strategy, teacher observations of performance in the classroom.

A sample set of materials from the Stieglitz Assessment of Phonemic Awareness follows on pages 73–77. These results are based on the administration of the SAPhA to a first-grade student named Mandy.

The results show that Mandy performed at a higher level than the comparison group on each of the four tasks. Her performance indicates that she has a strong foundation of phonemic awareness skills prerequisite to learning how to read and write. With corroborating evidence such as data from the results of using the Dictated Story Assessment Strategy and classroom observations, the teacher concluded that Mandy is functioning at a beginning reader level. In other words, she is well on her way to becoming a fluent reader.

SAMPLE OF STUDENT PERFORMANCE
ON THE SAPHA

The Stieglitz Assessment of Phonemic Awareness (SAPhA)

Student's Name: __Mandy_____ Sex: __F__ Age: __6__ years __2__ months

School: __Henry Barnard_____ School System: __Rhode Island College__ Grade Placement: __1__

Examiner: __Ezra Stieglitz_____ Date of Test: __9/21_____

CONTENT	SUMMARY OF INDIVIDUAL SCORE	MEAN SCORE*
Part 1. Rhyming Words	__17__/20	15/20
Comments:		
Part 2. Blending Speech Sounds into Words	__24__/30	20/30
Comments:		
Part 3. Isolating Speech	__11__/15	9/15
Comments:		
Part 4. Complete Segmentation of Phonemes	__22__/22	12/22
Comments:		

Student's Level of Reading Acquisition
(Refer to page 72 for description of levels.)

_____ Emergent   _____ Transitional   __✔__ Beginning   _____ Above Beginning Level

Additional comments:

The results show that Mandy performed at a higher level than the comparison group on each of the four tasks. Her performance indicates that she has a strong foundation of phonemic awareness skills prerequisite to learning how to read and write.

*Correct responses of kindergarten children performing task (Yopp, 1988).

PART 1: RHYMING WORDS

Purpose of Task

To recognize whether pairs of words rhyme

Level of Task

Simplest

EXAMINER INSTRUCTIONS: Place a + sign on the line next to each word pair when a correct response is given and a − sign for an incorrect response. If necessary, a word pair can be repeated once. Stop testing after three consecutive errors.

STUDENT DIRECTIONS: Read the following passage to the student.

"I am going to play a word game with you. Do you know what a rhyming word is? [Provide description below if child's response in unsatisfactory.]

"Rhymes are words that sound the same at the end. For example, the words *top, hop, mop,* **and** *stop* **rhyme because they sound the same at the end. All these words end with the sound /op/. But the words** *coat* **and** *fire* **do not rhyme because they do not sound the same at the end.**

"I am going to say two words and I want you to tell me if they rhyme. Let's try a few for practice. Listen carefully.

"Do *cat* **and** *mat* **rhyme?**

"Do *eye* **and** *nail* **rhyme?**

[If necessary, provide student with additional examples.] **"Now let's try these.** [Begin with item 1.]"

PRACTICE: A. cat   mat   _____ + _____

B. eye   nail   _____ + _____

1. fun	sun	+	11. walk	talk	+
2. pet	box	−	12. coat	cone	+
3. comb	car	+	13. write	pipe	+
4. toy	boy	+	14. long	song	+
5. rat	run	+	15. wall	will	−
6. bug	rug	+	16. tap	tip	−
7. go	do	+	17. blue	glue	+
8. hit	hot	+	18. hook	look	+
9. beet	seat	+	19. train	rain	+
10. sing	ring	+	20. sock	pot	+

Score _____ 17 _____ /20 correct responses

PART 2: BLENDING SPEECH SOUNDS INTO WORDS

Purpose of Task

To listen to speech sounds and then blend these sounds into words

Level of Task

Easy

EXAMINER INSTRUCTIONS: Segment each word according to how it is presented on the record sheet. Pronounce each segment without making it too obvious what the word is. Emphasize the sounds and not the letters in each word.

Place a **+** sign on the line next to each word identified correctly. If an incorrect answer is given, record the student's actual response on this line. For example, if the examiner says /c/–/u/–/p/ and the student's response is *cap,* record the student's incorrect response on this line. Write **DK** (don't know) when it becomes apparent that the word is unknown or the student says that he or she does not know the word.

If necessary, the segmentation of a word can be repeated once. Stop testing after three consecutive errors.

STUDENT DIRECTIONS: Read the following passage to the student.

"Let's play another word game.

"I will say words in a secret language. Your job is to guess the word I am saying. I will break the word into parts. When you say the parts together, you will know what the secret word is. For example, if I say these sounds /m/–/e/, I am saying the word *me.* **Or, if I say, /p/–/e/–/n/, I am saying the word** *pen.*

"Let's try a few for practice. Tell what word we would have if these sounds were put together. Listen carefully.

"If I say /i/–/t/, what word am I saying?

"If I say /m/–/eet/, what word am I saying?

"If I say /t/–/a/–/n/, what word am I saying?

[If necessary, provide student with additional examples.] **"Now let's try these.** [Begin with item 1.]"

PRACTICE: A. i–t   _____DK_____

B. m–eet   _____– me_____

C. c–a–n   _____+_____

1. b–e	+	11. h–am	+	21. n–a–p	+
2. i–f	+	12. r–ed	+	22. c–a–ke	+
3. s–o	– snow	13. p–ill	+	23. b–oi–l	– oil
4. u–p	+	14. f–un	+	24. sh–ou–t	+
5. w–ay	+	15. s–oup	+	25. t–ee–th	+
6. t–o	+	16. ch–air	+	26. f–a–s–t	+
7. h–igh	+	17. m–ost	– ghost	27. s–w–i–m	+
8. a–te	+	18. k–ind	+	28. r–i–ch	– reach
9. e–gg	+	19. t–ent	+	29. b–l–a–ck	+
10. sh–e	– sheet	20. y–ard	– yarn	30. j–u–m–p	+

Score _____24_____ /30 correct responses

PART 3: ISOLATING SPEECH SOUNDS

Purpose of Task

To isolate speech sounds in the beginning, middle, and end positions of words

Level of Task

Higher Level

EXAMINER INSTRUCTIONS: Place a **+** sign on the line next to each word when the sound is correctly identified. If an incorrect answer is given, record the student's actual response on this line. For example, if the examiner asks for the final sound in the word *net* and the student says /d/, record the student's incorrect response on this line. Write **DK** (don't know) when it becomes apparent that the sound is unknown or the student says that he or she does not know the sound.

   If necessary, a word can be repeated once. Stop testing after three consecutive errors.

STUDENT DIRECTIONS: Read the following passage to the student.

"I am going to say some words. I want you to say the sound found at the beginning of the word, in the middle of the word, or at the end of the word. For example, if I say the word *bat,* and ask for the sound at the beginning of the word, the answer is /b/. Or if I say the word *sip,* and ask for the sound in the middle of the word, the answer is /i/. Finally, if I say the word *pail,* and ask for the sound at the end of the word, the answer is /l/.

"Let's try a few for practice. Listen carefully.

   "What is the sound at the beginning of this word? *hen*

   "What is the sound in the middle of this word? *boat*

   "What is the sound at the end of this word? *rug*

[If necessary, provide student with additional examples.] "**Now let's try these.** [Begin with item 1.]"

PRACTICE: A. **man**   _____ – n _____

            B. boat   _____ – oat _____

            C. rug   _____ + _____

Beginning		Middle		End	
1. sun	+	6. pail	+	11. net	– ot
2. dog	+	7. bed	+	12. lip	+
3. team	+	8. kite	– ah	13. car	+
4. jar	+	9. gum	+	14. track	– ack
5. ship	+	10. moon	– n	15. fish	+

Score _____ 11 _____ /15 correct responses

PART 4: COMPLETE SEGMENTATION OF PHONEMES

Purpose of Task

To segment the sounds of words, each two or three phonemes in length

Level of Task

More Difficult

EXAMINER INSTRUCTIONS: Place a **+** sign on the line next to each word when the word is segmented correctly. If an incorrect answer is given, record the student's actual response on this line. For example, if the student segments the word *with* as /w/–/i/–**/d/**, record the student's incorrect response on this line. Write **DK** (don't know) when the student does not attempt to segment a word.

If necessary, a word can be repeated once. Also, the examiner may use an object such as a pen or pencil to demonstrate the separate sounds in a word. For example, in the practice word *wig*, the examiner should tap the pencil as each of the three sounds is made. Then, at the discretion of the examiner, the student could do the same with this object as he or she attempts to segment the words in this part. Stop testing after three consecutive errors.

STUDENT DIRECTIONS: Read the following passage to the student.

"Now we're going to play a different word game. I am going to say a word and I want you to break the word apart. You are going to tell me each sound in the word in the order that you hear them. For example, if I say the word *to*, you should say /t/–/o/. Or, if I say the word *old*, you should say /o/–/l/–/d/. [The examiner should emphasize the sounds and not the letters in each word.]

"Let's begin with these for practice.

   "What sounds do you hear in the word *so*?

   "What sounds do you hear in the word *at*?

   "What sounds do you hear in the word *wig*?

[If necessary, provide student with additional examples.] **"Now let's try these.** [Begin with item 1.]"

PRACTICE: A. so   ____**+**____

   B. at   ____**+**____

   C. wig   ___**+**____

1. see	__**+**__	9. they	__**+**__	16 mop	__**+**__
2. day	__**+**__	10. pain	__**+**__	17. let	__**+**__
3. if	__**+**__	11. five	__**+**__	18. good	__**+**__
4. my	__**+**__	12. joke	__**+**__	19. stay	__ **– stay** __
5. no	__**+**__	13. hill	__**+**__	20. cheap	__**+**__
6. add	__**+**__	14. can	__ **– c–an** __	21. them	__**+**__
7. boy	__**+**__	15. heat	__**+**__	22. wash	__**+**__
8. zoo	__**+**__				

Score   ____**20**____ /22 correct responses

Refer to pages 70–77 for additional information on how to administer and score the SAPhA.

Specific Analysis of Word Recognition Miscues

In the initial administration of the SIRI, the examiner completed a general analysis of word recognition miscues, including the identification of full versus half miscues, to determine a student's reading levels. The two scoring systems described below provide the examiner with the opportunity to conduct a more thorough analysis of a student's word recognition miscues. The first system is based on a review of miscue types, such as nonword substitutions, whole word substitutions, and omissions; the second system is based on an in-depth analysis of accountable miscues. A sample case study follows the description of these two scoring systems.

Directions for Examining Miscue Types

To collect data on miscue types, begin with the lowest-level passage attempted by the student. Review each miscue to determine its type. The different varieties of miscues are listed on the Categories of Accountable Miscues in Word Recognition form provided for each passage. (Refer to Table 2.1 on page 22 for a description of each miscue type.)

When this task is completed, enter the total of each miscue type on this form. After miscue category data are collected for each passage attempted, compile the results and transfer them to the Summary Sheet of Accountable Miscues on page 309.

Look for patterns in the types of miscues made by the student and for possible assessment implications. For example, the student who makes many whole word substitutions, such as *car* for *automobile,* is maintaining the basic word meaning but is disregarding graphic cues. In another case, the student who has many word insertions that disrupt the meaning of the text may not be using semantic and syntactic cues adequately (Wilson & Cleland, 1989, pp. 118–119).

Directions for Conducting an In-Depth Analysis

The reading miscue analysis system described below is an adaptation of a procedure developed by Argyle (1989). Most diagnosticians should find it easy to use this version of a miscue analysis system.

To conduct an in-depth analysis of accountable miscues, identify twenty to twenty-five miscues made by the student. Miscues selected for analysis can come from a single selection or from a combination of passages. However, keep in mind that combining word recognition miscues made across a series of passages of increasing difficulty can lead to misinterpretation. According to Harris and Sipay (1990), this misinterpretation can occur because "most of the miscues are likely to occur at the frustration level, and if they greatly outnumber those made below that level and differ in type, the data could be misleading." These authors, therefore, suggest that diagnosticians make "separate analyses on miscues that occur on texts that are difficult for the child and those made on material that is of a more suitable level of difficulty" (p. 244).

Record information on the Summary Sheet for Recording and Analyzing Miscues found on pages 310–311. At the top of this sheet, enter the source of student miscues (form of Graded Reading Passages Test) and the grade level of the passage. Then enter the student's estimated reading level for each passage selected and the number of miscues analyzed at each level. In the spaces provided, write in the student's miscue in the first column. Then in the column next to it, write in the correct word as it appeared in the text. Proceed until all the miscues and text are entered on this sheet.

Now begin the analysis of each miscue by asking, Is the meaning of the passage changed by the miscue? There are three possible responses in Part A of the miscue review: no change, partial change, or complete change. The illustration in Figure 3.4 on pages 80–81 shows how the miscues are analyzed. (Also refer to Figure 3.3 on page 79.) For example, *important* for *essential* represents no change in meaning. Therefore, the first column is checked, and nothing is recorded in the second and third columns. *Teeth* for *tooth* represents a partial change in meaning, and *begin* for *being* exemplifies

FIGURE 3.3

Sample recording and record of David's miscue types on the sixth-grade passage of the Graded Reading Passages Test (Form A)

Teeth to Spare (6)

          important ⓵⁄₂ **a** ⓵⁄₂
Good dental care is essential to the

p ①   **presment** ①
prese~~r~~vation of our teeth. Once a permanent

tooth is lost . . . that's it! Only a false tooth

can fill the gap. Sharks don't need to be
controlled ①
concerned about their teeth as we do because
teeth ①**actually** ⓵⁄₂
they are ‸given an endless supply. A shark

always has a full mouth of teeth. When a tooth

is lost, it is replaced by another one. The tiger

shark, as an example, is said to grow twenty-

four thousand teeth over a ten-year period.
             a ①
Teeth are attached to the shark's jaws in
elveral ①**rule** ①
several rows. Usually, only the outermost
       functured ①   **specials** ①
rows of teeth are functional. Some species of

sharks have as many as forty rows of teeth.

Each row is slightly larger than the last, with
   outside ⓵⁄₂ **begin** ①
the outermost rows being the largest. New
   organized ①
teeth originate in an area behind the jaws and
        a ①
move outward as they form and harden. As

the teeth in the front begin to wear down or
     the ⓵⁄₂
are lost when a shark attacks its prey, they
 each ⓵⁄₂   **Size** ①
are ‸replaced by those behind. Since new teeth
 contrally ①**through** ①
form continually, there is a conveyer belt
    teeth ⓵⁄₂ **replacingment** ①
system of tooth replacement. The shark,

therefore, always has a set of razor-sharp teeth

to use at will.

CATEGORIES OF ACCOUNTABLE MISCUES IN WORD RECOGNITION	
Full Miscues	*Number*
Nonword Substitutions	4
Whole Word Substitutions	11
Omissions	
Insertions	
Reversals	
Repetitions	
Pronounced by Examiner	1
Half Miscues	*Number*
Whole Word Substitutions	5
Omissions	
Insertions	2

Based on an example provided by Martha Johnston.

FIGURE 3.4

Sample summary sheet for recording and analyzing David's miscues

Summary Sheet for Recording and Analyzing Miscues

Form of Graded Reading Passages Test: **A**

Grade Level of Passage	Estimated Reading Level (Independent, Instructional, Frustration)	Miscue Numbers (e.g., 1–7)
6	Frustration	1–23

Miscue Number	Reader's Miscue	Text	PART A — Is the meaning changed by the miscue?			PART B — Is the miscue graphically similar to the text?		
			No Change	Partial Change	Complete Change	Begin-ning	Middle	End
1	important	essential	✓			—	—	—
2	a	the	✓			—	—	—
3	—	preservation			✓			
4	presment	permanent			✓	✓	—	✓
5	controlled	concerned			✓	✓	—	✓
6	teeth	they			✓	✓	—	—
7	actually	—	✓					
8	a	in			✓	—	—	—
9	selveral	several			✓	✓	✓	✓
10	rule	rows			✓	✓	—	—
11	functured	functional			✓	✓	✓	—
12	specials	species			✓	✓	✓	—
13	outside	outermost		✓		✓	—	—
14	begin	being			✓	✓	—	—
15	organized	originate			✓	✓	✓	—
16	a	and			✓	✓	—	—
17	the	a	✓			—	—	—
18	each	—	✓					
19	size	since			✓	✓	—	✓

Miscue Number	Reader's Miscue	Text	PART A — Is the meaning changed by the miscue?			PART B — Is the miscue graphically similar to the text?		
			No Change	Partial Change	Complete Change	Beginning	Middle	End
20	contrally	continually			✓	✓	—	✓
21	through	there			✓	✓	—	—
22	teeth	tooth		✓		✓	—	✓
23	replacingment	replacement			✓	✓	✓	✓
24								
25								
	Number of Miscues Checked		5	2	16	16	5	7
	Number of Miscues Listed		23	23	23	xxx	xxx	xxx
	Number of Miscues Analyzed		xxx	xxx	xxx	20	20	20
		Percent*	21.7	8.7	69.6	80.0	25.0	35.0

*Percent for Part A = Number of Miscues Checked ÷ Number of Miscues Listed

Percent for Part B = Number of Miscues Checked ÷ Number of Miscues Analyzed

(Round off to nearest tenth of a percent [e.g., 87.38 = 87.4 or 76.65 = 76.7].)

a complete change in meaning. Because the student did not respond to *preservation* and had to have this word pronounced for him, a check mark is placed in the Complete Change column.

Then ask the question, Is the miscue graphically similar to the text in the beginning, middle, or end of the word? This is Part B of the miscue analysis. For the miscue *outside* for *outermost*, as an example, there is a graphic similarity at the beginning but not in the middle or at the end. So, a check mark is placed in the first column and minus signs are recorded in columns two and three. However, if the student had said *ou* (as in *cow*) for *outermost*, then a plus sign would still be placed in the first column for the graphically similar beginning, but nothing would be recorded in the second and third columns because the miscue did not have middle and end parts. Note, too, that nothing is recorded in the graphically similar columns for insertions and words pronounced by the examiner. Once the miscue information is recorded, total the columns, determine percentages according to the directions at the bottom of the form, and look for general patterns in the results.

Occasionally, the diagnostician may encounter a miscue that is difficult to analyze. For example, accountable repetitions (when three or more words are repeated) are usually unsuitable for this type of analysis. When this occurs, skip the miscue and find another one to analyze.

Sample Case

Let's look at David's performance to illustrate how the two miscue scoring systems described above can provide relevant diagnostic information about a student's word recognition strategies. David is a 15-year-old student in tenth grade. He participates in a special reading program. The reading specialist administered Form A of the

Graded Reading Passages Test, which David read orally, to obtain an estimate of his reading levels. The results showed that David can read fourth-grade material with ease (independent level), fifth-grade material with assistance (instructional level), and sixth-grade material with difficulty (frustration level).

The diagnostician then read passages 6, 7, 8, and 9 from Form C to David to determine his listening comprehension level. The results showed that David can understand ninth-grade material read to him at a satisfactory level (70 percent on the Comprehension Check). It seems, therefore, that even though David is reading well below his grade placement, he has the potential to read and understand text written close to his grade placement.

Afterwards, David's teacher decided to conduct a specific analysis of his miscues on this test. Figure 3.3 shows her analysis of the types of miscues David made on the sixth-grade, Form A, passage as he read it orally.

David's teacher reviewed the examiner's passage record form for the sixth-grade selection. In her analysis of this material, she placed David's miscues in the following categories:

FULL MISCUES

Nonword Substitutions	Whole Word Substitutions
presment for *permanent*	*controlled* for *concerned*
selveral for *several*	*teeth* for *they*
funtured for *functional*	*a* for *in*
replacingment for *replacement*	*rule* for *rows*
	specials for *species*
	begin for *being*
	organized for *originate*
	a for *and*
	size for *since*
	centrally for *continually*
	through for *there*

Pronounced by Examiner

preservation

HALF MISCUES

Whole Word Substitutions	Insertions
important for *essential*	*actually*
a for *the*	*each*
outside for *outermost*	
the for *a*	
teeth for *tooth*	

The teacher then entered the number of each type of accountable miscue on the Categories of Accountable Miscues form for this passage (see Figure 3.3). The examiner then compiled miscue data from all passages attempted and transferred it to the Summary Sheet of Accountable Miscues (page 309).

A review of the sixth-grade passage data shows that, overall, David made more lower-quality miscues (full miscues) than higher-quality miscues (half miscues)— the type of miscues that alter the meaning of the text. He was really struggling with this passage and demonstrated poor use of word recognition strategies to master the content. A review of the compiled data for all passages attempted would reveal whether David made more higher-quality miscues on the lower-level passages.

An in-depth analysis of David's accountable miscues was conducted to shed more light on his reading problem (see Figure 3.4). Some general observations can be made as a result of reviewing the data in the Reader's Miscue column. These results reveal that the majority of David's miscues are real words. This can be regarded as a strength because David is using his knowledge of oral language to produce real words that he knows as he reads. Another strength is his persistence in pronouncing words. David's teacher had to pronounce only one word for him (*preservation*). However, a more disturbing aspect of David's reading behavior occurs in the category of meaning change (Part A). Close to 70 percent of his miscues changed the meaning of the passage. We can assume from this result that it would be difficult for David to understand fully the message presented by the author.

A review of the graphic similarity data (Part B) reveals that David can apply phonic skills. He has strength in utilizing beginning sounds and some skill with ending sounds. However, David appears to have difficulty with the middle parts of words. This behavior is usually exhibited by students with vowel deficit problems.

David's exhibited behaviors are characteristic of underpredictive readers. These students, according to Phinney (1988),

> don't use what they already know about language . . . to help them predict. They consider the text itself at the most superficial visual level. They believe that reading is a difficult and exacting task, that they must read every word precisely as it is on the page and that they must decode a word from left to right, letter by letter. . . . Underpredictive readers don't understand that the basic purpose for reading is to gain meaning from text. . . . Their comprehension is as patchy as their oral reading: they latch onto words and phrases and try to put together something from the bits and pieces, or they simply say they don't remember what happened. (pp. 55–58)

Phinney feels that an instructional program for underpredictive readers should focus on "the big picture, on ideas, and overall meanings" (p. 60). The cloze procedure is one technique that can be used to capitalize on David's phonic strengths (initial and final sounds) to improve his skill in predicting meaning and using vowels in context. For this procedure, cloze passages should be written so that ". . . what precedes the blank provides strong clues for predicting a meaningful insert" (p. 60). Also, the first and last sentences of this cloze exercise should be left intact. A sample activity from the story "The Emperor's New Clothes" is presented below. It is assumed that the student has already read the story and is familiar with the plot.

> *Directions:* "This passage is taken from the beginning of the story. As you can see, some of the words from this story are missing. First, remember what happened in this story. Then, see if you can use the letter clues to help you figure out the missing words. Write in words that make sense on the lines provided."

Many years ago there lived an Emperor. He was so fond of new

cl_____es that he spent all his m_____ey on them. He wanted to be

beautifully dr_____ed. The Emperor liked to go out w_____ing to show

off his new clothes. He spent many hours in his wardrobe trying on new clothes.

Specific Analysis of Comprehension Errors

Initially, the examiner checked comprehension of each passage to determine placement in reading material. As a follow-up, further analysis of the comprehension data can reveal important information about a student's skill in understanding the material at the literal, interpretive, and critical/creative levels of comprehension.

Directions

Begin by reviewing the comprehension assessment data for the lowest-level passage attempted by the student. Remember the symbol for each comprehension category (L = literal, I = interpretive, and C = critical/creative), and note how many items were attempted in free or probed recall for each of these categories. Any comprehension item scored by the teacher, including a "don't know" response, is counted as an item attempted.

Record these data in the first column of the Categories of Comprehension Errors form provided for each passage. Then tally the number of errors made in each of these categories, and write this information in the second column of this form.

After data are collected and recorded for each passage attempted, compile the results and transfer them to the Summary Sheet for Categories of Comprehension Errors on page 312. Finally, determine and record in the third column the percentage of errors in each comprehension category, and look for general patterns in the results.

Sample Case

Let's look at the performance of Maria, a 14-year-old student in ninth grade, to illustrate how the scoring system described above can provide important diagnostic information about a student's comprehension performance. Maria was referred to the reading specialist by her English teacher. This teacher reported that Maria had difficulty understanding material from the literature anthology text used in class. Conversations held by the reading specialist with Maria's science, social studies, and mathematics teachers did not reveal any problems in these other content areas.

The reading specialist decided to administer both an expository and narrative form of the SIRI. The results showed that Maria's instructional level on the expository test was eighth-grade level and her instructional level on the narrative test was fifth-grade level. As a result of this discrepancy in the two instructional levels, the reading specialist decided to analyze Maria's comprehension errors.

A review of the data recorded on the Summary Sheet for Categories of Comprehension Errors illustrated in Figure 3.5 shows that Maria has good comprehension of expository text. In contrast, Maria appears to have more difficulty understanding narrative discourse. Not only is her instructional level for this type of prose two grade levels lower than for expository discourse but the results on the record sheet reveal some difficulty with comprehension of narrative passages beyond the literal level.

Information from the SIRI may help to explain why Maria is more successful in subjects that require expository reading and less successful in a subject that demands mastery of narrative material. Of course, additional information is required to pinpoint the cause of Maria's difficulty with narrative text. For example, further diagnosis may reveal that Maria has limited knowledge of various literary elements and devices common to narrative-type text. She may require direct instruction in such literary elements as plot, theme, setting, and characterization, or such literary devices as flashback and point of view. Instruction in these areas could provide Maria with the skills she needs to understand narrative text beyond the literal level.

Summarizing the Results: Using the Synthesis of Information Rubric

The information gathered from administering the SIRI should be used to form conclusions about students' reading behaviors. Such conclusions are noted on the SIRI Synthesis of Information Rubric found on pages 248–252. The results recorded on this form provide the examiner with a good summary of a student's reading strengths and weaknesses.

In order to complete this rubric, the examiner should first collect, analyze, and review all test data. The ratings recorded on this form should be based on the results of administering the various components of the SIRI (procedures for initial admin-

FIGURE 3.5

Sample record of Maria's comprehension performance on the Graded Reading Passages Test

	EXPOSITORY		
	Free and Probed Recall		
	Items Attempted (Free & Probed)	Number of Errors	% of Errors* (Col. 2/Col. 1)
Literal	9	2	22.2
Interpretive	6	2	33.3
Critical/Creative	3	1	33.3

	NARRATIVE		
	Free and Probed Recall		
	Items Attempted (Free & Probed)	Number of Errors	% of Errors* (Col. 2/Col. 1)
Literal	12	3	25.0
Interpretive	3	2	66.7
Critical/Creative	3	3	100.0

*Round off to nearest tenth of a percent.

istration and diagnostic options). *The Dictated Story Assessment Strategy Record Form found on pages 245–247 should be used when a student is functioning on an emergent literacy level.*

The examiner should respond to as many of the items on the rubric as possible. There may be some items on which the examiner is unable to rate a student. For example, a student can be rated on Silent Comprehension only if the diagnostic option Finding a Silent Reading Comprehension Level is utilized.

The identification of patterns can help teachers form conclusions about a student's reading performance. When feasible, rely on data collected from more than one source when rating the student. For example, information gathered from the Interest in Reading section of the Reading Reflections Interview and the Level of Interest scale accompanying each passage on the Graded Rading Passages Test should be used to record ratings on Reading Interests, and the results of both the Graded Words in Context Test and the Graded Reading Passages Test should be used to rate a student's level of oral fluency. Patterns are more apt to be revealed and validated if teachers go beyond the initial procedures and employ some of the diagnostic alternatives available in the SIRI.

Generally, when rating each item, more value should be placed on a student's performance at the independent and instructional levels than at the frustration level because behaviors at the frustration level may not accurately reflect a student's overall performance. Obviously, the examiner should use his or her best judgment when making decisions based on the student's reading levels.

Let's refer back to the student David, whose case was discussed on pages 81–83. Initial testing showed a low instructional level (5 years below his grade 10 placement). The examiner utilized several diagnostic options to obtain additional information. An analysis of the data revealed more about David's reading behaviors. This review showed that David (1) had difficulty with word middles, (2) failed to use context to determine word meanings, and (3) had a listening level 4 years above his instructional level. Conclusions such as these are used as a basis for rating the student on the following items from the SIRI Synthesis of Information Rubric (pages 248–252):

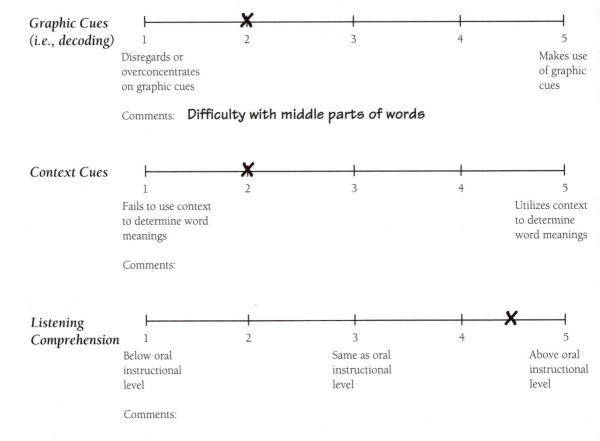

*Graphic Cues
(i.e., decoding)*

| 1 | 2 | 3 | 4 | 5 |

Disregards or
overconcentrates
on graphic cues

Makes use
of graphic
cues

Comments: **Difficulty with middle parts of words**

Context Cues

| 1 | 2 | 3 | 4 | 5 |

Fails to use context
to determine word
meanings

Utilizes context
to determine
word meanings

Comments:

*Listening
Comprehension*

| 1 | 2 | 3 | 4 | 5 |

Below oral
instructional
level

Same as oral
instructional
level

Above oral
instructional
level

Comments:

Periodically, as alternate forms of the SIRI are administered to monitor progress, growth in reading performance should be noted on this rubric and stored in the student's portfolio.

The assessment strategies described in Section Three illustrate how the SIRI can be used to obtain a wealth of information about a reader's strengths and weaknesses. However, with the end of testing, the teacher's job is only partially done. The effort expended on testing will have been wasted unless the results can be used to develop a plan for instruction—one that meets a student's specific needs. This plan should capitalize on a student's reading strengths and compensate for any weaknesses. It is only when insights from test results are used to help students improve in reading that teachers can finally say, "It was definitely worth the effort!"

Section Four

Student's Test Materials for Initial Administration and for Diagnostic Options

Initial Administration

Graded Words in Context Test: Form A   89

Graded Reading Passages Test: Form A—Expository   98

Graded Words in Context Test: Form B   107

Graded Reading Passages Test: Form B—Narrative   116

Photographs for Dictated Story Assessment Strategy   125

Graded Words in Context Test: Form A

(Examiner's record form appears on pages 183–192.)

PP

1. Look **at** this old car!
2. You can ride **in** my car.
3. This **dog** is not old.
4. You can come, **but** your pet can't.
5. This is a **red** book.
6. Can you **get** me a pet?
7. I **like** his little dog.
8. It is time **to** go home.
9. Can you **ride** on a bear?
10. I **want** a big book.

PR

1. We want you to **sit** down.
2. I like to **eat** fish.
3. I **may** want to run with you.
4. She will **take** the boy to the game.
5. They have **two** fish at home.
6. She **saw** a boy read a big book.
7. He will run **away** from the bear.
8. Is your **mother** at home?
9. The **little** boy is in your car.
10. Who **found** your cat?

ON

1. The green **bus** will take me to my house.
2. We want you to **stay** with us today.
3. The school is **far** from her house.
4. I like to **hear** the rain fall.
5. Can you read this book **again?**
6. I will surprise my **sister** with this trick.
7. We get **off** at this bus stop.
8. We take the bus to **town.**
9. I **wish** I had a pet to play with.
10. A fox **isn't** nice to a rabbit.
11. I will **give** this plant to my friend.
12. Tell me a **story** about a bear.
13. There are more **than** three fish in the water.
14. A lion can live in a **zoo.**
15. How **long** will it take you to bake a cake?
16. I jump out of bed in the **morning.**
17. I want to play **another** game.
18. I can open the door with my **hand.**
19. This is the **right** way to go to school.
20. Can I **please** have some water?

TW

1. The water in the lake is very **low.**
2. Will the little **deer** find her mother?
3. A **few** children hid under the table.
4. Some children are **afraid** of the dark.
5. He took a **rest** in his bed after dinner.
6. The school is a **mile** from her house.
7. The boy said, "You have **such** a nice smile."
8. **I'd** like to see my friend next week.
9. She has many books to **carry** to school.
10. Look at the **puppy** run up the hill!
11. The **owl** is a bird with two big eyes.
12. There were **seven** fish in the lake.
13. The **quick** rabbit ran faster than the mouse.
14. The top of this **mountain** is very high.
15. Grandma will **visit** us next week.
16. When will your sister **follow** us to school?
17. I heard a story about a bad **dragon.**
18. Is there **anyone** in this room who has a snake?
19. I know a **farmer** who has many animals.
20. He reads to his children every **evening.**

TH

1. The farmer had a nice **crop** of corn.
2. Give it to me at once, or I will **force** you to!
3. A car cannot run without a **motor**.
4. He was late to school as **usual**.
5. We went to the zoo **yesterday**.
6. She will like you more if you don't **bother** her.
7. You will really **enjoy** this magic show.
8. We will learn about the **history** of our country.
9. A rabbit likes to **nibble** on a carrot.
10. If you are not careful, this cat will **scratch** you.
11. Which **parent** will visit the school today?
12. Some children watch too much **television**.
13. The man found a gray **whisker** growing on his chin.
14. I do my best to **treat** my pets well.
15. I spilled paint on your pants by **accident**.
16. I **dare** you to take that frog to school.
17. Did you **understand** the answer to that question?
18. I write everything down in my **notebook**.
19. Your magic tricks will **amaze** everyone.
20. The man in the green shirt looks so **familiar**.

FO

1. Did you understand the **plot** of this story?
2. "Name" and "game" are two words that **rhyme**.
3. There was an **uproar** when the lion escaped from his cage.
4. The **bold** girl protected her friend from danger.
5. It is in **fashion** to wear this kind of shoe.
6. Do you know how much **property** he owns on this street?
7. I was too sleepy to be **aware** of how cold it was.
8. I bought a **cookbook** with 9 recipes for making fish.
9. A bad cold often makes a person sound **hoarse**.
10. He has a friend who will **represent** him in court.
11. It is hard to climb a mountain with a steep **slope**.
12. She earned a high or **excellent** grade on this test.
13. A **telegraph** is used to send a message to someone.
14. This pearl came from an **oyster**.
15. She was **fortunate** to have won the contest.
16. Reading is my favorite **subject** in school.
17. This **taxi** will take you to the airport.
18. It is lots of fun to ride a sled **downhill**.
19. If you eat too much, your weight will **increase**.
20. Children are usually frightened by a **thunderstorm**.

FI

1.   The terrible king tried to **conquer** the world.
2.   If you are not careful, this saw will **injure** you.
3.   Many crops can be grown on a large **plantation**.
4.   He wore a gold watch on his **wrist**.
5.   I am filled with **gratitude** for the favor you did.
6.   Sweets can **attract** flies at a picnic.
7.   One day we had a **delightful** ride in the country.
8.   Can you **furnish** this room with only two chairs?
9.   An **emerald** is a bright green stone or jewel.
10. The **manufacturer** of this car also makes trucks.
11. She was **shrewd** to buy a house ten years ago.
12. This pill is a good **treatment** for that illness.
13. It is **obvious** that two and two make four.
14. He was happy to earn a **satisfactory** grade in spelling.
15. Your **assignment** for tomorrow is to read Chapter 5.
16. The **brightness** of the sun can damage your eyes.
17. A cloudy, rainy day is a **dreary** day.
18. Our earth is but a small part of the **universe**.
19. We are learning to **somersault** in gym class.
20. The dinosaur is an example of a **prehistoric** animal.

SI

1. The mistakes you made on this test are only **minor** ones.
2. We feel **sympathy** toward people who are ill.
3. It is quite **evident** that they are twins.
4. Many people were hurt in the **collision** of the two trains.
5. An **igloo** is a hut built of blocks of ice.
6. It is wise to eat only a **minimum** of candy.
7. An election year is a busy time for a **politician.**
8. It was always an **ordeal** to take me to the dentist.
9. Offer more money and he will **yield** to your plan!
10. I can't **comprehend** a story with many hard words.
11. This difficult puzzle is sure to **frustrate** you.
12. I study hard for every **examination** in science.
13. The old man was a **legendary** figure in his sport.
14. The ball hit me so hard, it knocked me **unconscious.**
15. I **slouch** in my favorite chair when I am tired.
16. Putting things off is her greatest **weakness.**
17. A note of **appreciation** was sent to everyone who helped.
18. There is an equal **quantity** of nuts and raisins in this cake.
19. The **wanderer** moved from city to city.
20. I felt much **embarrassment** when I slipped and fell.

SE

1. They stopped to drink water at **an oasis** in the desert.
2. There are no houses for sale in this **vicinity**.
3. Keep the information about the spies **confidential**!
4. Both students earned **identical** grades of "A" on the test.
5. The President of the United States is a **prominent** person.
6. After much **repetition**, she memorized her part for the play.
7. A person who studies animal life is a **zoologist**.
8. The coin collector examined the rare coin to see if it was **authentic**.
9. His stage fright was a **disadvantage** each time he had to give a speech.
10. The scientists studied the **hibernation** habits of bears.
11. The expensive carpets gave the room a **luxurious** look.
12. The shy thief had an **unsuspecting** look on his face.
13. This story is a **translation** of a tale written in French.
14. It will be a real **breakthrough** when a cure for this illness is found.
15. The results of the test were used to **evaluate** her writing skills.
16. He looks so **sophisticated** in his three-piece suit.
17. Storms seem to occur with more **frequency** in March.
18. I like to eat a lettuce, tomato, and **mayonnaise** sandwich.
19. There is a great **resemblance** between the mother and her daughter.
20. Do you agree with his **interpretation** of that poem?

EI

1. A soap opera is like a never-ending **serial**.
2. The police were informed of the **urgency** of his plea for help.
3. Orange juice is my favorite **beverage**.
4. The children enjoyed the **novelty** of staying up late.
5. It was a poor **assumption** to think that the test would be easy.
6. The criminal surrendered to the police **voluntarily**.
7. Is it possible to observe the **transformation** of a caterpillar into a butterfly?
8. They were **optimistic** about the team's chance to win.
9. A **perishable** food such as fish should be refrigerated.
10. The blue team beat the green team **convincingly**.
11. Skill in writing is the main **qualification** for this job at the newspaper.
12. The worker's complaint about low pay was heard by the **grievance** committee.
13. The father said that the birth of his daughter was an **exhilarating** experience.
14. They drove many miles to hear her lecture because they knew she was so **knowledgeable**.
15. Because the student scored well on the test, there was the **implication** that he would succeed.
16. The injured man started a **rehabilitation** program for his broken leg.
17. I live in Florida and am **unaccustomed** to snow.
18. The **habitual** smoker decided to stop smoking.
19. An eclipse of the sun is a **phenomenal** event.
20. It is **monotonous** to play the same game ten times.

Graded Reading Passages Test: Form A—Expository

(Examiner's record form appears on pages 195–212.)

ON

Clouds in the Sky

Look up in the sky. What do you see? There are clouds. Some can look white. Others can look dark and gray.

On a sunny day we may see nice, big ones. The sun can shine through and make them look white.

On another day we may see many clouds. They are all over the sky. It looks like it will rain. The sun cannot shine through as well. This makes the clouds look dark and gray.

TW

Hide and Seek

Many children like to play "hide and seek." Hide and seek did not begin as a game. It started many years ago in a far away land.

Hide and seek was something grown-ups did each year when winter was over. People were tired of the cold and long nights. They wanted to know if spring was on the way.

Grown-ups would leave their village and go into the woods. They tried to find or "seek out" birds and flowers. It was important to return with a bird or flower. If one did, this was a sign that spring had really started.

TH

Hangnails

What is a hangnail? First of all, a hangnail is not really a nail. It is a tough, little piece of skin that hangs loosely at the side of your fingernail.

You get a hangnail when the skin around your nail gets a little dry. Then a piece of skin might start peeling off. Soon the piece of skin starts rubbing against your other fingers or against objects that you touch. The rubbing bothers the hangnail and makes the skin red and sore.

What do you do with a hangnail? Don't pick it. Don't bite it off. That will only make it worse. Instead, cut it off with scissors or nail clippers.

You can avoid getting hangnails by taking good care of your hands and nails. After washing your hands, dry them well. Use lotion to keep dry skin smooth.

Source: Reprinted from "What Is a Hangnail?" in *3-2-1 Contact Magazine,* April 1988, p. 5. Copyright © Sesame Workshop, 1988.

FO

Smelly Stickers

How do smelly stickers work? Almost any smell you can think of, from pizza to peanut butter, can be captured and put on a scratch and sniff sticker. But there's more to them than meets the nose!

Take a look at a sticker. All you see is a picture of something. But hundreds of thousands of super-small containers are glued to that sticker. Inside each container is a little bit of fragrance. The smell may come from the object pictured or it may have been made in a laboratory with chemicals.

When you scratch the sticker, you break open some of the containers. That releases the smell. But don't scratch too hard. You only need to open a few to catch the scent and your sticker will last a lot longer.

Some smells can't be captured. So far, they can't put the smell of a hamburger on a sticker. But wouldn't you rather smell the real thing . . . just before you bite into a double cheeseburger?

Source: Reprinted from "How Do Smelly Stickers Work?," in *3-2-1 Contact Magazine,* March 1988, p. 33. Copyright © Sesame Workshop, 1988.

FI

Samantha's Famous Letter

Samantha Smith was a girl with a dream. She dreamed of a world at peace. Samantha worried that differences between the United States and the Soviet Union might lead to war.

Early in 1983, she decided to write a letter to the leader of the Soviet Union. At the time, Samantha was eleven years old and in fifth grade. She had no idea that this letter would make her famous.

Samantha asked the Soviet leader how he might "help not to have a war." She was quite surprised when she received an answer. In his letter to her, the Soviet leader said that his people wanted peace. The letter also included an invitation to visit his country. He wanted Samantha to come and see for herself how much the Soviet people wanted peace.

During her two week visit, she was greeted by large groups of young people. She made speeches about peace and made many friends.

On her return, Samantha was honored for what she had done. She received the praise of many people for her efforts to make the world a better place to live.

SI

Teeth to Spare

Good dental care is essential to the preservation of our teeth. Once a permanent tooth is lost . . . that's it! Only a false tooth can fill the gap.

Sharks don't need to be concerned about their teeth as we do because they are given an endless supply. A shark always has a full mouth of teeth. When a tooth is lost, it is replaced by another one. The tiger shark, as an example, is said to grow twenty-four thousand teeth over a ten-year period.

Teeth are attached to the shark's jaws in several rows. Usually, only the outermost rows of teeth are functional. Some species of sharks have as many as forty rows of teeth. Each row is slightly larger than the last, with the outermost rows being the largest. New teeth originate in an area behind the jaws and move outward as they form and harden. As the teeth in the front begin to wear down or are lost when a shark attacks its prey, they are replaced by those behind. Since new teeth form continually, there is a conveyer belt system of tooth replacement. The shark, therefore, always has a set of razor-sharp teeth to use at will.

SE

Old Toys

Generations of children have been fascinated with toys. The science of archeology has helped us to learn about the favorite toys of children of long ago.

Archeologists have unearthed tombs of Egyptian children who lived at the time of the pyramids thousands of years ago. In the tombs they discovered tiny cooking utensils, wooden dolls, and toy animals.

Toy animals were also popular among the ancient Greeks. Young Greeks liked to play with wooden animals. Some of these animals were built with movable parts. Tails could be made to wag by simply pulling a string. There is even evidence that babies in ancient Greece played with rattles.

Children in ancient China enjoyed playing with marbles made of iron. Kite flying was also popular.

During the Middle Ages, young people played with tiny toy soldiers or knights. The knights were dressed in suits of shining armor. They were mounted on beautiful toy horses, ready to ride into battle.

Today, there are many kinds of electronic toys to delight young people. These include video games and electric trains. Yet, alongside these "modern" toys are many old favorites such as dolls, animals, and rattles. These old favorites have stood the test of time and have remained popular with children everywhere.

EI

A Price That's Too Good May Be Bad

Many products are sold in supermarkets and drugstores. Some are quite familiar to us because we hear about them on television or see them in advertisements. These products are easy to recognize because they are national brands. Other products that are similar to the national brands but that don't get the same press are known as store brands or private-label products.

One supermarket sold its own version of an all-purpose cleaner. The store brand product was similar in appearance to the popular national brand. Its chemical composition was exactly the same as the national brand's. Best of all, the store brand was about half the price of the national product it was imitating.

But from its introduction eight years ago, the store brand version of this all-purpose cleaner gathered dust on the shelf. Sales were so low that production was eventually stopped. Why was this so? The consumer just did not trust the lower price. When the price was too low, the consumer believed the store brand could not be as good.

So just how cheap is too cheap? One expert says it is unwise to price food products more than twenty percent below, and non-food products more than twenty-five percent below national brand equivalents. The greater the distance from the national brand, the more apt the consumer is to think, "Gee, they must have taken it out in the quality."

NI

Sticking Around with Velcro

One day in 1948 a man and his dog were walking through a field when he noticed his woolen pants were covered with burrs—tiny, bristly weed balls that were hard to remove. Unlike most people who just pluck off the burrs and forget them, this man, inventor George de Maestral, paused to figure out what made this annoying idiosyncrasy of nature stick so stubbornly.

Looking at a burr under a microscope, he discovered that each of the burr's tiny stems ended in a hook, which had caught on the loops in the fabric of his pants.

This inventor borrowed on nature's idea, and made it into a useful product we now use every day. He manufactured it out of nylon, with tiny hooks on one side, and tiny loops on the other. He dubbed the invention Velcro from an acronym for the "vel" of velvet-like soft loops and the "cro" of crochet, which is the French word for hook.

Today, Velcro is made from nylon most of the time. However, when greater sticking power is required, stainless steel and metal alloys are used. Besides replacing the need for shoelaces and zippers, this versatile fastener has earned the notice of engineers and scientists worldwide. NASA uses Velcro to secure objects and even astronauts against the antigravity of space travel. The medical field not only relies on Velcro to fasten blood-pressure cuffs, but used it to bind together two halves of an artificial heart. And the automobile and aerospace industries actually use Velcro to hold together car parts and airplane wings!

Like nature's burrs, it appears that Velcro is going to stick around for a long time.

Graded Words in Context Test: Form B

(Examiner's record form appears on pages 212–222.)

PP

1. There are **no** blue cats.
2. Where is **the** big bear?
3. Can **he** read this book?
4. I **will** help you read this book.
5. I **have** a blue car.
6. Come **and** play a game.
7. Can you play **with** me?
8. This **man** will help you.
9. Who will jump down **from** there?
10. Is **that** a good game?

PR

1. Can **all** of you read a book?
2. She **has** a pet dog.
3. I ride to **work** in a car.
4. We want you to **put** the dog in the car.
5. I want to ride in your **new** car.
6. I want you to **call** the man with the dog.
7. Stop at the big **tree**!
8. Can you help **them** play that game?
9. Go with **green** and stop with red.
10. Will the dog jump out of the **window**?

ON

1. The fish is **wet**.
2. I can **hop** up and down.
3. I **miss** my mother.
4. Where is your green **coat**?
5. This book is about a **horse**.
6. This **shoe** is too big.
7. Do you know **which** car is green?
8. Put the ball in the **black** box.
9. I like to eat good **food**.
10. He cut his **leg**.
11. This game is **better**.
12. She is a **kind** woman.
13. Put the plant on the **table**.
14. I found her **money**.
15. It is **dark** at night.
16. Can you **guess** how old I am?
17. I **never** found my frog.
18. The big dog likes to **bark**.
19. You **should** like each other.
20. Happy **birthday** to you!

TW

1. Please help me **set** the table.
2. We will **pull** the horse with a rope.
3. There are many trees in a **forest.**
4. Did you find a good **job?**
5. She will **meet** you at the zoo.
6. How far can a **crow** fly?
7. There are **eight** frogs in the lake.
8. **You'll** find the book on this table.
9. There are many letters in the **mail** today.
10. Please help me **hang** this picture.
11. I will **send** you a picture of your friend.
12. The tire is on the **wheel.**
13. A **cowboy** rides on a horse.
14. It is not nice to **scare** a friend.
15. We have a **number** of girls in our class.
16. We used food to **trap** the mouse.
17. A **kitchen** is a room where food is cooked.
18. Can you ask a good **question?**
19. You must have a **pass** when you leave the room.
20. He feels **unhappy** on a rainy day.

TH

1. Please help me **chop** some wood for the fire.
2. I **expect** to be there at noon.
3. Cut your meat with this **knife**.
4. I heard the **visitor** ring the doorbell.
5. She likes to have **lettuce** on her sandwich.
6. I **insist** that you wash your hands before eating.
7. He will **fry** the chicken in oil.
8. Are you joking or are you **serious**?
9. They make a nice **husband** and wife.
10. Cake is made with **sugar**.
11. You should **complain** about that broken window.
12. The food is in the **refrigerator**.
13. Did you hear the **alarm** ring?
14. A frog can have a long **tongue**.
15. Please place the **kettle** on the stove.
16. The prince and **princess** rode away on a horse.
17. What is the **difference** between a bee and a bird?
18. You should always **obey** your mother.
19. A blanket is **useful** on a cold night.
20. Please send her an **immediate** answer.

FO

1. The old man needed to walk with a **cane**.
2. It takes much **wisdom** to be the leader of a country.
3. It is your **duty** to take the garbage out this week.
4. I will **publish** your story in the school newspaper.
5. Don't **argue** with him about who won the game.
6. It pays to be **cautious** when driving a car on an icy road.
7. I don't like the buzzing sound of a **mosquito** in my ear.
8. Smoking is a bad **habit**.
9. Coffee can have a **bitter** taste.
10. We know that this painting is an **original** and not a fake.
11. The nurse wore a white **uniform**.
12. Ted becomes **jealous** when his mother plays with his younger sister.
13. This old coin was very **valuable**.
14. An **honest** person does not steal money from others.
15. Our country is a great **nation**.
16. It takes much **patience** to learn how to ride a bicycle.
17. Jane saw a beautiful **flake** of snow on her window.
18. Dan took his **raincoat** with him because it was a cloudy day.
19. Children can **entertain** themselves by playing with blocks.
20. I followed her **suggestion** and bought a car with four doors.

FI

1. He lived in a small **shack** in the woods.
2. The workers unloaded the **baggage** from the airplane.
3. She lost ten points on the test because of an **error** in addition.
4. She stacked the cans of carrots in the kitchen **cabinet**.
5. The **legal** age to drive in some states is sixteen.
6. He looked **weird** in that monster costume.
7. The hunter followed the **series** of animal tracks in the mud.
8. Our team will lose if you **fumble** the football.
9. I like it when the weather forecast is **accurate**.
10. This factory has lots of **machinery**.
11. He entered the hospital for an **operation** on his leg.
12. The teacher was asked to **dismiss** her class early today.
13. The team never lost hope of **eventual** victory.
14. Stay away from **poisonous** snakes!
15. The sound of a dripping faucet can be a **nuisance**.
16. The fake coin he bought was found to be **worthless**.
17. This statue is an important **landmark** to the people of our town.
18. She planned to **organize** her students into three groups.
19. He was told to **investigate** the scene of the crime.
20. The **conclusion** of this mystery is exciting.

SI

1. The **infant** baby was only three days old.
2. Children need healthy food to **nourish** their bodies.
3. I like to visit the circus to see the **acrobat.**
4. She sprinkled **perfume** on her wrist.
5. It was his turn to **monitor** the children in the hallway.
6. I felt some **fatigue** after running a mile.
7. The famous **historian** wrote an interesting book on the Civil War.
8. Can you **recommend** him for a job?
9. Please give him a **boost** so that he can climb over the fence.
10. You can store three suits in this **garment** bag.
11. The weather can **differ** from one moment to the next.
12. I cannot understand this chapter because there are too many **technical** words.
13. She is the best **candidate** for the mayor of this city.
14. I **sympathize** greatly with the runner who lost the race.
15. The **probable** cost of this trip is two hundred dollars.
16. I understand how you feel about the **tragic** loss of your friend.
17. Snow in the desert is a rare **occurrence.**
18. I enjoyed watching the **violinist** play her instrument.
19. The nurse tried to **elevate** the man's head so that he could sit up and read.
20. The scientist was honored for her great **accomplishment.**

SE

1. It was by accident that his name was **omitted** from the list.
2. Because of the thick fog, **visibility** was poor.
3. An argument between two countries can lead to a **conflict**.
4. I do not like to **inhale** smoke from your pipe.
5. It is nice to be alone and have a few minutes of **privacy**.
6. I'll take a room in this hotel, **regardless** of the price.
7. The results of this poorly designed study are **questionable**.
8. Do you know how to **analyze** the results of this study?
9. This book is about President Lincoln's **disapproval** of slavery.
10. I feel uncomfortable when the **humidity** is high.
11. The **glamorous** actress attracted large crowds of people.
12. There was a feeling of **uncertainty** in the room as the election results were announced.
13. The company grew under her **leadership**.
14. He enjoyed jogging up and down the **boulevard** each morning.
15. Mary's wrong answer **eliminated** her from the contest.
16. The **simultaneous** arrival of the two guests was unplanned.
17. Everyone should have a **fundamental** knowledge of English grammar.
18. I like to spread **margarine** on my bread.
19. A college education is a **requirement** for this job.
20. I am sorry for any **inconvenience** caused by my late arrival.

EI

1. A coat can be made of **synthetic** fiber instead of real wool.
2. Such poor behavior is **unworthy** of a leader.
3. He became **bankrupt** when he lost all his money.
4. The **xylophone** is her favorite musical instrument.
5. She was the only one **authorized** to receive top-secret information.
6. The weak army was **vulnerable** to attack in two places.
7. The workers attended the **testimonial** for the retiring president of the company.
8. The happy man always had the look of **optimism** on his face.
9. You are **prohibited** from smoking in this restaurant.
10. She became a **celebrity** after the release of her first movie.
11. The millionaire was the **wealthiest** man in town.
12. The hungry lion attacked the animal with great **ferocity**.
13. The **excavation** of the old riverbed revealed dinosaur bones.
14. **Legislation** was passed to increase the tax on gasoline.
15. If you want your egg to be soft-boiled, **immerse** it in boiling water for about one minute.
16. He ordered a **replacement** part for his broken bicycle.
17. The racing car jumped forward when the driver stepped on the **accelerator**.
18. Helping to prevent people from being cruel to animals is a **humane** thing to do.
19. The brownish-colored bread or **pumpernickel** tasted very good.
20. Jack has a **miscellaneous** collection of stones, shells, and coins.

Graded Reading Passages Test: Form B—Narrative

(Examiner's record form appears on pages 223–240.)

ON

A Snowy Day

Bill and Kim looked out the window. They were very happy. It was snowing. They wanted to go out to play.

Bill and Kim could not wait to build something with the snow. When they went outside, they made two large balls. They put one on top of the other. Then they made one small ball. They put it on the very top. Then Bill and Kim used some sticks and stones. Now they were done.

TW

The Boy and the Fox

One day a boy saw a fox sleeping on top of a rock.

The boy said out loud, "If I kill the fox, I can always sell her skin. I can use the money to buy and plant bean seeds. Then I will sell the beans and use the money to buy the field across the way."

"I will then plant bean seeds in my own field. People will see my beans and say, 'Oh, what nice beans this boy has.' Then I will say, 'Keep away from my beans.' They won't listen to me, so I will shout to them loudly, 'Keep away from my beans.'"

The boy shouted so loudly that the fox woke up and ran away. In the end, the boy was left with nothing.

Source: Adapted from Wiggin, K. D., and Smith, N. A. (Eds.) (1952). *Tales of laughter: A third fairy book* (p. 462). Garden City, NY: Doubleday.

TH

The Crow and the Pitcher

A crow flew many miles in search of water. She finally found a water pitcher. When the crow put its beak into the mouth of the tall pitcher, she found that it held only a little water. She could not reach far enough down to get at it. The crow tried and tried. Finally, she gave up.

Then a thought came to her. Not far from the pitcher sat a pile of pebbles. She flew to the pile and with her beak took a pebble and dropped the pebble into the pitcher. She flew back and forth, dropping pebble after pebble into the pitcher.

As the crow worked, the water rose nearer and nearer to the top. She kept casting pebbles into the pitcher until she was able to dip her beak into the pitcher. Then she quenched her thirst.

FO

The Two Farmers

Once there were two farmers, David and Joseph, who decided to form a partnership. They agreed to buy a field together.

David said to Joseph, "Now we must share the crop as is fair and right. Suppose you take the roots and I take the tops of the plants?" Joseph agreed to this plan. That year the two farmers planted corn. However, when they harvested the crop, David got all the corn and Joseph got nothing but roots and rubbish.

David noticed the displeased look on Joseph's face and said, "This year I have benefited. Next year it will be your turn. You shall have the top and I will have to put up with the root."

When spring came, David asked Joseph, "Would you prefer to plant carrots this year?"

"Fine! That's a better food than corn," answered Joseph.

But when the crop was harvested, David got the carrot roots, while Joseph got the carrot greens. Joseph was so angry that he decided to end the partnership.

Source: Adapted from Wiggin, K. D., and Smith, N. A. (Eds.) (1952). *Tales of laughter: A third fairy book* (p. 31). Garden City, NY: Doubleday.

FI

The Horse's Mouth

There was a fellow who had a strange way of doing business. Whenever he shopped for an item, he would get the seller to believe that there was something wrong with it. He used this trick to lower the price.

One day he wanted to buy a horse from a dealer. A fine looking animal was led out of the stable. The horse appeared to be in excellent condition.

"Oh," the man said. "This horse has a fine head. But it is astonishing how much that head reminds me of a horse my father owned twenty years ago."

Passing along the animal, he continued: "And those hind legs are good and what a beautiful fine tail! I declare it is marvelous how much they remind me of a horse my father owned twenty years ago."

He then opened the mouth. Looking at the teeth, he said, "My goodness! It must be the same horse!"

Although it really wasn't the same horse, the man had succeeded in fooling the dealer. The dealer now believed that this was a twenty-year-old horse. As a result, the man was able to buy this young, good-looking animal for much less than it was really worth.

Source: Adapted from Twain, Mark. (1956). The horse's mouth. In James Tidwell (Ed.), *A treasury of American folk humor* (pp. 34–35). New York: Crown.

SI

The Story of an Old Attic

Late one rainy November afternoon, Mary Dillon lay on her stomach in the musty attic of the old farmhouse. She was absorbed in the story of a haunted house found in one of the old yellowed magazines stacked there. Finishing the story, she closed her eyes for a short rest.

When she awoke, it was pitch dark. The rain was still falling with a steady patter on the roof. The attic was a pleasant place in the daytime, but after dark, and after one had been reading a ghost story, it was definitely otherwise.

As she sat up uneasily, Mary heard something move in front of her. She quickly grabbed a flashlight resting at her side, fumbled with the switch, and pointed the beam of light in the direction of the sound. Suddenly, Mary encountered a pair of glowing eyes staring back at her out of the darkness. Ghosts had eyes just like that! She felt her red hair rising on end. The eyes slowly approached her, and Mary was fascinated, frozen with fear. She tried to cry out, but no sound came from her throat.

"Meow," said Dusty, the family cat, whose throat was in perfectly good order, and whose eyes were as bright as cat's eyes should be. Snatching Dusty in her arms, Mary hurried downstairs.

Source: Adapted from De Witt, D. H. (1914). The old attic. In *St. Nicholas: An Illustrated Magazine for Young Folks, 41,* 474.

SE

Who?

It was a warm summer Sunday—June 20, 1980, to be exact. It was one of those lazy days when even the flies don't want to move. My grandmother and I were in the kitchen carefully wrapping chocolate bars (instead of cigars) to give to friends, in celebration of my soon-to-be sibling's birth.

Over the sound of someone's lawn mower, Grandmother was, as usual, humming a little song. Grandmom's perfume mixed strangely with the smell of freshly cut grass, forming a bittersweet aroma. Over the drone of the lawn mower and my grandmother's humming, I could faintly hear the elated shouts of children fresh into summer vacation.

Suddenly, it came—like a sneeze from an unsuspecting victim, like a bullet from a gun. The phone rang and these thoughts went through my head at four times the speed of light: DAD . . . HOSPITAL . . . MOM . . . BABY . . . PHONE. As if moving by its own choosing, my hand grasped the receiver and brought it to my waiting face. The ringing stopped, unable to complete its song. From the bulbous object came my father's happy voice, "Hello, Jamie?"

"Yes," I heard myself reply.

"Michael's here," he cried triumphantly.

"Michael?" I asked. "Michael who?"

Source: Used by permission of the author, Benjamin Reese. First published in *Merlyn's Pen: Fiction, Essays, and Poems by America's Teens*, vol. 3, no. 4, April/May 1988.

EI

Getting the Point

As a naive five-year-old, I was not suspicious when my father, the very center of my toddler universe, took me for a ride one sunny Wednesday afternoon.

We had an appointment with someone, he hurriedly explained, who had lollipops. This sounded good to me, since anyone with candy was a pleasure to visit.

We walked hand-in-hand into an austere office building and were directed to a sterile-looking room with four cubicles. I was comfortably settled on my father's lap in one of the cubicles when a friendly-looking man in a white coat joined us. The man sat down in front of us and reached for what I imagined to be an enviable stash of candy.

But what was this? A very large, extremely pointed object was in his hand. I looked at my father, and at that instant spotted guilt and trepidation on his face. From this I took my cue and panicked. My foot shot out into the man's abdomen. He grunted, doubled over for a second, and worst of all, replaced his smile with a scowl.

Before I could engineer an escape, my father—my hero—grabbed me tight while the man rapidly thrust the intravenous needle toward a vein in my arm. I braced myself for intense pain, but surprisingly, it really didn't hurt much.

Realizing that my overreaction had probably seriously jeopardized my opportunity for candy, I tried to salvage my dignity. Calmly, I stepped down off my father's lap, held my head high, and sauntered bravely out of the room.

The lollipop was strawberry.

NI

The Visitor

   I had been travelling alone on horseback through a singularly dreary tract of country; and eventually discovered myself, as the shades of evening foreclosed, within view of the melancholy house. I know not how it was—but, with the first glimpse of the building, a sense of insufferable gloom pervaded my spirit.

   I analyzed the scene before me—upon the bleak walls, upon the vacant eye-like windows, and upon a few white trunks of decayed trees. What was it—I paused to contemplate—what was it that so unnerved me in the contemplation of this dwelling?

   Noticing these things, I rode over a short causeway to the house where a servant in waiting took my horse. I entered the archway of the hall and an attendant then led me in silence through many dark and intricate passages in my progress to the studio of his master. The attendant now threw open a door and ushered me into the presence of his master.

   The room in which I found myself was very large and lofty. The windows were long, narrow, and pointed. Dark draperies hung upon the walls and the furniture was comfortless, antique, and tattered. Many books and musical instruments lay scattered about, but failed to give any vitality to the scene. I felt that I breathed an atmosphere of sorrow. An air of deep and irredeemable gloom hung over and pervaded all.

   Upon my entrance, a man rose from a sofa on which he had been reclining and greeted me.

Source: Adapted from Poe, E. A. (1938). The fall of the house of Usher. In *The complete tales and poems of Edgar Allan Poe* (pp. 231–245). New York: The Modern Library.

Photographs for Dictated Story Assessment Strategy

(Examiner's record form appears on pages 245–247.)

1	Mangy Camel
2	A Big Hit
3	The Flood
4	Sand Castle
5	The Daredevil
6	Man and Beast
7	Basketball Game
8	The Crowd
9	Thrill Ride
10	Fire

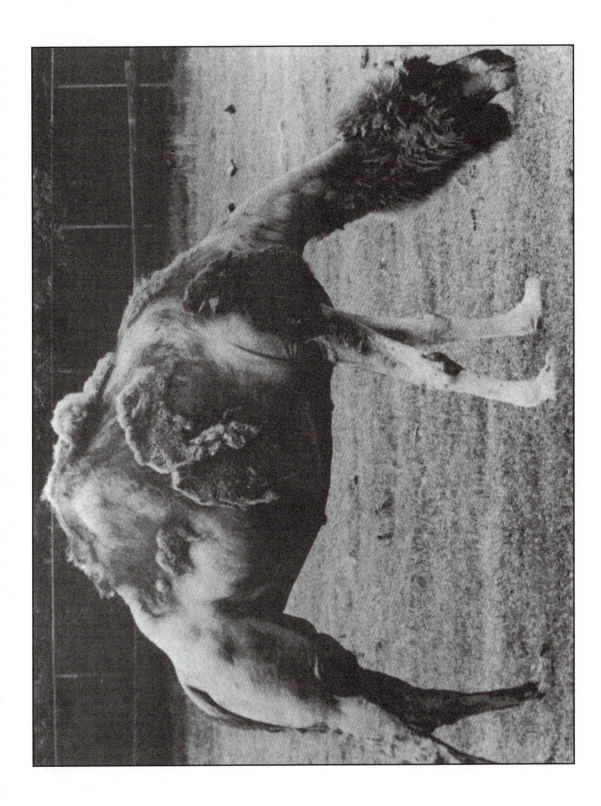

Photograph #1: Mangy Camel

What do you see in this photograph?

Why is there a fence in this photograph?

Where do you think this camel lives?

What is this camel doing? How can you tell?

How does this camel look different from other camels you have seen?

Would you like to visit this camel? Why?

Photo courtesy of Jack Hanson.

Photograph #2: A Big Hit

What do you see in this photograph?

Where was this photograph taken?

What is the boy holding in his hand?

What is the object above his head?

What is he trying to do? Why is he trying to do this?

What might happen if the boy smashed the star with his stick?

What do you think happened after this photograph was taken?

Photograph #3: The Flood

What do you see in this photograph?

During what time of the year was this photograph taken? How do you know?

Where was this photograph taken? How do you know?

Why is there lots of water in this photograph?

What are the people in the rowboat doing?

What was this place like one month before the photograph was taken?

How would you feel if you lived in the white-colored house? Why?

Would you like to visit the place in this photograph? Why?

Photo courtesy of AP.

Photograph #4: Sand Castle

What do you see in this photograph?

Where are the people in this photograph?

What did they build?

How did they build this sand castle (or whatever object identified by the student)?

Is it easy or hard to build a sand castle? Why?

How long will this sand castle last? Will it be there when the people return to the beach the next day?
How do you know?

What else can people do at the beach?

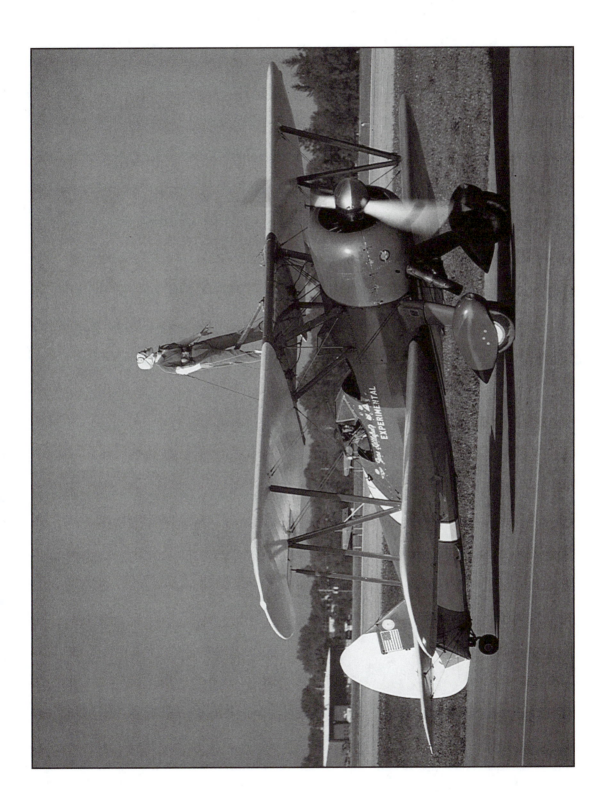

Photograph #5: *The Daredevil*

What do you see in this photograph?

Where was this photograph taken?

Who is in this photograph?

Describe the airplane in this photograph.

Where is the man/woman standing?

Why is he/she doing this?

What do you think happened ten minutes after this photograph was taken?

Would you like to be the man/woman in this photograph? Why?

6

Photograph #6: Man and Beast

What do you see in this photograph?

What kind of animal is in this photograph?

What is the man doing?

Why is he doing this?

What might happen if he stopped holding on to the animal?

What is this man's occupation? (What does he do to earn a living?)

Would you like to do what the man in the photograph is doing? Why?

7

Photograph #7: Basketball Game

What do you see in this photograph?

What are the people doing?

What kind of clothes are they wearing?

Who has the ball?

What is she doing with the ball?

What are the other players trying to do?

How would you describe the looks on their faces?

Who do you think is going to win? Why?

Photograph #8: The Crowd

What do you see in this photograph?

Who is in this photograph?

What are the people wearing?

Where was this photograph taken? How do you know?

How do the people in this photograph feel? How can you tell?

What are they doing?

What do you think they are looking at?

What do you think happened before this photograph was taken?

What do you think happened after this photograph was taken?

Photo courtesy of *The Providence Journal-Bulletin*. Used with permission of The Providence Journal Company.

9

Photograph #9: Thrill Ride

What do you see in this photograph?

Where was this photograph taken?

What are the people in this photograph doing?

How do the people feel at this moment? How do you know?

Why are some of the people holding their hands up in the air?

What do you think is going to happen to these people in the next three minutes?

Would you like to do what the people in the photograph are doing? Why?

What is your favorite amusement/theme park ride? Why?

Photograph #10: Fire

What do you see in this photograph?

How many firefighters are there in this photograph?

What are these firefighters trying to do?

Where is the fire?

How are the firefighters trying to put out the fire?

Why do the firefighters need a ladder?

Would you like to be near the top of the ladder in this photograph? Why?

Photo courtesy of *The Providence Journal-Bulletin.* Used with permission of The Providence Journal Company.

Diagnostic Options

Graded Words in Isolation Test: Form A   148

Graded Words in Isolation Test: Form B   152

Practice Passages   156

Graded Reading Passages Test: Form C—Expository   158

Graded Reading Passages Test: Form D—Narrative   167

Student's Test Materials for Diagnostic Options

Graded Words in Isolation Test: Form A

(Examiner's record form appears on pages 258–262.)

PP	PR	ON
1. at	1. sit	1. bus
2. in	2. eat	2. stay
3. dog	3. may	3. far
4. but	4. take	4. hear
5. red	5. two	5. again
6. get	6. saw	6. sister
7. like	7. away	7. off
8. to	8. mother	8. town
9. ride	9. little	9. wish
10. want	10. found	10. isn't
		11. give
		12. story
		13. than
		14. zoo
		15. long
		16. morning
		17. another
		18. hand
		19. right
		20. please

TW	*TH*
1. low	1. crop
2. deer	2. force
3. few	3. motor
4. afraid	4. usual
5. rest	5. yesterday
6. mile	6. bother
7. such	7. enjoy
8. I'd	8. history
9. carry	9. nibble
10. puppy	10. scratch
11. owl	11. parent
12. seven	12. television
13. quick	13. whisker
14. mountain	14. treat
15. visit	15. accident
16. follow	16. dare
17. dragon	17. understood
18. anyone	18. notebook
19. farmer	19. amaze
20. evening	20. familiar

	FO		*FI*
1.	plot	1.	conquer
2.	rhyme	2.	injure
3.	uproar	3.	plantation
4.	bold	4.	wrist
5.	fashion	5.	gratitude
6.	property	6.	attract
7.	aware	7.	delightful
8.	cookbook	8.	furnish
9.	hoarse	9.	emerald
10.	represent	10.	manufacturer
11.	slope	11.	shrewd
12.	excellent	12.	treatment
13.	telegraph	13.	obvious
14.	oyster	14.	satisfactory
15.	fortunate	15.	assignment
16.	subject	16.	brightness
17.	taxi	17.	dreary
18.	downhill	18.	universe
19.	increase	19.	somersault
20.	thunderstorm	20.	prehistoric

SI

1. minor
2. sympathy
3. evident
4. collision
5. igloo
6. minimum
7. politician
8. ordeal
9. yield
10. comprehend
11. frustrate
12. examination
13. legendary
14. unconscious
15. slouch
16. weakness
17. appreciation
18. quantity
19. wanderer
20. embarrassment

SE

1. oasis
2. vicinity
3. confidential
4. identical
5. prominent
6. repetition
7. zoologist
8. authentic
9. disadvantage
10. hibernation
11. luxurious
12. unsuspecting
13. translation
14. breakthrough
15. evaluate
16. sophisticated
17. frequency
18. mayonnaise
19. resemblance
20. interpretation

EI

1. serial
2. urgency
3. beverage
4. novelty
5. assumption
6. voluntarily
7. transformation
8. optimistic
9. perishable
10. convincingly
11. qualification
12. grievance
13. exhilarating
14. knowledgeable
15. implication
16. rehabilitation
17. unaccustomed
18. habitual
19. phenomenal
20. monotonous

Graded Words in Isolation Test: Form B

(Examiner's record form appears on pages 263–267.)

PP	PR	ON
1. no	1. all	1. wet
2. the	2. has	2. hop
3. he	3. work	3. miss
4. will	4. put	4. coat
5. have	5. new	5. horse
6. and	6. call	6. shoe
7. with	7. tree	7. which
8. man	8. them	8. black
9. from	9. green	9. food
10. that	10. window	10. leg
		11. better
		12. kind
		13. table
		14. money
		15. dark
		16. guess
		17. never
		18. bark
		19. should
		20. birthday

TW

1. set
2. pull
3. forest
4. job
5. meet
6. crow
7. eight
8. you'll
9. mail
10. hang
11. send
12. wheel
13. cowboy
14. scare
15. number
16. trap
17. kitchen
18. question
19. pass
20. unhappy

TH

1. chop
2. expect
3. knife
4. visitor
5. lettuce
6. insist
7. fry
8. serious
9. husband
10. sugar
11. complain
12. refrigerator
13. alarm
14. tongue
15. kettle
16. princess
17. difference
18. obey
19. useful
20. immediate

FO	FI
1. cane	1. shack
2. wisdom	2. baggage
3. duty	3. error
4. publish	4. cabinet
5. argue	5. legal
6. cautious	6. weird
7. mosquito	7. series
8. habit	8. fumble
9. bitter	9. accurate
10. original	10. machinery
11. uniform	11. operation
12. jealous	12. dismiss
13. valuable	13. eventual
14. honest	14. poisonous
15. nation	15. nuisance
16. patience	16. worthless
17. flake	17. landmark
18. raincoat	18. organize
19. entertain	19. investigate
20. suggestion	20. conclusion

SI	*SE*	*EI*
1. infant	1. omitted	1. synthetic
2. nourish	2. visibility	2. unworthy
3. acrobat	3. conflict	3. bankrupt
4. perfume	4. inhale	4. xylophone
5. monitor	5. privacy	5. authorized
6. fatigue	6. regardless	6. vulnerable
7. historian	7. questionable	7. testimonial
8. recommend	8. analyze	8. optimism
9. boost	9. disapproval	9. prohibited
10. garment	10. humidity	10. celebrity
11. differ	11. glamorous	11. wealthiest
12. technical	12. uncertainty	12. ferocity
13. candidate	13. leadership	13. excavation
14. sympathize	14. boulevard	14. legislation
15. probable	15. eliminated	15. immerse
16. tragic	16. simultaneous	16. replacement
17. occurrence	17. fundamental	17. accelerator
18. violence	18. margarine	18. humane
19. elevate	19. requirement	19. pumpernickel
20. accomplishment	20. inconvenience	20. miscellaneous

Practice Passages

(Examiner's record form appears on pages 268–271.)

*PRACTICE
ON*

The Fall Is Nice

It is fall. The leaves are falling. How fast they fall.

Let's catch all the leaves we can. There are red ones. There are brown ones. There are yellow ones. We like the red leaves the most.

Let's make a big pile right here. Then we can run and jump in them. It is fun to play in the leaves. We like fall.

*PRACTICE
TH*

The First Paper Maker

Do you know who the first paper maker was? It was the wasp.

A wasp needs paper in order to build a nest. To make a nest, a wasp must fly from place to place until he has found the right kind of wood. He tears off little pieces with his mouth. He lays these pieces side by side, just as you may lay sticks.

At last, he gathers them in a little bundle, and flies with them to his nest. Then he begins to chew the wood. As he chews it, he wets it with a kind of gum that runs from his mouth. While the chewed wood is still soft and wet, the wasp spreads it out as thin flakes. The flakes soon dry and then they are paper. He uses this paper to build the cells of his nest. While this is good paper to build nests with, it is not good paper to write on.

Source: Story adapted from Baldwin, J. (1897). *School reading by grades: Third year* (pp. 45–47). New York: American Book Company.

Graded Reading Passages Test: Form C—Expository

(Examiner's record form appears on pages 272–289.)

ON

Light

Where does light come from? You know it comes from the sun. It comes from the stars too. A fire makes light. A lamp makes light. What is the same about all these things? They are all hot.

Have you ever been in a place with no light at all? Most places have some light. Think of your room at night. Can you see a little bit when your lamp is out? If you can, there is some light getting in.

Without light, we could not see. We see things only when light falls on them.

TW

Our Best Friends

Many people have pets. Do you ever wonder how animals came to live with people?

Long ago, all animals were wild. People then hunted for food. They hunted many kinds of animals. They grew to like those that were smart, friendly, or useful. Horses were once food. So were rabbits and some birds. Today they are pets.

Wolves often followed hunters. They wanted some of the meat. Some were taken in to live with the hunters. Dogs come from the wolf family. They are the oldest pets.

Most pets come from families of wild animals that live in groups. One well known pet does not fit this picture. When you pet it, it makes a strange sound. This pet is the cat.

TH

The Ant Lion

If you were an ant, you would not want to meet an ant lion. Ant lions feed on ants. They trap them in holes that they dig in dry, loose soil.

The ant lion is an insect. It digs its hole by walking backwards in a circle. As it walks, it pushes its tail into the soil. This moves the dirt up over its wide back. By jerking its head, the ant lion throws the soil off to the side. The ant lion walks in smaller and smaller circles. At last, it reaches the center of its cone-shaped hole. The ant lion then hides in the soil at the bottom.

An unlucky ant walking on the edge slides down the soft sides of the hole. The waiting ant lion traps the ant in its jaws. The juices from the ant's body then become the ant lion's meal.

FO

Pop Goes the Kernel

You put a handful of kernels in. You plug in the popper. As they heat up, the kernels start to explode. Before you know it, that little pile of kernels has become a big bowl of popcorn.

What makes popcorn pop? The answer to that question has to do with what a kernel is made of and how it is put together.

The tough yellowish shell of a kernel covers a starchy inside. The secret to the popping, though, is the water. The tightly packed center of the kernel is moist. As the water heats up, it pushes against the walls of the kernel. Pressure builds up until, POP, the walls burst. The starchy center puffs out into bubbles that form the soft white part of the popcorn.

Popcorn fills about forty times more space than the unpopped kernels do, but it weighs less. Can you guess why? It's because something is missing.

FI

The Spirit to Win

When, at the age of four, Wilma Rudolph lost the ability to walk, she could not have dreamed that she would one day be the fastest woman runner in the world. But that is just what happened.

Wilma was born in Clarksville, Tennessee. When she was four years old, she was struck by polio. This crippling disease left Wilma's left leg paralyzed.

With constant exercise, Wilma's muscles regained some of their strength. After two years, Wilma was able to take a step or two. Every day, she pushed herself to go farther. When she was eight, she could walk with the aid of a leg brace. Wilma was not satisfied with that, though. She kept working. At eleven, she could walk without the brace. At thirteen, she joined the school basketball team. By fifteen, she was a star player and a member of the track team.

At sixteen, she ran in the Olympics and won a bronze medal. Four years later, in the 1960 Olympics, she won three gold medals. She was then voted the top amateur athlete in the United States. Wilma Rudolph's spirit and determination made her a winner in every way.

SI

Time Zones

When it is noon in New York, it is nine o'clock in Los Angeles. We know this because time zones divide the globe into neat time slots. But time zones are not natural elements. How and why did they come about?

Time zones developed from a railroad scheduling nightmare in the mid-1800s. At that time, people set their clocks by the sun. When the sun appeared to be directly overhead, they would set their clocks to noon. But what looked like overhead to one person did not to another. Also, because of the earth's rotation, the sun was overhead at different times in different places. So no one agreed on the time. This caused real problems for people attempting to catch trains and for people attempting to schedule them. The railroads pushed for some kind of standard time system.

Finally, a decision was made to divide the earth into twenty-four hour time zones, to match the twenty-four hours in a day. The width in each time zone was made equal to the distance the sun travels in one hour. Within each zone, the time would be the same, with noon occurring when the sun was over the middle of the zone.

The United States switched from sun time to official time on November 18, 1883. In some places on that day, noon came twice!

SE

The Game of Frisbee

On beaches, in parks, across backyards, people toss these plastic disks to one another. Playing Frisbee is as common now as playing catch. But until the 1960s, it was unheard of. Where did the Frisbee come from?

Well, its name comes from the Frisbee Pie Company. Frisbee Pies, which were made in Connecticut, were sold in metal pie plates with the company name stamped into them. In the early part of the century, some college students who liked the pies found that the plates were also enjoyable. They flipped the empty tins to one another in an outdoor game very much like you-know-what.

In 1948, a man named Fred Morrison, who had at one time had fun tossing pie pans, created a plastic flying saucer that could be played with in the same way. Plastic was a new product at the time. It made a much safer toy than the hard metal tins, and it could be molded into shapes that flew better. Morrison called his original flying saucers Pluto Platters.

He started out selling them on street corners. Then he got together with a new toy company named Wham-O. Wham-O improved the design of the disks. They also changed the name to Frisbee and sponsored Frisbee tournaments all over the country to promote Frisbee as a sport. The game caught on fast, and it looks as though it's here to stay.

EI

To Buy or Not to Buy

As a consumer, or buyer, you have been in a tremendous number of stores in your life. Have you ever given a thought to how those stores are arranged?

Carefully considered choices are made about where to display each type of merchandise. Where should the basic items go? How can you be made to notice items that you may not be looking for, and how can you be persuaded to make an unplanned purchase? These are questions that a store planner must answer.

Think about the stores that most people go into frequently: drugstores and supermarkets. Where are the basic items such as prescriptions, dairy products, produce, and meat situated? They are usually toward the back, forcing you to pass by numerous other products that may catch your eye.

There is even a whole category of products that are displayed where you are most likely to notice them: at the checkout counter. They are referred to as impulse items. The thinking is that when you spot one of these inexpensive items, you will decide you want it. Some common impulse items are magazines, candy, and batteries.

In a technique called scrambled merchandising, stores sometimes offer the same item in several places. For example, batteries might be placed in the hardware section as well as near the register. Seasons, too, affect the placement of merchandise. In summer, picnic supplies might stand in the busy front section of the store, while in November and December, holiday decorations occupy that space. So, when you walk into a drugstore next summer, remember that it is no accident that the sunglasses are right up in front.

NI

The Pencil—A Lasting Impression

Lincoln wrote part of the Gettysburg Address with one, and one of these instruments can draw a line thirty-five miles long. The device we call the pencil has had a long and glorious evolution dating back to the 1500s.

It took a hurricane to uncover the world's first mineral deposit of graphite, and thus make possible the invention of the pencil. After the storm, farmers found black material underneath an uprooted tree. These farmers found it useful to mark their sheep. Playwrights were happy to find a less messy method than feather pen and ink to record their stories. The first pencils were eventually wrapped in rope or encased in metal until the Germans invented a way to enclose the graphite in wood, the method we still use today.

For a long time, scientists thought the material they were writing with was actually lead, because of its similar appearance. However, in the late eighteenth century they discovered that the "lead" was actually a form of carbon. So, as a result of this discovery, scientists graciously renamed the material "graphite" from the Greek word meaning "to write."

Today's manufacturers mark their pencils with numbers ranging from one to four to identify the hardness of the graphite the pencil contains. This advancement was made possible by a Frenchman who developed a process of mixing graphite with clay to vary the texture.

Soon afterward, another breakthrough was made, without which pencils may have been written out of our history. When the known mineral deposits of graphite were beginning to diminish, an American discovered a way to manufacture graphite using coke.

However, most writers would agree that we are all most indebted to an American by the name of Hyman Lipman, who patented his idea of attaching erasers to pencils in 1858, five years before Lincoln authored the Gettysburg Address.

Graded Reading Passages Test: Form D—Narrative

(Examiner's record form appears on pages 290–307.)

ON

A Day by the Lake

Pat stood by the lake. A soft wind blew. Across the grass, ducks swam near the shore. There were big ducks and baby ducks.

Two stood on the grass near Pat. Pat opened a paper bag. She put her hand in it. It came out full of bits of bread. She dropped some bread around her on the ground. She threw some on the water. The ducks swam to it.

They quacked and ate the bread. Pat laughed and threw some more bread.

TW

The Lesson

There were once some children who were always fighting. Their father tried to get them to stop. They would not listen. They could not get along together. Finally, the father asked his children to do something to teach them a lesson. The father asked, "Bring me a bunch of sticks."

The children did as they were told. One child held out the bunch of sticks. The father said, "Try to break the bunch of sticks." The child tried. He could not break the bunch of sticks. Each child took a turn. No one could break the bunch of sticks. The father then handed one stick to each child. "Now try to break your stick," said the man.

Each child easily broke a stick in two. The father then said, "Take a lesson from the sticks, my children. Only together are they not able to be broken."

TH

The Blind Woman

A woman who had become blind called a doctor. She promised that if he could cure her, she would reward him well. If he failed, he would get nothing. The doctor agreed.

He went often to the woman's apartment. He would pretend to treat her eyes. But he would also steal furniture and other objects. Little by little, he took all her belongings. Finally, he used his skill to cure her and asked for his money.

Every time he asked for his payment, the woman made up a reason for not paying him. Eventually he took her to court. The woman said to the judge, "I did promise to pay the doctor if he gave me back my sight. However, how can I be cured? If I truly could see, wouldn't I see furniture and other belongings in my house?"

FO

The Promise

Long ago, in a distant land beside the sea, people often spotted mermaids. The mermaids had fantastic treasures. Sometimes the mermaids would swim to shore. They would spread their treasures around them on the sand. If anyone came near, however, they would jump back in the sea.

One day, two little girls walking on a beach spied a mermaid. To their surprise, she did not swim away when she saw them. Instead, she smiled and called them over. She gave each a bundle of treasure. "Do not open them until you get home," she warned. The girls promised not to. Then off they went, happy and excited.

One girl soon grew impatient. When she was out of sight of the mermaid, she decided to open her gift. To her disappointment, she found only ashes and dust.

The other girl kept her promise. She did not look inside until she got home. In her bundle she found gold, silver, and sparkling jewels. Her family was delighted, and they never forgot their good fortune.

FI

A Surprise for Miss Stern

Ricky Glen loved the outdoors. He always carried with him as much of his favorite environment as he could.

Last Tuesday, a shining early spring day, he carried a bit too much of it into Miss Stern's classroom. As usual, Miss Stern had Ricky leave his nature collection on her desk during class. That day it included a stick with a light brown papery ball attached to it. It was that strange ball that caused the trouble.

All was fine until one o'clock, when Miss Stern said, "Now take out your math books." Perhaps it was the warm sun shining onto the desk that started the whole thing. Whatever it was, that ball began to wiggle and shake. Twenty amazed pairs of eyes stared as hundreds of tiny green specks jumped from it. They hopped around on Miss Stern's desk. They even hopped on Miss Stern. Bolting for the door, she yelled, "Ricky! What is the meaning of this!"

"They're baby grasshoppers, Miss Stern!"

The words, "Get rid of those tiny insects, Ricky!" faded down the hallway with Miss Stern.

Ricky scooped the babies from Miss Stern's desk, the flower pots, the floor, and the windowsills. He gathered them all up in a box and carried them outside—all, that is, except the ones that rode out in Miss Stern's hair.

SI

The Strange Day

On that crisp Monday morning in late October, Jane's alarm sounded at seven, as usual. Jane pulled herself out of bed and proceeded to get ready for school. It was as ordinary a morning as a morning can be. Jane showered, ate breakfast, got dressed, patted the cat good-bye, and headed out the door. That's when things began to look a bit out of the ordinary.

Why was it so quiet? Usually the sidewalks were dotted with kids going to school, but today Jane emerged as the sole pedestrian. Even cars were scarce.

By the time she reached the school, Jane was feeling decidedly uneasy. There, she encountered the strangest thing of all. Not a soul was in sight, and the school doors were locked tight. What was going on? Her senses reeling, Jane leaned her head against the locked door.

A minute later, Jane nearly jumped out of her skin when a deep voice boomed, "What are you doing here so early?" Spinning around, she found herself facing Mr. Cheston, the school janitor. Her heart hammering, Jane screeched, "Where is everyone?" Mr. Cheston leaned closer and said in a low voice, "You forgot to set your clock back, didn't you?"

As his words penetrated, Jane went limp and echoed, "Clock?" "That's right," laughed Mr. Cheston heartily. "Daylight saving time is over. You're an hour ahead of the rest of us!"

SE

Up, Up, and Away

Though the sun had set long ago, the heavy air stuck to my skin like a damp cloth. The July sky blazed with stars so bright they rivaled the gaudy reds, greens, and yellows that turned night on the ground into a weird artificial day. Shouts, laughter, music, screams of terror and delight, dings, rings, and hums filled the air.

Transported by the exotic scent of popcorn and cotton candy, Jeff and I wrestled our way through the crowd to my favorite ride. We climbed aboard and the attendant banged the safety bar into place. The seat swung back and forth as the big wheel began to turn, carrying us back and up, up, a hundred feet into the night sky.

As we climbed, the noise fell away and the scene below us grew and grew, till it looked like a picture in a book, complete and removed from us. The wheel paused, with Jeff and me swinging madly at the top, and I inhaled the dreamy scene mingled with the cool, fresh air of the higher altitudes. Suddenly we dropped back to earth. My heart and stomach leaped to my throat, and I shouted in spite of myself. There isn't a better way to spend a summer night.

EI

Stage Fright

Civic duty, volunteerism, getting involved—whatever you call it, one of these noble descriptive phrases motivated my brief but memorable venture into the world of acting.

It all began innocently. My school's drama club was to present an original play about the Roman Empire. It seemed the entire student body was participating; so who was I to resist the lure of stardom?

So the process ensued—auditions, rehearsals, and finally, the night of the fated fiasco itself. I was to serve as the narrator, introducing the cast and events to the audience. A rather innocuous role I assumed. How was I to know an overzealous cleaning man had unwittingly "staged" a surprise for my first and only "stage left"?

When the time approached for my debut, I realized my breathing had quickened and my stomach had become queasy. Stage fright had set in. But worst of all, a frog-sized lump was lodged in my throat. How was I to narrate anything?

Not to worry. As I took my first step toward the limelight, my knees locked and my feet slid out from under. With all the grace of an elephant, I made my entrance and exit almost simultaneously, sliding on my toga across the overwaxed stage. A sprained ankle relieved me of my duties as narrator. And so ended my glorious career as an entertainer—although I did receive a standing ovation as the cast carried me out on a stretcher for the final curtain call. Mom would have been proud—if she'd stayed.

NI

The White Trail

The sleds were singing their eternal lament to the creaking of the harnesses and the tinkling bells of the leaders, but the men and dogs were tired and made no sound. The trail was heavy with new-fallen snow, and they had traveled far, and the runners, burdened with quarters of frozen moose, clung to the unpacked surface and resisted with a stubborness almost human. Darkness was coming on, but there was no camp in the vicinity that evening. The snow fell gently through the still air, not in flakes, but in tiny frost crystals. It was very warm—barely ten degrees below zero—and the men did not mind.

The dogs had become fatigued early in the afternoon, but they now began to show new vigor. Among the intelligent ones there was a certain restlessness—an impatience, a sniffling of snouts and raising of ears, and these became irritated with their more sluggish brothers, urging them on with numerous sly nips on their hindquarters. Those, thus scolded, perked up and assisted in spreading the excitement. At last, the leader of the foremost sled uttered a short whine of satisfaction, crouching lower in the snow and throwing himself against the collar. The rest followed suit. There was a tightening of muscles in the harness; the sleds leaped forward, and the men clung to the gee-poles, violently accelerating their pace to escape going under the runners. The weariness of the day fell from them, and they whooped encouragement to the dogs. The animals responded with joyous yelps. They were swinging through the gathering darkness at a rattling gallop.

Source: Adapted from London, J. (1982). An odyssey of the north. In *Jack London: Novels and stories* (pp. 333–364). New York: Literary Classics of the United States.

Examiner's Record Forms and Quick Lists of Instructions for Initial Administration and for Diagnostic Options

Initial Administration

Summary of Student Performance Sheet   179

Reading Reflections Interview Form   180

Quick List of Instructions for Administering the Graded Words
   in Context Test   182

Graded Words in Context Test: Form A   183

Quick List of Instructions for Administering the Graded Reading
   Passages Test   193

Graded Reading Passages Test: Form A—Expository   195

Graded Words in Context Test: Form B   213

Graded Reading Passages Test: Form B—Narrative   223

Story Retelling Form to Assess Sense of Story Structure
   and Comprehension   241

Quick List of Instructions for Administering the Dictated Story
   Assessment Strategy   243

Dictated Story Assessment Strategy Record Form   245

SIRI Synthesis of Information Rubric   248

Summary of Student Performance Sheet

Student's Name: _____ Sex: _____ Age: _____ years _____ months

School: _____ School System: _____ Grade Placement: _____

Examiner: _____ Date(s) of Administration: _____

Graded Words in Context Form: _____ Oral Reading Form(s): _____

Listening Comprehension Form(s): _____

Graded Words in Isolation Form: _____ Silent Reading Form(s): _____

GRADED WORDS TESTS

GRADE LEVEL	PERCENT CORRECT	
	Context	Isolation
PP		
P		
1		
2		
3		
4		
5		
6		
7		
8		

GRADED READING PASSAGES TEST

EXPOSITORY

Grade Level	Word Recognition	Oral Comp.	List. Comp. (%)	Prior Knowledge (1–5)	Interest (1–5)
1					
2					
3					
4					
5					
6					
7					
8					
9					

NARRATIVE

Grade Level	Word Recognition	Oral Comp.	List. Comp. (%)	Prior Knowledge (Y–N)	Interest (1–5)
1					
2					
3					
4					
5					
6					
7					
8					
9					

ESTIMATED READING LEVELS

	GRADE LEVELS	
	Expository	Narrative
Independent		
Instructional*		
Frustration		
Listening		

*List as one grade level or range of two grade levels (e.g., 5–6).

☐ Shaded areas are used to record results of diagnostic options.

Reading Reflections Interview Form

Student's Name: _____ Sex: _____ Age: _____ years _____ months

School: _____ School System: _____ Grade Placement: _____

Interviewer: _____ Date of Interview: _____

INTERVIEWER INSTRUCTIONS: During the interview, feel free to probe to elicit as much information about the student's knowledge of the reading process, perceptions of reading and his or her reading ability, and interest in reading. General probe questions such as, Can you tell me more about that? or, Anything else? may be used and, when asked, should be recorded on this form.

Throughout the interview, look for patterns of responses. This can serve as the basis for answering the summary questions listed at the end of this form.

STUDENT DIRECTIONS: Read the following directions to the student.

"I will be asking you some questions to find out what you think and feel about reading. There are no right or wrong answers. Just do the best you can to answer each question. As you are answering these questions, I will be taking some notes. This is to help me remember what you have said. Let's begin with this question."

Knowledge of Reading

1. What is reading? _____

_____

_____

2. Why do people read? _____

_____

_____

3. Can you read if you don't have a book? (Additional prompt: What else can a person read besides a book?) _____

_____

_____

Perceptions of Reading and Reading Ability

4. How did you learn to read? _____

_____

_____

5. Are you a good reader? How do you know? _____

_____

_____

6. How does a teacher decide which students are good readers?

_____

7. What does a person have to learn to be a good reader?

_____

_____

Interest in Reading

8. Are there some things you *like* about reading? Please explain.

_____

_____

9. Are there some things you *don't like* about reading? Please explain.

_____

_____

10. Finish this sentence: If I could choose anything to read, I would like to read about . . . (Prompt student to add to this sentence by saying: "Can you think of anything *else* you would like to read about?"

_____

_____

_____

SUMMARY

What does the student know about the nature of reading?

What are the student's perceptions of reading and his or her reading ability?

What are the student's reading interests?

Additional comments:

Quick List of Instructions for Administering the Graded Words in Context Test

(Refer to pages 15–16, 19–20 in Section Two for more information about how to establish rapport and administer the Graded Words in Context Test.)

1. Have a copy of the appropriate form to record the results of the Graded Words in Context Test (see pages 183–192 or 213–222).

2. Have a student's copy of the Graded Words in Context Test (see pages 183–192 or 213–222).

3. As a rule of thumb, begin with the sentence set that is two grade levels below the student's actual grade placement or two grade levels below a student's grade equivalent score on a recently administered norm-referenced test.

4. Give the following directions to the student:

   "I have some sentences that I want you to read to me. Some of these sentences will be easy for you to read, and others may be more difficult. Try hard to read all the words in each sentence. If there are words you don't know, try to figure them out. Do the best you can. As you are reading these sentences, I will be taking some notes. This is to help me remember what you have read. Do you have any questions? Let's begin with this sentence."

5. Open the test booklet to the appropriate page.

6. Point to the first sentence and have the student begin reading to you.

7. When a target word is pronounced correctly, place a + on the line to the left of the sentence on the record form. If the target word is missed, place a – on the line to the left of the sentence.

8. Use the coding system found on pages 19–20 for recording miscues with target words only.

9. Stop after two target words in a sentence set are missed.

10. Begin with the next lower sentence set and continue until every target word in a sentence set is pronounced correctly.

11. Record the percentage of correct target word responses on the line provided at the bottom of each sentence set (e.g., 95 percent) on the examiner's record form. When two target words are missed and testing is discontinued before the set is completed, write *inc.* (incomplete) on this line.

12. Record the results on the Summary of Student Performance Sheet provided on page 179.

Graded Words in Context Test: Form A

(Student's test materials appear on pages 89–97.)

Preprimer

1. at   _____   Look **at** this old car.

2. in   _____   You can ride **in** my car.

3. dog   _____   This **dog** is not old.

4. but   _____   You can come, **but** your pet can't.

5. red   _____   This is a **red** book.

6. get   _____   Can you **get** me a pet?

7. like   _____   I **like** his little dog.

8. to   _____   It is time **to** go home.

9. ride   _____   Can you **ride** on a bear?

10. want   _____   I **want** a big book.

            _____   %

Primer

1. sit   _____   We want you to **sit** down.

2. eat   _____   I like to **eat** fish.

3. may   _____   I **may** want to run with you.

4. take   _____   She will **take** the boy to the game.

5. two   _____   They have **two** fish at home.

6. saw   _____   She **saw** a boy read a big book.

7. away   _____   He will run **away** from the bear.

8. mother   _____   Is your **mother** at home?

9. little   _____   The **little** boy is in your car.

10. found   _____   Who **found** your cat?

             _____   %

Grade 1

1.	bus	_____	The green **bus** will take me to my house.
2.	stay	_____	We want you to **stay** with us today.
3.	far	_____	The school is **far** from her house.
4.	hear	_____	I like to **hear** the rain fall.
5.	again	_____	Can you read this book **again**?
6.	sister	_____	I will surprise my **sister** with this trick.
7.	off	_____	We get **off** at this bus stop.
8.	town	_____	We take the bus to **town.**
9.	wish	_____	I **wish** I had a pet to play with.
10.	isn't	_____	A fox **isn't** nice to a rabbit.
11.	give	_____	I will **give** this plant to my friend.
12.	story	_____	Tell me a **story** about a bear.
13.	than	_____	There are more **than** three fish in the water.
14.	zoo	_____	A lion can live in a **zoo.**
15.	long	_____	How **long** will it take you to bake a cake?
16.	morning	_____	I jump out of bed in the **morning.**
17.	another	_____	I want to play **another** game.
18.	hand	_____	I can open the door with my **hand.**
19.	right	_____	This is the **right** way to go to school.
20.	please	_____	Can I **please** have some water?
		_____	%

Grade 2

1.	low	_____	The water in the lake is very **low.**
2.	deer	_____	Will the little **deer** find her mother?
3.	few	_____	A **few** children hid under the table.
4.	afraid	_____	Some children are **afraid** of the dark.
5.	rest	_____	He took a **rest** in his bed after dinner.
6.	mile	_____	The school is a **mile** from her house.
7.	such	_____	The boy said, "You have **such** a nice smile."
8.	I'd	_____	**I'd** like to see my friend next week.
9.	carry	_____	She has many books to **carry** to school.
10.	puppy	_____	Look at the **puppy** run up the hill!
11.	owl	_____	The **owl** is a bird with two big eyes.
12.	seven	_____	There were **seven** fish in the lake.
13.	quick	_____	The **quick** rabbit ran faster than the mouse.
14.	mountain	_____	The top of this **mountain** is very high.
15.	visit	_____	Grandma will **visit** us next week.
16.	follow	_____	When will your sister **follow** us to school?
17.	dragon	_____	I heard a story about a bad **dragon.**
18.	anyone	_____	Is there **anyone** in this room who has a snake?
19.	farmer	_____	I know a **farmer** who has many animals.
20.	evening	_____	He reads to his children every **evening.**
		_____	%

Grade 3

1. crop   _____   The farmer had a nice **crop** of corn.

2. force   _____   Give it to me at once, or I will **force** you to!

3. motor   _____   A car cannot run without a **motor**.

4. usual   _____   He was late to school as **usual**.

5. yesterday   _____   We went to the zoo **yesterday**.

6. bother   _____   She will like you more if you don't **bother** her.

7. enjoy   _____   You will really **enjoy** this magic show.

8. history   _____   We will learn about the **history** of our country.

9. nibble   _____   A rabbit likes to **nibble** on a carrot.

10. scratch   _____   If you are not careful, this cat will **scratch** you.

11. parent   _____   Which **parent** will visit the school today?

12. television   _____   Some children watch too much **television**.

13. whisker   _____   The man found a gray **whisker** growing on his chin.

14. treat   _____   I do my best to **treat** my pets well.

15. accident   _____   I spilled paint on your pants by **accident**.

16. dare   _____   I **dare** you to take that frog to school.

17. understand   _____   Did you **understand** the answer to that question?

18. notebook   _____   I write everything down in my **notebook**.

19. amaze   _____   Your magic tricks will **amaze** everyone.

20. familiar   _____   The man in the green shirt looks so **familiar**.

                     _____   %

Grade 4

1.	plot	_____	Did you understand the **plot** of this story?
2.	rhyme	_____	"Name" and "game" are two words that **rhyme**.
3.	uproar	_____	There was an **uproar** when the lion escaped from his cage.
4.	bold	_____	The **bold** girl protected her friend from danger.
5.	fashion	_____	It is in **fashion** to wear this kind of shoe.
6.	property	_____	Do you know how much **property** he owns on this street?
7.	aware	_____	I was too sleepy to be **aware** of how cold it was.
8.	cookbook	_____	I bought a **cookbook** with 9 recipes for making fish.
9.	hoarse	_____	A bad cold often makes a person sound **hoarse**.
10.	represent	_____	He has a friend who will **represent** him in court.
11.	slope	_____	It is hard to climb a mountain with a steep **slope**.
12.	excellent	_____	She earned a high or **excellent** grade on this test.
13.	telegraph	_____	A **telegraph** is used to send a message to someone.
14.	oyster	_____	This pearl came from an **oyster**.
15.	fortunate	_____	She was **fortunate** to have won the contest.
16.	subject	_____	Reading is my favorite **subject** in school.
17.	taxi	_____	This **taxi** will take you to the airport.
18.	downhill	_____	It is lots of fun to ride a sled **downhill**.
19.	increase	_____	If you eat too much, your weight will **increase**.
20.	thunderstorm	_____	Children are usually frightened by a **thunderstorm**.
		_____	%

Grade 5

1.   conquer   _____   The terrible king tried to **conquer** the world.

2.   injure   _____   If you are not careful, this saw will **injure** you.

3.   plantation   _____   Many crops can be grown on a large **plantation.**

4.   wrist   _____   He wore a gold watch on his **wrist.**

5.   gratitude   _____   I am filled with **gratitude** for the favor you did.

6.   attract   _____   Sweets can **attract** flies at a picnic.

7.   delightful   _____   One day we had a **delightful** ride in the country.

8.   furnish   _____   Can you **furnish** this room with only two chairs?

9.   emerald   _____   An **emerald** is a bright green stone or jewel.

10. manufacturer   _____   The **manufacturer** of this car also makes trucks.

11. shrewd   _____   She was **shrewd** to buy a house ten years ago.

12. treatment   _____   This pill is a good **treatment** for that illness.

13. obvious   _____   It is **obvious** that two and two make four.

14. satisfactory   _____   He was happy to earn a **satisfactory** grade in spelling.

15. assignment   _____   Your **assignment** for tomorrow is to read Chapter 5.

16. brightness   _____   The **brightness** of the sun can damage your eyes.

17. dreary   _____   A cloudy, rainy day is a **dreary** day.

18. universe   _____   Our earth is but a small part of the **universe.**

19. somersault   _____   We are learning to **somersault** in gym class.

20. prehistoric   _____   The dinosaur is an example of a **prehistoric** animal.

_____   %

Grade 6

1. minor   _____   The mistakes you made on this test are only **minor** ones.

2. sympathy   _____   We feel **sympathy** toward people who are ill.

3. evident   _____   It is quite **evident** that they are twins.

4. collision   _____   Many people were hurt in the **collision** of the two trains.

5. igloo   _____   An **igloo** is a hut built of blocks of ice.

6. minimum   _____   It is wise to eat only a **minimum** of candy.

7. politician   _____   An election year is a busy time for a **politician**.

8. ordeal   _____   It was always an **ordeal** to take me to the dentist.

9. yield   _____   Offer more money and he will **yield** to your plan!

10. comprehend   _____   I can't **comprehend** a story with many hard words.

11. frustrate   _____   This difficult puzzle is sure to **frustrate** you.

12. examination   _____   I study hard for every **examination** in science.

13. legendary   _____   The old man was a **legendary** figure in his sport.

14. unconscious   _____   The ball hit me so hard, it knocked me **unconscious**.

15. slouch   _____   I **slouch** in my favorite chair when I am tired.

16. weakness   _____   Putting things off is her greatest **weakness**.

17. appreciation   _____   A note of **appreciation** was sent to everyone who helped.

18. quantity   _____   There is an equal **quantity** of nuts and raisins in this cake.

19. wanderer   _____   The **wanderer** moved from city to city.

20. embarrassment _____   I felt much **embarrassment** when I slipped and fell.

_____   %

Grade 7

1.	oasis	_____	They stopped to drink water at an **oasis** in the desert.
2.	vicinity	_____	There are no houses for sale in this **vicinity**.
3.	confidential	_____	Keep the information about the spies **confidential**!
4.	identical	_____	Both students earned **identical** grades of "A" on the test.
5.	prominent	_____	The President of the United States is a **prominent** person.
6.	repetition	_____	After much **repetition**, she memorized her part for the play.
7.	zoologist	_____	A person who studies animal life is a **zoologist**.
8.	authentic	_____	The coin collector examined the rare coin to see if it was **authentic**.
9.	disadvantage	_____	His stage fright was a **disadvantage** each time he had to give a speech.
10.	hibernation	_____	The scientists studied the **hibernation** habits of bears.
11.	luxurious	_____	The expensive carpets gave the room a **luxurious** look.
12.	unsuspecting	_____	The shy thief had an **unsuspecting** look on his face.
13.	translation	_____	This story is a **translation** of a tale written in French.
14.	breakthrough	_____	It will be a real **breakthrough** when a cure for this illness is found.
15.	evaluate	_____	The results of the test were used to **evaluate** her writing skills.
16.	sophisticated	_____	He looks so **sophisticated** in his three-piece suit.
17.	frequency	_____	Storms seem to occur with more **frequency** in March.
18.	mayonnaise	_____	I like to eat a lettuce, tomato, and **mayonnaise** sandwich.
19.	resemblance	_____	There is a great **resemblance** between the mother and her daughter.
20.	interpretation	_____	Do you agree with his **interpretation** of that poem?
		_____	%

Grade 8

1. serial _____ A soap opera is like a never-ending **serial**.

2. urgency _____ The police were informed of the **urgency** of his plea for help.

3. beverage _____ Orange juice is my favorite **beverage**.

4. novelty _____ The children enjoyed the **novelty** of staying up late.

5. assumption _____ It was a poor **assumption** to think that the test would be easy.

6. voluntarily _____ The criminal surrendered to the police **voluntarily**.

7. transformation _____ Is it possible to observe the **transformation** of a caterpillar into a butterfly?

8. optimistic _____ They were **optimistic** about the team's chance to win.

9. perishable _____ A **perishable** food such as fish should be refrigerated.

10. convincingly _____ The blue team beat the green team **convincingly**.

11. qualification _____ Skill in writing is the main **qualification** for this job at the newspaper.

12. grievance _____ The worker's complaint about low pay was heard by the **grievance** committee.

13. exhilarating _____ The father said that the birth of his daughter was an **exhilarating** experience.

14. knowledgeable _____ They drove many miles to hear her lecture because they knew she was so **knowledgeable**.

15. implication _____ Because the student scored well on the test, there was the **implication** that he would succeed.

16. rehabilitation _____ The injured man started a **rehabilitation** program for his broken leg.

17. unaccustomed _____ I live in Florida and am **unaccustomed** to snow.

18. habitual _____ The **habitual** smoker decided to quit smoking.

19. phenomenal _____ An eclipse of the sun is a **phenomenal** event.

20. monotonous _____ It is **monotonous** to play the same game ten times.

_____ %

Quick List of Instructions for Administering the Graded Reading Passages Test

(Refer to pages 20–31 in Section Two for more information about how to administer the Graded Reading Passages Test.)

1. Select the prose type (narrative or expository).

2. Have a copy of the appropriate form to record the results of the Graded Reading Passages Test (see pages 195–212 for Form A—Expository; and pages 223–240 for Form B—Narrative).

3. Use the student's base level score on the Graded Words in Context Test to determine the level at which to begin administering the Graded Reading Passages Test.

4. Give the following directions to the student:

   "**I am going to have you read some material to me out loud. Some of these passages will be easy for you to read, and others may be more difficult. Try hard to pronounce as many of the words as possible. Also, try to remember what you are reading. When you have finished, I will take the booklet away and ask you some questions.** (Free Recall option: **When you are finished, I will take the booklet away and ask you to tell me what you remember about the passage.**) **I will again be taking notes. This is to help me remember what you have read. Do you understand? Let's begin with this passage.**"

5. Open the test booklet to the appropriate page and place the booklet in front of the student.

6. Refer to the duplicated copy of the examiner's record form for the selected passage on the Graded Reading Passages Test. Read the introductory statement at the top of the page to the student.

7. Have the pupil read the passage out loud, beginning with the title. (It is recommended that the examiner use a tape recorder when administering this test.)

8. As the student is reading the material aloud, use the Marking System for Oral Reading Miscues presented in Table 2.1 on page 22 to record miscues in word recognition on the examiner's record form.

9. Roughly score performance in word recognition as the student progresses through the passages. (A more accurate scoring of miscues takes place after testing, when a tape recording of the session is played back.)

10. When the student has finished reading a passage, remove the manual and begin the comprehension check. Decide whether to use probed recall, free recall, or a combination of the two procedures to check comprehension of each selection.

    a. If *probed recall* is used, ask the questions listed on the record form.

    b. If the *free recall* technique is used, ask, "**What can you tell me about the passage you have just read?**" Record in the free recall column on the record form the questions from the probed recall that are addressed during the free recall, or retelling, of the article.

    To assist the examiner, a Story Retelling Form to Assess Sense of Story Structure is provided on pages 241–242.

11. Responses to questions are entered on the passage record form. If a question is answered correctly, place a + on the line in the probed recall column to the right of the printed question (or in the free recall column if this procedure is used). If a question is missed, place a – on the line to the right. Half credit can be given as well. If a student does not respond to a question or does not know the answer, enter DK (don't know) on the line to the right of the question.

12. After the student finishes reading an *expository* selection, show the pupil the Prior Knowledge scale and have the student determine a self-perceived level of prior knowledge for the passage just read. Record the student's response on the form. After the student finishes reading a *narrative* selection, ask, "Have you ever read this story before?" Record the student's answer on the form.

13. Then, point to the Level of Interest scale, read the question, and have the student determine a self-perceived level of interest. Record the student's response on the scale.

14. Quickly score the comprehension segment of the passage test by totaling the number of literal and interpretive comprehension errors, and enter the number on the Total Comprehension Errors line on the record form.

15. Let **x** mark the spot on the comprehension side of this scale to show the error count and equivalent reading level for the passage read.

16. Use the results of the first selection read to determine whether the next highest or lowest passage should be read by the student.

17. Have the student read as many selections as needed to gather enough information to delineate the range of reading levels: independent, instructional, or frustration.

18. Record the results on the Summary of Student Performance Sheet provided on page 179.

Graded Reading Passages Test: Form A—Expository

(Student's test materials appear on pages 98–106.)

 Clouds in the Sky (1)

INTRODUCTION: Please read this article to learn something about clouds.

Clouds in the Sky

Look up in the sky. What do you see?

There are clouds. Some can look white. Others

can look dark and gray.

On a sunny day we may see nice, big ones.

The sun can shine through and make them look

white.

On another day we may see many clouds.

They are all over the sky. It looks like it will

rain. The sun cannot shine through as well.

This makes the clouds look dark and gray.

Accountable Miscues

Full Miscues: _____ × 1 = _____

Half Miscues: _____ × $\frac{1}{2}$ = _____

TOTAL _____

COMPREHENSION CHECK

	Probed Recall	*Free Recall*

L 1. What is the color of clouds on a cloudy day? _____ _____

(gray) (dark and gray)

L 2. Why do clouds look white on a sunny day? _____ _____

(The sun shines through and makes them look white.)

L 3. On what kind of a day might we see big clouds? _____ _____

(on a nice day) (sunny day)

L 4. Why do clouds look dark and gray on a cloudy day? _____ _____

(because the sun cannot shine through as well)

I 5. Why can't we see the sun on a day when the clouds look dark and gray? _____ _____

(because the sun is covered by the clouds)

C 6. Do you like clouds when they are white or gray? Why? _ _ _ _

(Accept any logical response, such as "I like them when they are white because this means I can play outside.")

Total Comprehension Errors _____

(L & I)

PRIOR KNOWLEDGE

How much did you know about why clouds are white and gray before reading this article?

I knew:

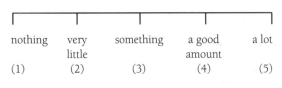

nothing	very little	something	a good amount	a lot
(1)	(2)	(3)	(4)	(5)

LEVEL OF INTEREST

How much did you like reading this article?

This article was:

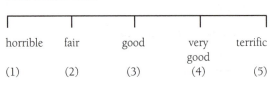

horrible	fair	good	very good	terrific
(1)	(2)	(3)	(4)	(5)

LEVELS OF WORD RECOGNITION AND COMPREHENSION

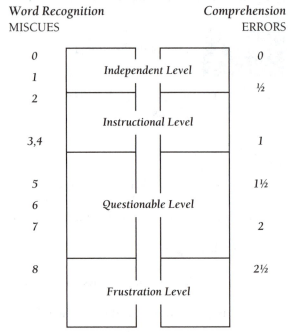

Word Recognition
MISCUES

Comprehension
ERRORS

MISCUES		ERRORS
0	Independent Level	0
1		½
2		
	Instructional Level	
3,4		1
5		1½
6	Questionable Level	
7		2
8		2½
	Frustration Level	

Clouds in the Sky (1)

CATEGORIES OF ACCOUNTABLE MISCUES IN WORD RECOGNITION

FULL MISCUES	NUMBER	HALF MISCUES	NUMBER
Nonword Substitutions		Whole Word Substitutions	
Whole Word Substitutions		Omissions	
Omissions		Insertions	
Insertions			
Reversals			
Repetitions			
Pronounced by Examiner			

CATEGORIES OF COMPREHENSION ERRORS

	FREE AND PROBED RECALL	
	Items Attempted (Free and Probed)	*Number of Errors*
Literal		
Interpretive		
Critical/Creative		

E   *Hide and Seek* (2)

INTRODUCTION: Have you ever played the game of "hide and seek"? Please read this article to learn about the first people to do hide and seek.

Note: If necessary, provide background information about how the game is played.

Hide and Seek

Many children like to play "hide and seek."

Hide and seek did not begin as a game. It

started many years ago in a far away land.

Hide and seek was something grown-ups

did each year when winter was over. People

were tired of the cold and the long nights. They

wanted to know if spring was on the way.

Grown-ups would leave their village and go

into the woods. They tried to find or "seek out"

birds and flowers. It was important to return

with a bird or flower. If one did, this was a sign

that spring had really started.

Accountable Miscues

Full Miscues: _____ × 1 = _____

Half Miscues: _____ × $\frac{1}{2}$ = _____

TOTAL _____

COMPREHENSION CHECK

		Probed Recall	Free Recall

L 1. When did hide and seek start?   _____   _____

(many years ago)

L 2. Many years ago, who did hide and seek?   _____   _____

(grown-ups)

L 3. During what time of the year did grown-ups do hide and seek?   _____   _____

(after winter)

(at the beginning of spring)

(springtime)

L 4. Name two things people looked for when they did hide and seek.   _____   _____

(birds and flowers)

I 5. Hide and seek was something grown-ups did each year. Why was it so important for them to do hide and seek?   _____   _____

(It was used to find out when spring had really started.)

(It was an important custom.)

C 6. Hide and seek is different today. Why is this so?   _ _   _ _

(It is no longer a ritual or custom.)

(We have better ways of determining the start of spring.)

(Because a long time ago it wasn't a game, but today it is a game.)

Total Comprehension Errors _____

(L & I)

PRIOR KNOWLEDGE

How much did you know about how hide and seek started before reading this article?

I knew:

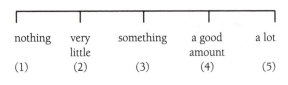

nothing	very little	something	a good amount	a lot
(1)	(2)	(3)	(4)	(5)

LEVEL OF INTEREST

How much did you like reading this article?

This article was:

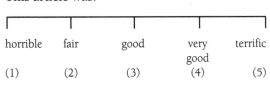

horrible	fair	good	very good	terrific
(1)	(2)	(3)	(4)	(5)

LEVELS OF WORD RECOGNITION AND COMPREHENSION

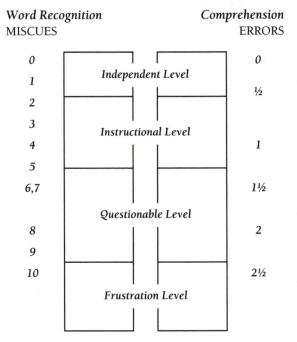

Hide and Seek (2)

CATEGORIES OF ACCOUNTABLE MISCUES IN WORD RECOGNITION

FULL MISCUES	NUMBER	HALF MISCUES	NUMBER
Nonword Substitutions		Whole Word Substitutions	
Whole Word Substitutions		Omissions	
Omissions		Insertions	
Insertions			
Reversals			
Repetitions			
Pronounced by Examiner			

CATEGORIES OF COMPREHENSION ERRORS

	FREE AND PROBED RECALL	
	Items Attempted (Free and Probed)	*Number of Errors*
Literal		
Interpretive		
Critical/Creative		

Hangnails (3)

INTRODUCTION: Please read this article to learn something about hangnails.

Hangnails

What is a hangnail? First of all, a hangnail is not really a nail. It is a tough, little piece of skin that hangs loosely at the side of your fingernail.

You get a hangnail when the skin around your nail gets a little dry. Then a piece of skin might start peeling off. Soon the piece of skin starts rubbing against your other fingers or against objects that you touch. The rubbing bothers the hangnail and makes the skin red and sore.

What do you do with a hangnail? Don't pick it. Don't bite it off. That will only make it worse. Instead, cut it off with scissors or nail clippers.

You can avoid getting hangnails by taking good care of your hands and nails. After washing your hands, dry them well. Use lotion to keep dry skin smooth.

Source: Reprinted from "What Is a Hangnail?" in *3-2-1 Contact Magazine,* April 1988, p. 5. Copyright © Sesame Workshop, 1988.

COMPREHENSION CHECK

		Probed Recall	Free Recall
L 1.	What is a hangnail?	___	___
	(A hangnail is a tough, little piece of skin that hangs loosely at the side of your fingernail.)		
L 2.	You get a hangnail when the skin around your nail gets to be what?	___	___
	(dry)		
L 3.	What shouldn't you do to a hangnail?	___	___
	(pick it) (bite it off)		
L 4.	How should a hangnail be removed?	___	___
	(with scissors or nail clippers)		
I 5.	Why can a hangnail hurt?	___	___
	(because the skin is red and sore from rubbing against something)		
C 6.	Why should a young child ask an adult to remove a hangnail?	_ _	_ _
	(Young children may not know how to use scissors or nail clippers properly.)		
	(for safety reasons)		

Total Comprehension Errors _____
(L & I)

Accountable Miscues

Full Miscues: _____ × 1 = _____

Half Miscues: _____ × $\frac{1}{2}$ = _____

TOTAL _____

PRIOR KNOWLEDGE

How much did you know about hangnails before reading this article?

I knew:

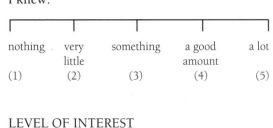

nothing	very little	something	a good amount	a lot
(1)	(2)	(3)	(4)	(5)

LEVEL OF INTEREST

How much did you like reading this article?

This article was:

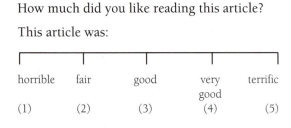

horrible	fair	good	very good	terrific
(1)	(2)	(3)	(4)	(5)

LEVELS OF WORD RECOGNITION AND COMPREHENSION

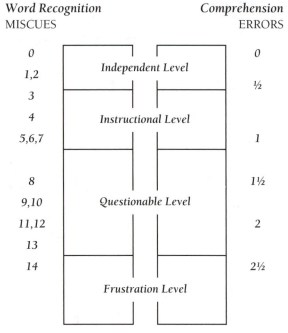

Word Recognition
MISCUES

Comprehension
ERRORS

MISCUES	Level	ERRORS
0 / 1,2 / 3	Independent Level	0 / ½
4 / 5,6,7	Instructional Level	1
8 / 9,10 / 11,12 / 13	Questionable Level	1½ / 2
14	Frustration Level	2½

Hangnails (3)

CATEGORIES OF ACCOUNTABLE MISCUES IN WORD RECOGNITION

FULL MISCUES	NUMBER	HALF MISCUES	NUMBER
Nonword Substitutions		Whole Word Substitutions	
Whole Word Substitutions		Omissions	
Omissions		Insertions	
Insertions			
Reversals			
Repetitions			
Pronounced by Examiner			

CATEGORIES OF COMPREHENSION ERRORS

	FREE AND PROBED RECALL	
	Items Attempted (Free and Probed)	*Number of Errors*
Literal		
Interpretive		
Critical/Creative		

Smelly Stickers (4)

INTRODUCTION: Please read this article to learn how scratch and sniff or smelly stickers work.

Smelly Stickers

How do smelly stickers work? Almost any smell you can think of, from pizza to peanut butter, can be captured and put on a scratch and sniff sticker. But there's more to them than meets the nose!

Take a look at a sticker. All you see is a picture of something. But hundreds of thousands of super-small containers are glued to that sticker. Inside each container is a little bit of fragrance. The smell may come from the object pictured or it may have been made in a laboratory with chemicals.

When you scratch the sticker, you break open some of the containers. That releases the smell. But don't scratch too hard. You only need to open a few to catch the scent and your sticker will last a lot longer.

Some smells can't be captured. So far, they can't put the smell of a hamburger on a sticker. But wouldn't you rather smell the real thing . . . just before you bite into a double cheeseburger?

Source: Reprinted from "How Do Smelly Stickers Work?," in *3-2-1 Contact Magazine,* March 1988, p. 33. Copyright © Sesame Workshop, 1988.

COMPREHENSION CHECK

		Probed Recall	Free Recall
L 1.	Name a smell mentioned in the article that can be put on a smelly sticker.	____	____
	(peanut butter)		
L 2.	Name a smell that has not been put on a smelly sticker.	____	____
	(hamburger) (cheeseburger)		
L 3.	There are hundreds of thousands of what glued to a smelly sticker?	____	____
	(containers)		
L 4.	What happens when you scratch a smelly sticker?	____	____
	(You break open some of the containers. This releases a smell.)		
I 5.	Janet has a smelly sticker. Her smelly sticker lost its smell much faster than Bill's. Why?	____	____
	(Janet scratched her smelly sticker too hard.)		
C 6.	Why do you think smelly stickers are made for people to buy?	– –	– –
	(for fun) (entertainment)		

Note: If pupil's answer is "to smell," probe with: "But why do people buy them?"

Total Comprehension Errors _____

(L & I)

Accountable Miscues

Full Miscues: _____ × 1 = _____

Half Miscues: _____ × $\frac{1}{2}$ = _____

TOTAL _____

PRIOR KNOWLEDGE

How much did you know about smelly stickers before reading this article?

I knew:

nothing	very little	something	a good amount	a lot
(1)	(2)	(3)	(4)	(5)

LEVEL OF INTEREST

How much did you like reading this article?

This article was:

horrible	fair	good	very good	terrific
(1)	(2)	(3)	(4)	(5)

LEVELS OF WORD RECOGNITION AND COMPREHENSION

Word Recognition
MISCUES

Comprehension
ERRORS

Word Recognition MISCUES	Level	Comprehension ERRORS
0	Independent Level	0
1,2		½
3,4		
5	Instructional Level	
6,7		1
8,9		
10		1½
11,12	Questionable Level	
13,14		2
15		
16		2½
	Frustration Level	

Smelly Stickers (4)
CATEGORIES OF ACCOUNTABLE MISCUES IN WORD RECOGNITION

FULL MISCUES	NUMBER	HALF MISCUES	NUMBER
Nonword Substitutions		Whole Word Substitutions	
Whole Word Substitutions		Omissions	
Omissions		Insertions	
Insertions			
Reversals			
Repetitions			
Pronounced by Examiner			

CATEGORIES OF COMPREHENSION ERRORS

	FREE AND PROBED RECALL	
	Items Attempted (Free and Probed)	*Number of Errors*
Literal		
Interpretive		
Critical/Creative		

Samantha's Famous Letter (5)

INTRODUCTION: This article is a true story about a young girl named Samantha Smith. Please read this article to find out what made her famous.

Samantha's Famous Letter

Samantha Smith was a girl with a dream. She dreamed of a world at peace. Samantha worried that differences between the United States and the Soviet* Union might lead to war.

Early in 1983, she decided to write a letter to the leader of the Soviet Union. At the time, Samantha was eleven years old and in fifth grade. She had no idea that this letter would make her famous.

Samantha asked the Soviet leader how he might "help not to have a war." She was quite surprised when she received an answer. In his letter to her, the Soviet leader said that his people wanted peace. The letter also included an invitation to visit his country. He wanted Samantha to come and see for herself how much the Soviet people wanted peace.

During her two week visit, she was greeted by large groups of young people. She made speeches about peace and made many friends.

On her return, Samantha was honored for what she had done. She received the praise of many people for her efforts to make the world a better place to live.

---

*Count the first mispronunciation of *Soviet* as an accountable miscue and disregard all other mispronunciations of that word.

Accountable Miscues

Full Miscues: _____ × 1 = _____

Half Miscues: _____ × $\frac{1}{2}$ = _____

TOTAL _____

COMPREHENSION CHECK

	Probed Recall	Free Recall

L 1. What are the names of two countries mentioned in this article? _____ _____

(United States & Soviet Union)

L 2. Why did Samantha write a letter to the leader of the Soviet Union? _____ _____

(She wanted his help in not having a war.)

(She wanted peace between the two countries.)

L 3. What did the leader of the Soviet Union say in his letter to Samantha? _____ _____

(He said that the Soviet people wanted peace.)

(He invited Samantha to visit his country.)

L 4. What happened to Samantha when she returned to the United States? _____ _____

(She was honored.)
(She received praise.)

I 5. What did the Soviet people think of Samantha? _____ _____

(They liked her.)

C 6. What can we all learn from someone like Samantha Smith? _ _ _ _

(Accept any logical response, such as "Speak out when you believe in something.")

Total Comprehension Errors _____

(L & I)

PRIOR KNOWLEDGE

How much did you know about Samantha Smith before reading this article?

I knew:

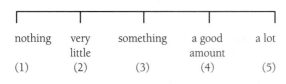

nothing	very little	something	a good amount	a lot
(1)	(2)	(3)	(4)	(5)

LEVEL OF INTEREST

How much did you like reading this article?

This article was:

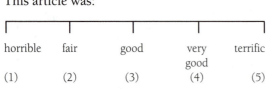

horrible	fair	good	very good	terrific
(1)	(2)	(3)	(4)	(5)

LEVELS OF WORD RECOGNITION AND COMPREHENSION

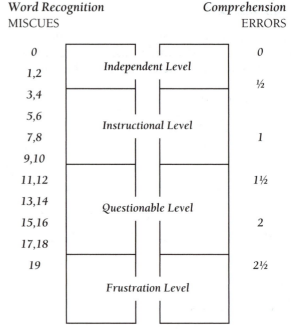

Word Recognition MISCUES		*Comprehension* ERRORS
0	Independent Level	0
1,2		½
3,4		
5,6	Instructional Level	
7,8		1
9,10		
11,12		1½
13,14	Questionable Level	
15,16		2
17,18		
19		2½
	Frustration Level	

Samantha's Famous Letter (5)

CATEGORIES OF ACCOUNTABLE MISCUES IN WORD RECOGNITION

FULL MISCUES	NUMBER	HALF MISCUES	NUMBER
Nonword Substitutions		Whole Word Substitutions	
Whole Word Substitutions		Omissions	
Omissions		Insertions	
Insertions			
Reversals			
Repetitions			
Pronounced by Examiner			

CATEGORIES OF COMPREHENSION ERRORS

	FREE AND PROBED RECALL	
	Items Attempted (Free and Probed)	*Number of Errors*
Literal		
Interpretive		
Critical/Creative		

Teeth to Spare (6)

INTRODUCTION: Please read this article to learn more about an animal who doesn't need to visit a dentist.

Teeth to Spare

Good dental care is essential to the preservation of our teeth. Once a permanent tooth is lost . . . that's it! Only a false tooth can fill the gap.

Sharks don't need to be concerned about their teeth as we do because they are given an endless supply. A shark always has a full mouth of teeth. When a tooth is lost, it is replaced by another one. The tiger shark, as an example, is said to grow twenty-four thousand teeth over a ten-year period.

Teeth are attached to the shark's jaws in several rows. Usually, only the outermost rows of teeth are functional. Some species of sharks have as many as forty rows of teeth. Each row is slightly larger than the last, with the outermost rows being the largest. New teeth originate in an area behind the jaws and move outward as they form and harden. As the teeth in the front begin to wear down or are lost when a shark attacks its prey, they are replaced by those behind. Since new teeth form continually, there is a conveyer belt system of tooth replacement. The shark, therefore, always has a set of razor-sharp teeth to use at will.

Accountable Miscues

Full Miscues: _____ × 1 = _____

Half Miscues: _____ × $\frac{1}{2}$ = _____

TOTAL _____

COMPREHENSION CHECK

Probed Recall   Free Recall

L 1. Why don't sharks have to be concerned about their teeth? _____ _____

(They have an endless supply.)

L 2. A shark has many teeth. How are these teeth placed in the shark's jaws? _____ _____

(in rows)

L 3. Which teeth are used the most? _____ _____

(The ones in the outermost rows.)

(The ones in the front.)

L 4. How do sharks lose their teeth? _____ _____

(They wear down.)

(They are lost when a shark attacks its prey.)

I 5. When a shark loses a tooth, how does it get another tooth to replace the one that was lost? _____ _____

(any correct description of the process detailed in article)

C 6. What would probably happen to the shark if it only had one set of permanent teeth? _ _ _ _

(It would probably die.)

Note: If pupil says, "It couldn't eat," probe with: "Then what would happen?"

Total Comprehension Errors _____
(L & I)

PRIOR KNOWLEDGE

How much did you know about how shark's teeth develop before reading this article?

I knew:

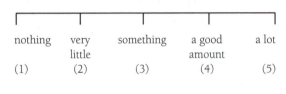

nothing	very little	something	a good amount	a lot
(1)	(2)	(3)	(4)	(5)

LEVEL OF INTEREST

How much did you like reading this article?

This article was:

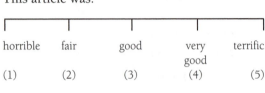

horrible	fair	good	very good	terrific
(1)	(2)	(3)	(4)	(5)

LEVELS OF WORD RECOGNITION AND COMPREHENSION

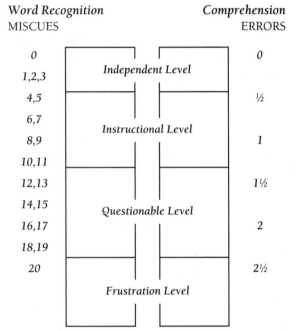

Word Recognition
MISCUES

Comprehension
ERRORS

MISCUES	Level	ERRORS
0		0
1,2,3	Independent Level	
4,5		½
6,7	Instructional Level	
8,9		1
10,11		
12,13		1½
14,15	Questionable Level	
16,17		2
18,19		
20		2½
	Frustration Level	

Teeth to Spare (6)

CATEGORIES OF ACCOUNTABLE MISCUES IN WORD RECOGNITION

FULL MISCUES	NUMBER	HALF MISCUES	NUMBER
Nonword Substitutions		Whole Word Substitutions	
Whole Word Substitutions		Omissions	
Omissions		Insertions	
Insertions			
Reversals			
Repetitions			
Pronounced by Examiner			

CATEGORIES OF COMPREHENSION ERRORS

	FREE AND PROBED RECALL	
	Items Attempted (Free and Probed)	Number of Errors
Literal		
Interpretive		
Critical/Creative		

Old Toys (7)

INTRODUCTION: Did you ever think that children of long ago liked to play with toys too? Please read this article to learn more about the toys these children enjoyed.

Old Toys

Generations of children have been fascinated with toys. The science of archeology has helped us to learn about the favorite toys of children of long ago.

Archeologists have unearthed tombs of Egyptian children who lived at the time of the pyramids thousands of years ago. In the tombs they discovered tiny cooking utensils, wooden dolls, and toy animals.

Toy animals were also popular among the ancient Greeks. Young Greeks liked to play with wooden animals. Some of these animals were built with movable parts. Tails could be made to wag by simply pulling a string. There is even evidence that babies in ancient Greece played with rattles.

Children in ancient China enjoyed playing with marbles made of iron. Kite flying was also popular.

During the Middle Ages, young people played with tiny toy soldiers or knights. The knights were dressed in suits of shining armor. They were mounted on beautiful toy horses, ready to ride into battle.

Today, there are many kinds of electronic toys to delight young people. These include video games and electric trains. Yet, alongside these "modern" toys are many old favorites such as dolls, animals, and rattles. These old favorites have stood the test of time and have remained popular with children everywhere.

Accountable Miscues

Full Miscues: _____ × 1 = _____

Half Miscues: _____ × $\frac{1}{2}$ = _____

TOTAL _____

COMPREHENSION CHECK

	Probed Recall	Free Recall

L 1. What did Egyptian children play with at the time of the pyramids? _____ _____

(cooking utensils)

(wooden dolls)

(toy animals)

I 2. What was special about some of the toys young Greeks played with? _____ _____

(They were built with movable parts.)

L 3. Kite flying was popular in what country? _____ _____

(China)

L 4. What did children from the Middle Ages play with? _____ _____

(toy soldiers)

(knights)

(toy horses)

I 5. What does this article tell us about children and toys? _____ _____

(Accept any logical response, such as "There are some toys that have been popular with children for generations.")

C 6. Based on the information in this article, what kinds of toys do you think children will be playing with five hundred years from today? _ _ _ _

(dolls, toy animals, etc.)

(The same kinds of toys that have been popular through the generations.)

Total Comprehension Errors _____

(L & I)

PRIOR KNOWLEDGE

How much did you know about the favorite toys of children of long ago before reading this article?

I knew:

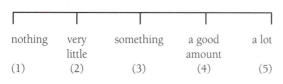

nothing	very little	something	a good amount	a lot
(1)	(2)	(3)	(4)	(5)

LEVEL OF INTEREST

How much did you like reading this article?

This article was:

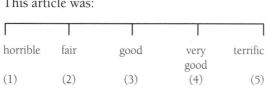

horrible	fair	good	very good	terrific
(1)	(2)	(3)	(4)	(5)

LEVELS OF WORD RECOGNITION AND COMPREHENSION

Word Recognition MISCUES		*Comprehension* ERRORS
0	Independent Level	0
1,2,3		½
4,5		
6,7	Instructional Level	
8,9		1
10,11		
12,13		1½
14,15	Questionable Level	
16,17		2
18,19		
20		2½
	Frustration Level	

Old Toys (7)

CATEGORIES OF ACCOUNTABLE MISCUES IN WORD RECOGNITION

FULL MISCUES	NUMBER	HALF MISCUES	NUMBER
Nonword Substitutions		Whole Word Substitutions	
Whole Word Substitutions		Omissions	
Omissions		Insertions	
Insertions			
Reversals			
Repetitions			
Pronounced by Examiner			

CATEGORIES OF COMPREHENSION ERRORS

	FREE AND PROBED RECALL	
	Items Attempted (Free and Probed)	Number of Errors
Literal		
Interpretive		
Critical/Creative		

A Price That's Too Good May Be Bad (8)

INTRODUCTION: Please read this article to find out why some people would rather pay more money for the same product.

A Price That's Too Good May Be Bad

Many products are sold in supermarkets and drugstores. Some are quite familiar to us because we hear about them on television or see them in advertisements. These products are easy to recognize because they are national brands. Other products that are similar to the national brands but that don't get the same press are known as store brands or private-label products.

One supermarket sold its own version of an all-purpose cleaner. The store brand product was similar in appearance to the popular national brand. Its chemical composition was exactly the same as the national brand's. Best of all, the store brand was about half the price of the national product it was imitating.

But from its introduction eight years ago, the store brand version of this all-purpose cleaner gathered dust on the shelf. Sales were so low that production was eventually stopped. Why was this so? The consumer just did not trust the lower price. When the price was too low, the consumer believed the store brand could not be as good.

So just how cheap is too cheap? One expert says it is unwise to price food products more than twenty percent below, and non-food products more than twenty-five percent below national brand equivalents. The greater the distance from the national brand, the more apt the consumer is to think, "Gee, they must have taken it out in the quality."

Source: Adapted from *The Wall Street Journal* (November 15, 1988), p. B1. Reprinted by permission of *The Wall Street Journal,* © 1988, Dow Jones & Company, Inc. All rights reserved worldwide.

Accountable Miscues

Full Miscues: _____ × 1 = _____

Half Miscues: _____ × $\frac{1}{2}$ = _____

TOTAL _____

COMPREHENSION CHECK

	Probed Recall	Free Recall

L 1. What is a national brand product?   ____   ____

(a familiar product that we hear about a lot in the media)

Note: Pupil might name a national brand product, such as Cheerios or Kleenex.

L 2. What is a store brand or private-label product?   ____   ____

(a supermarket's own version of a national brand product)

I 3. What does the author of this article think about the quality of some store brand products?   ____   ____

(They are just as good as their national brand equivalents.)

L 4. What was the difference in price between the national brand and store brand versions of the two all-purpose cleaners?   ____   ____

(The store brand version was about half the price.)

I 5. Why is the title of this article "A Price That's Too Good May Be Bad"?   ____   ____

(Accept any logical response, such as "Shoppers feel that a lower price is an indication of poorer quality.")

C 6. You are the owner of a supermarket. You set the price of a national brand of shampoo at $2.00. How much should you charge for the equivalent store brand version of this product?   __ __   __ __

(not less than $1.50)

Total Comprehension Errors _____

(L & I)

PRIOR KNOWLEDGE

How much did you know about shopping for national brand and store brand products before reading this article?

I knew:

nothing	very little	something	a good amount	a lot
(1)	(2)	(3)	(4)	(5)

LEVEL OF INTEREST

How much did you like reading this article?

This article was:

horrible	fair	good	very good	terrific
(1)	(2)	(3)	(4)	(5)

LEVELS OF WORD RECOGNITION AND COMPREHENSION

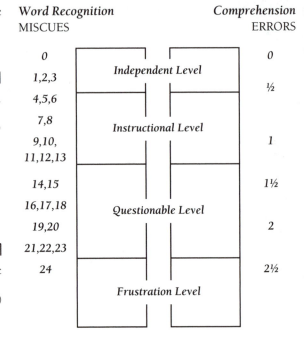

Word Recognition MISCUES		Comprehension ERRORS
0	Independent Level	0
1,2,3		½
4,5,6		
7,8	Instructional Level	
9,10, 11,12,13		1
14,15		1½
16,17,18	Questionable Level	
19,20		2
21,22,23		
24		2½
	Frustration Level	

A Price That's Too Good May Be Bad (8)

CATEGORIES OF ACCOUNTABLE MISCUES IN WORD RECOGNITION

FULL MISCUES	NUMBER	HALF MISCUES	NUMBER
Nonword Substitutions		Whole Word Substitutions	
Whole Word Substitutions		Omissions	
Omissions		Insertions	
Insertions			
Reversals			
Repetitions			
Pronounced by Examiner			

CATEGORIES OF COMPREHENSION ERRORS

	FREE AND PROBED RECALL	
	Items Attempted (Free and Probed)	*Number of Errors*
Literal		
Interpretive		
Critical/Creative		

Sticking Around with Velcro (9)

INTRODUCTION: Please read this article to learn about George de Maestral and his invention.

Sticking Around with Velcro

One day in 1948 a man and his dog were walking through a field when he noticed his woolen pants were covered with burrs—tiny, bristly weed balls that were hard to remove. Unlike most people who just pluck off the burrs and forget them, this man, inventor George de Maestral,* paused to figure out what made this annoying idiosyncrasy of nature stick so stubbornly.

Looking at a burr under a microscope, he discovered that each of the burr's tiny stems ended in a hook, which had caught on the loops in the fabric of his pants.

This inventor borrowed on nature's idea, and made it into a useful product we now use every day. He manufactured it out of nylon, with tiny hooks on one side, and tiny loops on the other. He dubbed the invention Velcro from an acronym for the "vel" of velvet-like soft loops and the "cro" of crochet, which is the French word for hook.

Today, Velcro is made from nylon most of the time. However, when greater sticking power is required, stainless steel and metal alloys are used. Besides replacing the need for shoelaces and zippers, this versatile fastener has earned the notice of engineers and scientists worldwide. NASA uses Velcro to secure objects and even astronauts against the antigravity of space travel. The medical field not only relies on Velcro to fasten blood-pressure cuffs, but used it to bind together two halves of an artificial heart. And the automobile and aerospace industries actually use Velcro to hold together car parts and airplane wings!

Like nature's burrs, it appears that Velcro is going to stick around for a long time.

Accountable Miscues

Full Miscues: _____ × 1 = _____

Half Miscues: _____ × $\frac{1}{2}$ = _____

TOTAL _____

COMPREHENSION CHECK

	Probed Recall	Free Recall

L 1. Where did George de Maestral get the idea for Velcro? _____ _____

(while walking through a field)

L 2. What is Velcro manufactured out of? _____ _____

(nylon)

I 3. How does Velcro work?_____ _____

(Accept any correct description of what makes Velcro work.)

L 4. Describe one way the medical field uses Velcro. _____ _____

(to fasten blood-pressure cuffs)

(to bind together two halves of an artificial heart)

I 5. How do we know from this article that Velcro can have great sticking power? _____ _____

(It can hold together car parts and airplane wings.)

C 6. Think of a unique way to use Velcro. _ _ _ _

(Accept any logical response, such as "On a saddle to keep a rider from falling off his or her horse.")

Total Comprehension Errors _____

(L & I)

---

*Disregard mispronunciation of this name.

PRIOR KNOWLEDGE

How much did you know about the invention of Velcro and what makes it work before reading this article?

I knew:

nothing	very little	something	a good amount	a lot
(1)	(2)	(3)	(4)	(5)

LEVEL OF INTEREST

How much did you like reading this article?

This article was:

horrible	fair	good	very good	terrific
(1)	(2)	(3)	(4)	(5)

LEVELS OF WORD RECOGNITION AND COMPREHENSION

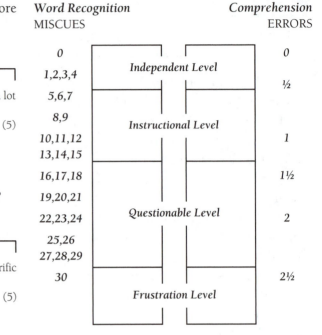

Word Recognition
MISCUES

0
1,2,3,4
5,6,7
8,9
10,11,12
13,14,15
16,17,18
19,20,21
22,23,24
25,26
27,28,29
30

Comprehension
ERRORS

0
½
1
1½
2
2½

Independent Level

Instructional Level

Questionable Level

Frustration Level

Sticking Around with Velcro (9)

CATEGORIES OF ACCOUNTABLE MISCUES IN WORD RECOGNITION

FULL MISCUES	NUMBER	HALF MISCUES	NUMBER
Nonword Substitutions		Whole Word Substitutions	
Whole Word Substitutions		Omissions	
Omissions		Insertions	
Insertions			
Reversals			
Repetitions			
Pronounced by Examiner			

CATEGORIES OF COMPREHENSION ERRORS

	FREE AND PROBED RECALL	
	Items Attempted (Free and Probed)	*Number of Errors*
Literal		
Interpretive		
Critical/Creative		

Graded Words in Context Test: Form B

(Student's test materials appear on pages 107–115.)

Preprimer

1.	no	_____	There are **no** blue cats.
2.	the	_____	Where is **the** big bear?
3.	he	_____	Can **he** read this book?
4.	will	_____	I **will** help you read this book.
5.	have	_____	I **have** a blue car.
6.	and	_____	Come **and** play a game.
7.	with	_____	Can you play **with** me?
8.	man	_____	This **man** will help you.
9.	from	_____	Who will jump down **from** there?
10.	that	_____	Is **that** a good game?
		_____	%

Primer

1.	all	_____	Can **all** of you read a book?
2.	has	_____	She **has** a pet dog.
3.	work	_____	I ride to **work** in a car.
4.	put	_____	We want you to **put** the dog in the car.
5.	new	_____	I want to ride in your **new** car.
6.	call	_____	I want you to **call** the man with the dog.
7.	tree	_____	Stop at the big **tree**!
8.	them	_____	Can you help **them** play that game?
9.	green	_____	Go with **green** and stop with red.
10.	window	_____	Will the dog jump out of the **window**?
		_____	%

Grade 1

1.	wet	_____	The fish is **wet.**
2.	hop	_____	I can **hop** up and down.
3.	miss	_____	I **miss** my mother.
4.	coat	_____	Where is your green **coat?**
5.	horse	_____	This book is about a **horse.**
6.	shoe	_____	This **shoe** is too big.
7.	which	_____	Do you know **which** car is green?
8.	black	_____	Put the ball in the **black** box.
9.	food	_____	I like to eat good **food.**
10.	leg	_____	He cut his **leg.**
11.	better	_____	This game is **better.**
12.	kind	_____	She is a **kind** woman.
13.	table	_____	Put the plant on the **table.**
14.	money	_____	I found her **money.**
15.	dark	_____	It is **dark** at night.
16.	guess	_____	Can you **guess** how old I am?
17.	never	_____	I **never** found my frog.
18.	bark	_____	The big dog likes to **bark.**
19.	should	_____	You **should** like each other.
20.	birthday	_____	Happy **birthday** to you!
		_____	%

Grade 2

1. set   _____   Please help me **set** the table.
2. pull   _____   We will **pull** the horse with a rope.
3. forest   _____   There are many trees in a **forest**.
4. job   _____   Did you find a good **job**?
5. meet   _____   She will **meet** you at the zoo.
6. crow   _____   How far can a **crow** fly?
7. eight   _____   There are **eight** frogs in the lake.
8. you'll   _____   **You'll** find the book on this table.
9. mail   _____   There are many letters in the **mail** today.
10. hang   _____   Please help me **hang** this picture.
11. send   _____   I will **send** you a picture of your friend.
12. wheel   _____   The tire is on the **wheel**.
13. cowboy   _____   A **cowboy** rides on a horse.
14. scare   _____   It is not nice to **scare** a friend.
15. number   _____   We have a **number** of girls in our class.
16. trap   _____   We used food to **trap** the mouse.
17. kitchen   _____   A **kitchen** is a room where food is cooked.
18. question   _____   Can you ask a good **question**?
19. pass   _____   You must have a **pass** when you leave the room.
20. unhappy   _____   He feels **unhappy** on a rainy day.

             _____   %

Grade 3

1. chop   _____   Please help me **chop** some wood for the fire.

2. expect   _____   I **expect** to be there at noon.

3. knife   _____   Cut your meat with this **knife**.

4. visitor   _____   I heard the **visitor** ring the doorbell.

5. lettuce   _____   She likes to have **lettuce** on her sandwich.

6. insist   _____   I **insist** that you wash your hands before eating.

7. fry   _____   He will **fry** the chicken in oil.

8. serious   _____   Are you joking or are you **serious**?

9. husband   _____   They make a nice **husband** and wife.

10. sugar   _____   Cake is made with **sugar**.

11. complain   _____   You should **complain** about that broken window.

12. refrigerator _____   The food is in the **refrigerator**.

13. alarm   _____   Did you hear the **alarm** ring?

14. tongue   _____   A frog can have a long **tongue**.

15. kettle   _____   Please place the **kettle** on the stove.

16. princess   _____   The prince and **princess** rode away on a horse.

17. difference   _____   What is the **difference** between a bee and a bird?

18. obey   _____   You should always **obey** your mother.

19. useful   _____   A blanket is **useful** on a cold night.

20. immediate   _____   Please send her an **immediate** answer.

_____   %

Grade 4

1.	cane	_____	The old man needed to walk with a **cane**.
2.	wisdom	_____	It takes much **wisdom** to be the leader of a country.
3.	duty	_____	It is your **duty** to take the garbage out this week.
4.	publish	_____	I will **publish** your story in the school newspaper.
5.	argue	_____	Don't **argue** with him about who won the game.
6.	cautious	_____	It pays to be **cautious** when driving a car on an icy road.
7.	mosquito	_____	I don't like the buzzing sound of a **mosquito** in my ear.
8.	habit	_____	Smoking is a bad **habit**.
9.	bitter	_____	Coffee can have a **bitter** taste.
10.	original	_____	We know that this painting is an **original** and not a fake.
11.	uniform	_____	The nurse wore a white **uniform**.
12.	jealous	_____	Ted becomes **jealous** when his mother plays with his younger sister.
13.	valuable	_____	This old coin was very **valuable**.
14.	honest	_____	An **honest** person does not steal money from others.
15.	nation	_____	Our country is a great **nation**.
16.	patience	_____	It takes much **patience** to learn how to ride a bicycle.
17.	flake	_____	Jane saw a beautiful **flake** of snow on her window.
18.	raincoat	_____	Dan took his **raincoat** with him because it was a cloudy day.
19.	entertain	_____	Children can **entertain** themselves by playing with blocks.
20.	suggestion	_____	I followed her **suggestion** and bought a car with four doors.
		_____	%

Grade 5

1.	shack	_____	He lived in a small **shack** in the woods.
2.	baggage	_____	The workers unloaded the **baggage** from the airplane.
3.	error	_____	She lost ten points on the test because of an **error** in addition.
4.	cabinet	_____	She stacked the cans of carrots in the kitchen **cabinet**.
5.	legal	_____	The **legal** age to drive in some states is sixteen.
6.	weird	_____	He looked **weird** in that monster costume.
7.	series	_____	The hunter followed the **series** of animal tracks in the mud.
8.	fumble	_____	Our team will lose if you **fumble** the football.
9.	accurate	_____	I like it when the weather forecast is **accurate**.
10.	machinery	_____	This factory has lots of **machinery**.
11.	operation	_____	He entered the hospital for an **operation** on his leg.
12.	dismiss	_____	The teacher was asked to **dismiss** her class early today.
13.	eventual	_____	The team never lost hope of **eventual** victory.
14.	poisonous	_____	Stay away from **poisonous** snakes!
15.	nuisance	_____	The sound of a dripping faucet can be a **nuisance**.
16.	worthless	_____	The fake coin he bought was found to be **worthless**.
17.	landmark	_____	This statue is an important **landmark** to the people of our town.
18.	organize	_____	She planned to **organize** her students into three groups.
19.	investigate	_____	He was told to **investigate** the scene of the crime.
20.	conclusion	_____	The **conclusion** of this mystery is exciting.
		_____	%

Grade 6

1. infant   _____   The **infant** baby was only three days old.

2. nourish   _____   Children need healthy food to **nourish** their bodies.

3. acrobat   _____   I like to visit the circus to see the **acrobat**.

4. perfume   _____   She sprinkled **perfume** on her wrist.

5. monitor   _____   It was his turn to **monitor** the children in the hallway.

6. fatigue   _____   I felt some **fatigue** after running a mile.

7. historian   _____   The famous **historian** wrote an interesting book on the Civil War.

8. recommend   _____   Can you **recommend** him for a job?

9. boost   _____   Please give him a **boost** so that he can climb over the fence.

10. garment   _____   You can store three suits in this **garment** bag.

11. differ   _____   The weather can **differ** from one moment to the next.

12. technical   _____   I cannot understand this chapter because there are too many **technical** words.

13. candidate   _____   She is the best **candidate** for the mayor of this city.

14. sympathize   _____   I **sympathize** greatly with the runner who lost the race.

15. probable   _____   The **probable** cost of this trip is two hundred dollars.

16. tragic   _____   I understand how you feel about the **tragic** loss of your friend.

17. occurrence   _____   Snow in the desert is a rare **occurrence**.

18. violinist   _____   I enjoyed watching the **violinist** play her instrument.

19. elevate   _____   The nurse tried to **elevate** the man's head so that he could sit up and read.

20. accomplishment   _____   The scientist was honored for her great **accomplishment**.

_____   %

Grade 7

1.	omitted	_____	It was by accident that his name was **omitted** from the list.
2.	visibility	_____	Because of the thick fog, **visibility** was poor.
3.	conflict	_____	An argument between two countries can lead to a **conflict**.
4.	inhale	_____	I do not like to **inhale** smoke from your pipe.
5.	privacy	_____	It is nice to be alone and have a few minutes of **privacy**.
6.	regardless	_____	I'll take a room in this hotel, **regardless** of the price.
7.	questionable	_____	The results of this poorly designed study are **questionable**.
8.	analyze	_____	Do you know how to **analyze** the results of this study?
9.	disapproval	_____	This book is about President Lincoln's **disapproval** of slavery.
10.	humidity	_____	I feel uncomfortable when the **humidity** is high.
11.	glamorous	_____	The **glamorous** actress attracted large crowds of people.
12.	uncertainty	_____	There was a feeling of **uncertainty** in the room as the election results were announced.
13.	leadership	_____	The company grew under her **leadership**.
14.	boulevard	_____	He enjoyed jogging up and down the **boulevard** each morning.
15.	eliminated	_____	Mary's wrong answer **eliminated** her from the contest.
16.	simultaneous	_____	The **simultaneous** arrival of the two guests was unplanned.
17.	fundamental	_____	Everyone should have a **fundamental** knowledge of English grammar.
18.	margarine	_____	I like to spread **margarine** on my bread.
19.	requirement	_____	A college education is a **requirement** for this job.
20.	inconvenience	_____	I am sorry for any **inconvenience** caused by my late arrival.
		_____	%

Grade 8

1.	synthetic	_____	A coat can be made of a **synthetic** fiber instead of real wool.
2.	unworthy	_____	Such poor behavior is **unworthy** of a leader.
3.	bankrupt	_____	He became **bankrupt** when he lost all his money.
4.	xylophone	_____	The **xylophone** is her favorite musical instrument.
5.	authorized	_____	She was the only one **authorized** to receive top-secret information.
6.	vulnerable	_____	The weak army was **vulnerable** to attack in two places.
7.	testimonial	_____	The workers attended the **testimonial** for the retiring president of the company.
8.	optimism	_____	The happy man always had the look of **optimism** on his face.
9.	prohibited	_____	You are **prohibited** from smoking in this restaurant.
10.	celebrity	_____	She became a **celebrity** after the release of her first movie.
11.	wealthiest	_____	The millionaire was the **wealthiest** man in town.
12.	ferocity	_____	The hungry lion attacked the animal with great **ferocity**.
13.	excavation	_____	The **excavation** of the old riverbed revealed dinosaur bones.
14.	legislation	_____	**Legislation** was passed to increase the tax on gasoline.
15.	immerse	_____	If you want your egg to be soft-boiled, **immerse** it in boiling water for about one minute.
16.	replacement	_____	He ordered a **replacement** part for his broken bicycle.
17.	accelerator	_____	The racing car jumped forward when the driver stepped on the **accelerator**.
18.	humane	_____	Helping to prevent people from being cruel to animals is a **humane** thing to do.
19.	pumpernickel	_____	The brownish-colored bread or **pumpernickel** tasted very good.
20.	miscellaneous	_____	Jack has a **miscellaneous** collection of stones, shells, and coins.
		_____	%

Graded Reading Passages Test: Form B—Narrative

(Student's test materials appear on pages 116–124.)

 A Snowy Day (1)

INTRODUCTION: Please read this story to find out what two children like to do.

A Snowy Day

Bill and Kim looked out the window. They were very happy. It was snowing. They wanted to go out to play.

Bill and Kim could not wait to build something with the snow. When they went outside, they made two large balls. They put one on top of the other. Then they made one small ball. They put it on the very top. Then Bill and Kim used some sticks and stones. Now they were done.

Accountable Miscues

Full Miscues: _____ × 1 = _____

Half Miscues: _____ × $\frac{1}{2}$ = _____

TOTAL _____

COMPREHENSION CHECK

	Probed Recall	Free Recall

L 1. What were the names of the two children in the story?   _____ _____

(Bill and Kim)

L 2. Why were Bill and Kim very happy?   _____ _____

(They saw it was snowing.)

L 3. How many balls of snow did Bill and Kim make?   _____ _____

(3)

L 4. Where did they put the small ball?   _____ _____

(on the top)

I 5. What do you think Bill and Kim built with the white flakes?   _____ _____

(a snowman)

C 6. Could this story have happened? What makes you think so?   _ _ _ _

(Accept any logical response, such as "Because the events sound real.")

Total Comprehension Errors _____

(L & I)

PRIOR KNOWLEDGE

Have you ever read this story before?

_____Yes _____ No

LEVEL OF INTEREST

How much did you like reading this story?

This story was:

horrible	fair	good	very good	terrific
(1)	(2)	(3)	(4)	(5)

LEVELS OF WORD RECOGNITION AND COMPREHENSION

Word Recognition   *Comprehension*
MISCUES   ERRORS

MISCUES		ERRORS
0		0
1	*Independent Level*	½
2		
3	*Instructional Level*	
4		1
5		
6	*Questionable Level*	1½
7		2
8		
9	*Frustration Level*	2½

A Snowy Day (1)

CATEGORIES OF ACCOUNTABLE MISCUES IN WORD RECOGNITION

FULL MISCUES	NUMBER	HALF MISCUES	NUMBER
Nonword Substitutions		Whole Word Substitutions	
Whole Word Substitutions		Omissions	
Omissions		Insertions	
Insertions			
Reversals			
Repetitions			
Pronounced by Examiner			

CATEGORIES OF COMPREHENSION ERRORS

	FREE AND PROBED RECALL	
	Items Attempted (Free and Probed)	*Number of Errors*
Literal		
Interpretive		
Critical/Creative		

The Boy and the Fox (2)

INTRODUCTION: Please read this story to find out what happens to a boy and a fox.

The Boy and the Fox

One day a boy saw a fox sleeping on top of a rock.

The boy said out loud, "If I kill the fox, I can always sell her skin. I can use the money to buy and plant bean seeds. Then I will sell the beans and use the money to buy the field across the way."

"I will then plant bean seeds in my own field. People will see my beans and say, 'Oh, what nice beans this boy has.' Then I will say, 'Keep away from my beans.' They won't listen to me, so I will shout to them loudly, 'Keep away from my beans.'"

The boy shouted so loudly that the fox woke up and ran away. In the end, the boy was left with nothing.

Source: Adapted from Wiggin, K. D., and Smith, N. A. (Eds.) (1952). *Tales of laughter: A third fairy book* (p. 462). Garden City, NY: Doubleday.

Accountable Miscues

Full Miscues: _____   × 1 = _____

Half Miscues: _____   × $\frac{1}{2}$ = _____

TOTAL _____

COMPREHENSION CHECK

		Probed Recall	Free Recall

L 1. Where was the fox sleeping?   _____ _____

(on top of a rock)

L 2. What did the boy want to do with the fox's skin?   _____ _____

(sell it)

L 3. What kind of seeds did the boy want to plant?   _____ _____

(bean seeds)

L 4. What did the boy want to do with the money from the beans?   _____ _____

(buy his own field and plant beans)

I 5. Were the people the boy was shouting at real? How do you know?   _____ _____

(No, because I can tell from the story that he was only imagining them.)

C 6. What can we learn from this story?   _ _ _ _

(Accept any logical response, such as "Don't count your chickens before they hatch" or the equivalent.)

Total Comprehension Errors _____
                                      (L & I)

PRIOR KNOWLEDGE

Have you ever read this story before?

_____ Yes _____ No

LEVEL OF INTEREST

How much did you like reading this story?

This story was:

horrible	fair	good	very good	terrific
(1)	(2)	(3)	(4)	(5)

LEVELS OF WORD RECOGNITION AND COMPREHENSION

Word Recognition MISCUES		Comprehension ERRORS
0		0
1	Independent Level	½
2,3		
4	Instructional Level	
5		1
6,7		
8		1½
9	Questionable Level	
10,11		2
12		
13		2½
	Frustration Level	

The Boy and the Fox (2)

CATEGORIES OF ACCOUNTABLE MISCUES IN WORD RECOGNITION

FULL MISCUES	NUMBER	HALF MISCUES	NUMBER
Nonword Substitutions		Whole Word Substitutions	
Whole Word Substitutions		Omissions	
Omissions		Insertions	
Insertions			
Reversals			
Repetitions			
Pronounced by Examiner			

CATEGORIES OF COMPREHENSION ERRORS

	FREE AND PROBED RECALL	
	Items Attempted (Free and Probed)	Number of Errors
Literal		
Interpretive		
Critical/Creative		

The Crow and the Pitcher (3)

INTRODUCTION: This story is about a crow with a big problem. Please read this story to find out how the crow solves her problem.

The Crow and the Pitcher

A crow flew many miles in search of water. She finally found a water pitcher. When the crow put its beak into the mouth of the tall pitcher, she found that it held only a little water. She could not reach far enough down to get at it. The crow tried and tried. Finally, she gave up.

Then a thought came to her. Not far from the pitcher sat a pile of pebbles. She flew to the pile and with her beak took a pebble and dropped the pebble into the pitcher. She flew back and forth, dropping pebble after pebble into the pitcher.

As the crow worked, the water rose nearer and nearer to the top. She kept casting pebbles into the pitcher until she was able to dip her beak into the pitcher. Then she quenched her thirst.

Accountable Miscues

Full Miscues: _____ × 1 = _____

Half Miscues: _____ × $\frac{1}{2}$ = _____

TOTAL _____

COMPREHENSION CHECK

	Probed Recall	Free Recall

L 1. What was the crow looking for? _____ _____

(water)

L 2. What did the crow find at the beginning of the story? _____ _____

(a water pitcher)

L 3. How much water did the crow find in the pitcher? _____ _____

(She found only a little.)

(She didn't find much water.)

I 4. What did the crow do to solve the problem of getting the water at the bottom of the pitcher? _____ _____

(Accept any logical description of how the pebbles were used.)

L 5. What did the crow do at the end of the story? _____ _____

(She quenched her thirst.)

(She was able to quench her thirst and save her life.)

C 6. What is the lesson we can learn from this story? __ __ __ __

(Accept any logical response, such as "It pays to be persistent.")

Total Comprehension Errors _____

(L & I)

PRIOR KNOWLEDGE

Have you ever read this story before?

_____Yes _____ No

LEVEL OF INTEREST

How much did you like reading this story?

This story was:

horrible	fair	good	very good	terrific
(1)	(2)	(3)	(4)	(5)

LEVELS OF WORD RECOGNITION AND COMPREHENSION

Word Recognition MISCUES		*Comprehension* ERRORS
0	Independent Level	0
1,2		½
3		
4,5	Instructional Level	
6		1
7		
8,9		1½
10		
11,12	Questionable Level	2
13		
14,15		
16	Frustration Level	2½

The Crow and the Pitcher (3)

CATEGORIES OF ACCOUNTABLE MISCUES IN WORD RECOGNITION

FULL MISCUES	NUMBER	HALF MISCUES	NUMBER
Nonword Substitutions		Whole Word Substitutions	
Whole Word Substitutions		Omissions	
Omissions		Insertions	
Insertions			
Reversals			
Repetitions			
Pronounced by Examiner			

CATEGORIES OF COMPREHENSION ERRORS

	FREE AND PROBED RECALL	
	Items Attempted (Free and Probed)	*Number of Errors*
Literal		
Interpretive		
Critical/Creative		

The Two Farmers (4)

INTRODUCTION: This story is about two farmers who agree to do something together. Please read to find out what happens to these farmers.

The Two Farmers

Once there were two farmers, David and Joseph, who decided to form a partnership. They agreed to buy a field together.

David said to Joseph, "Now we must share the crop as is fair and right. Suppose you take the roots and I take the tops of the plants?" Joseph agreed to this plan. That year the two farmers planted corn. However, when they harvested the crop, David got all the corn and Joseph got nothing but roots and rubbish.

David noticed the displeased look on Joseph's face and said, "This year I have benefited. Next year it will be your turn. You shall have the top and I will have to put up with the root."

When spring came, David asked Joseph, "Would you prefer to plant carrots this year?"

"Fine! That's a better food than corn," answered Joseph.

But when the crop was harvested, David got the carrot roots, while Joseph got the carrot greens. Joseph was so angry that he decided to end the partnership.

Source: Adapted from Wiggin, K. D., and Smith, N. A. (Eds.) (1952). *Tales of laughter: A third fairy book* (p. 31). Garden City, NY: Doubleday.

Accountable Miscues

Full Miscues: _____ × 1 = _____

Half Miscues: _____ × $\frac{1}{2}$ = _____

TOTAL _____

COMPREHENSION CHECK

		Probed Recall	Free Recall

L 1. What were the names of the two characters in this story?   _____ _____

(David and Joseph)

L 2. What did David and Joseph agree to do together?   _____ _____

(They decided to form a partnership; to own a field together.)

L 3. What did the farmers plant the first year?   _____ _____

(corn)

I 4. Joseph was upset about how the corn crop was divided. Why was he upset?   _____ _____

(because the part of the corn he received was useless)

L 5. What happens at the end of this story?   _____ _____

(Joseph decides to end the partnership.)

C 6. Would you ever become a partner with someone like David? Why?   _ _ _ _

(No, because I wouldn't trust him.)

Total Comprehension Errors _____

(L & I)

PRIOR KNOWLEDGE

Have you ever read this story before?

_____Yes _____ No

LEVEL OF INTEREST

How much did you like reading this story?

This story was:

horrible	fair	good	very good	terrific
(1)	(2)	(3)	(4)	(5)

LEVELS OF WORD RECOGNITION AND COMPREHENSION

Word Recognition MISCUES		*Comprehension* ERRORS
0		0
1,2	Independent Level	
3,4		½
5,6		
7	Instructional Level	1
8,9		
10,11		1½
12		
13,14	Questionable Level	2
15,16		
17		
18	Frustration Level	2½

The Two Farmers (4)

CATEGORIES OF ACCOUNTABLE MISCUES IN WORD RECOGNITION

FULL MISCUES	NUMBER	HALF MISCUES	NUMBER
Nonword Substitutions		Whole Word Substitutions	
Whole Word Substitutions		Omissions	
Omissions		Insertions	
Insertions			
Reversals			
Repetitions			
Pronounced by Examiner			

CATEGORIES OF COMPREHENSION ERRORS

	FREE AND PROBED RECALL	
	Items Attempted (Free and Probed)	*Number of Errors*
Literal		
Interpretive		
Critical/Creative		

The Horse's Mouth (5)

INTRODUCTION: This story is about a man who had a strange way of doing business. Please read to find out if you would ever want to sell something to this man.

The Horse's Mouth

There was a fellow who had a strange way of doing business. Whenever he shopped for an item, he would get the seller to believe that there was something wrong with it. He used this trick to lower the price.

One day he wanted to buy a horse from a dealer. A fine looking animal was led out of the stable. The horse appeared to be in excellent condition.

"Oh," the man said. "This horse has a fine head. But it is astonishing how much that head reminds me of a horse my father owned twenty years ago." Passing along the animal, he continued: "And those hind legs are good and what a beautiful fine tail! I declare it is marvelous how much they remind me of a horse my father owned twenty years ago."

He then opened the mouth. Looking at the teeth, he said, "My goodness! It must be the same horse!"

Although it really wasn't the same horse, the man had succeeded in fooling the dealer. The dealer now believed that this was a twenty-year-old horse. As a result, the man was able to buy this young, good-looking animal for much less than it was really worth.

Source: Story adapted from Twain, Mark. (1956). The horse's mouth. In James Tidwell (Ed.), *A treasury of American folk humor* (pp. 34–35). New York: Crown.

Accountable Miscues

Full Miscues: _____ ×   1 = _____

Half Miscues: _____ × $\frac{1}{2}$ = _____

TOTAL _____

COMPREHENSION CHECK

Probed Recall   *Free Recall*

L 1. This story is about a man who had a strange way of doing business. What did he like to do in order to lower the cost of anything that he wanted to buy?   ____   ____

(He would find fault with something he wanted to buy.)

(He would use a trick to lower the price.)

L 2. The man said the horse reminded him of something. What did he say the horse reminded him of?   ____   ____

(a horse his father owned twenty years ago)

L 3. How do we know from the story that the horse was in excellent condition?   ____   ____

(fine head) (beautiful tail) (etc.)

I 4. Why did the man look at the horse's teeth and say, "I guess it's the same horse"?   ____   ____

(He wanted the dealer to believe that it was an old horse and, therefore, that it should be sold to him at a lower price.)

L 5. At the end of the story, how old did the dealer believe the horse was?   ____   ____

(20)

C 6. Would you ever want to sell anything to someone who is like the man in the story? Why?   __ __   __ __

(No, because I wouldn't trust him.)

(He would try to trick me.)

Total Comprehension Errors _____

(L & I)

PRIOR KNOWLEDGE

Have you ever read this story before?

_____Yes _____ No

LEVEL OF INTEREST

How much did you like reading this story?

This story was:

horrible	fair	good	very good	terrific
(1)	(2)	(3)	(4)	(5)

LEVELS OF WORD RECOGNITION AND COMPREHENSION

Word Recognition
MISCUES

Comprehension
ERRORS

MISCUES	Level	ERRORS
0		0
1,2,3	Independent Level	
4,5		½
6,7		
8,9	Instructional Level	1
10,11		
12,13		1½
14,15		
16,17	Questionable Level	2
18,19		
20		2½
	Frustration Level	

The Horse's Mouth (5)

CATEGORIES OF ACCOUNTABLE MISCUES IN WORD RECOGNITION

FULL MISCUES	NUMBER	HALF MISCUES	NUMBER
Nonword Substitutions		Whole Word Substitutions	
Whole Word Substitutions		Omissions	
Omissions		Insertions	
Insertions			
Reversals			
Repetitions			
Pronounced by Examiner			

CATEGORIES OF COMPREHENSION ERRORS

	FREE AND PROBED RECALL	
	Items Attempted (Free and Probed)	Number of Errors
Literal		
Interpretive		
Critical/Creative		

The Story of an Old Attic (6)

INTRODUCTION: Have you ever been afraid of the dark? Please read this story to find out what happens to Mary Dillon.

The Story of an Old Attic

Late one rainy November afternoon, Mary Dillon lay on her stomach in the musty attic of the old farmhouse. She was absorbed in the story of a haunted house found in one of the old yellowed magazines stacked there. Finishing the story, she closed her eyes for a short rest.

When she awoke, it was pitch dark. The rain was still falling with a steady patter on the roof. The attic was a pleasant place in the daytime, but after dark, and after one had been reading a ghost story, it was definitely otherwise.

As she sat up uneasily, Mary heard something move in front of her. She quickly grabbed a flashlight resting at her side, fumbled with the switch, and pointed the beam of light in the direction of the sound. Suddenly, Mary encountered a pair of glowing eyes staring back at her out of the darkness. Ghosts had eyes just like that! She felt her red hair rising on end. The eyes slowly approached her, and Mary was fascinated, frozen with fear. She tried to cry out, but no sound came from her throat.

"Meow," said Dusty, the family cat, whose throat was in perfectly good order, and whose eyes were as bright as cat's eyes should be. Snatching Dusty in her arms, Mary hurried downstairs.

Source: Adapted from De Witt, D. H. (1914). The old attic. In *St. Nicholas: An Illustrated Magazine for Young Folks, 41,* 474.

Accountable Miscues

Full Miscues: _____ × 1 = _____

Half Miscues: _____ × $\frac{1}{2}$ = _____

TOTAL _____

COMPREHENSION CHECK

		Probed Recall	Free Recall
L 1.	Where does this story take place?	____	____
	(in the attic of an old farmhouse)		
L 2.	Mary Dillon was reading a story in a magazine. What was this story about?	____	____
	(a haunted house) (ghosts)		
L 3.	Mary pointed something in the direction of the mysterious sound? What did she point?	____	____
	(a flashlight) (beam of light)		
L 4.	Who was in the attic with Mary?	____	____
	(her cat)		
I 5.	How did Mary feel at the end of this story?	____	____
	(relieved) (happy)		
C 6.	Could this story have happened? What makes you think so?	– –	– –
	(Accept any logical response, such as "because the events sound real.")		

Total Comprehension Errors _____

(L & I)

PRIOR KNOWLEDGE

Have you ever read this story before?

_____Yes _____ No

LEVEL OF INTEREST

How much did you like reading this story?

This story was:

horrible	fair	good	very good	terrific
(1)	(2)	(3)	(4)	(5)

LEVELS OF WORD RECOGNITION AND COMPREHENSION

Word Recognition
MISCUES

Comprehension
ERRORS

MISCUES	Level	ERRORS
0	**Independent Level**	0
1,2,3		½
4,5		
6,7	**Instructional Level**	
8,9		1
10,11,12		
13,14		1½
15,16	**Questionable Level**	
17,18,19		2
20		
21	**Frustration Level**	2½

The Story of an Old Attic (6)

CATEGORIES OF ACCOUNTABLE MISCUES IN WORD RECOGNITION

FULL MISCUES	NUMBER	HALF MISCUES	NUMBER
Nonword Substitutions		Whole Word Substitutions	
Whole Word Substitutions		Omissions	
Omissions		Insertions	
Insertions			
Reversals			
Repetitions			
Pronounced by Examiner			

CATEGORIES OF COMPREHENSION ERRORS

	FREE AND PROBED RECALL	
	Items Attempted (Free and Probed)	*Number of Errors*
Literal		
Interpretive		
Critical/Creative		

Who? (7)

INTRODUCTION: This story presents a description of a happy event. Please read to find out the nature of this happy event.

Who?

It was a warm summer Sunday—June 20, 1980, to be exact. It was one of those lazy days when even the flies don't want to move. My grandmother and I were in the kitchen carefully wrapping chocolate bars (instead of cigars) to give to friends, in celebration of my soon-to-be sibling's birth.

Over the sound of someone's lawn mower, Grandmother was, as usual, humming a little song. Grandmom's perfume mixed strangely with the smell of freshly cut grass, forming a bittersweet aroma. Over the drone of the lawn mower and my grandmother's humming, I could faintly hear the elated shouts of children fresh into summer vacation.

Suddenly, it came—like a sneeze from an unsuspecting victim, like a bullet from a gun. The phone rang and these thoughts went through my head at four times the speed of light: DAD . . . HOSPITAL . . . MOM . . . BABY . . . PHONE. As if moving by its own choosing, my hand grasped the receiver and brought it to my waiting face. The ringing stopped, unable to complete its song. From the bulbous object came my father's happy voice, "Hello, Jamie?"

"Yes," I heard myself reply.

"Michael's here," he cried triumphantly.

"Michael?" I asked. "Michael who?"

Source: Used by permission of the author, Benjamin Reese. First published in *Merlyn's Pen: Fiction, Essays, and Poems by America's Teens*, vol. 3, no. 4, April/May 1988.

Accountable Miscues

Full Miscues: _____ × 1 = _____

Half Miscues: _____ × $\frac{1}{2}$ = _____

TOTAL _____

COMPREHENSION CHECK

		Probed Recall	Free Recall

L 1. When does this story take place? _____ _____

(in the summer)

(June 20, 1980)

L 2. What were Jamie* and his grandmother doing? _____ _____

(wrapping chocolate bars)

L 3. What was Jamie waiting for? _____ _____

(a call from his father to announce the birth of a sibling)

I 4. What did the author mean when he said to himself, "Suddenly, it came. Like a sneeze from an unsuspecting victim, like a bullet from a gun"? If the student responds "The ringing phone," ask, "How did the author feel about this phone call?" _____ _____

(great surprise)

I 5. How did Jamie react to his father's phone call? _____ _____

(He did not connect the name Michael with the birth of a new brother.)

C 6. Can you remember when you felt like the character in the story? Describe what happened when you felt this way. _ _ _ _

(Accept any logical response, such as "I felt this way when I entered a contest and won the first prize.")

Total Comprehension Errors _____

(L & I)

*This character could be male or female.

PRIOR KNOWLEDGE

Have you ever read this story before?

_____Yes _____ No

LEVEL OF INTEREST

How much did you like reading this story?

This story was:

horrible	fair	good	very good	terrific
(1)	(2)	(3)	(4)	(5)

LEVELS OF WORD RECOGNITION AND COMPREHENSION

Word Recognition MISCUES		Comprehension ERRORS
0		0
1,2	Independent Level	
3,4		½
5,6		
7,8	Instructional Level	1
9,10		
11,12		1½
13,14	Questionable Level	
15,16		2
17,18		
19		2½
	Frustration Level	

Who? (7)

CATEGORIES OF ACCOUNTABLE MISCUES IN WORD RECOGNITION

FULL MISCUES	NUMBER	HALF MISCUES	NUMBER
Nonword Substitutions		Whole Word Substitutions	
Whole Word Substitutions		Omissions	
Omissions		Insertions	
Insertions			
Reversals			
Repetitions			
Pronounced by Examiner			

CATEGORIES OF COMPREHENSION ERRORS

	FREE AND PROBED RECALL	
	Items Attempted (Free and Probed)	Number of Errors
Literal		
Interpretive		
Critical/Creative		

Getting the Point (8)

INTRODUCTION: Please read this story about a five-year-old's first experience.

Getting the Point

As a naive five-year-old, I was not suspicious when my father, the very center of my toddler universe, took me for a ride one sunny Wednesday afternoon.

We had an appointment with someone, he hurriedly explained, who had lollipops. This sounded good to me, since anyone with candy was a pleasure to visit.

We walked hand-in-hand into an austere office building and were directed to a sterile-looking room with four cubicles. I was comfortably settled on my father's lap in one of the cubicles when a friendly-looking man in a white coat joined us. The man sat down in front of us and reached for what I imagined to be an enviable stash of candy.

But what was this? A very large, extremely pointed object was in his hand. I looked at my father, and at that instant spotted guilt and trepidation on his face. From this I took my cue and panicked. My foot shot out into the man's abdomen. He grunted, doubled over for a second, and worst of all, replaced his smile with a scowl.

Before I could engineer an escape, my father—my hero—grabbed me tight while the man rapidly thrust the intravenous needle toward a vein in my arm. I braced myself for intense pain, but surprisingly, it really didn't hurt much.

Realizing that my overreaction had probably seriously jeopardized my opportunity for candy, I tried to salvage my dignity. Calmly, I stepped down off my father's lap, held my head high, and sauntered bravely out of the room.

The lollipop was strawberry.

Accountable Miscues

Full Miscues: _____ × 1 = _____

Half Miscues: _____ × $\frac{1}{2}$ = _____

TOTAL _____

COMPREHENSION CHECK

Probed Recall   *Free Recall*

L 1. What is the age of the child in this story?   _____ _____

(5)

I 2. Why is the title of the story "Getting the Point"?   _____ _____

(It is about a child's first experience with the point of a needle.)

L 3. At first, the five-year-old was happy to see the man in the white coat. Why?   _____ _____

(He or she was expecting to get a lollipop or candy.)

L 4. How did the father feel?   _____ _____

(guilty)

I 5. Who is telling this story?   _____ _____

(a person who was the five-year-old described in this story)

Note: If student responds, "The child who got the shot," ask, "Is the five-year-old telling the story? Who is?"

C 6. This story is about a five-year-old child. Do you think most five-year-olds would enjoy reading this story? Why?   _ _ _ _

(Accept any logical response, such as "This story is too difficult for a five-year-old to read. It is written for an older person to enjoy.")

Total Comprehension Errors _____

(L & I)

PRIOR KNOWLEDGE

Have you ever read this story before?

_____Yes _____ No

LEVEL OF INTEREST

How much did you like reading this story?

This story was:

horrible	fair	good	very good	terrific
(1)	(2)	(3)	(4)	(5)

LEVELS OF WORD RECOGNITION
AND COMPREHENSION

Word Recognition   *Comprehension*
MISCUES   ERRORS

Miscues	Level	Errors
0	Independent Level	0
1,2		½
3,4		
5,6	Instructional Level	
7,8,9		1
10,11,12		
13,14		
15,16,17		1½
18,19	Questionable Level	
20,21,22		2
23,24,25		
26,27,28		2½
29	Frustration Level	

Getting the Point (8)

CATEGORIES OF ACCOUNTABLE MISCUES IN WORD RECOGNITION

FULL MISCUES	NUMBER	HALF MISCUES	NUMBER
Nonword Substitutions		Whole Word Substitutions	
Whole Word Substitutions		Omissions	
Omissions		Insertions	
Insertions			
Reversals			
Repetitions			
Pronounced by Examiner			

CATEGORIES OF COMPREHENSION ERRORS

	FREE AND PROBED RECALL	
	Items Attempted (Free and Probed)	*Number of Errors*
Literal		
Interpretive		
Critical/Creative		

The Visitor (9)

INTRODUCTION: Many times the author of a story will try to establish a certain mood or feeling. The following passage was taken from a longer story. Please read this passage to determine the mood or feeling expressed by the author.

The Visitor

I had been traveling alone on horseback through a singularly dreary tract of country; and eventually discovered myself, as the shades of evening foreclosed, within view of the melancholy house. I knew not how it was—but, with the first glimpse of the building, a sense of insufferable gloom pervaded my spirit.

I analyzed the scene before me—upon the bleak walls, upon the vacant eye-like windows, and upon a few white trunks of decayed trees. What was it—I paused to contemplate—what was it that so unnerved me in the contemplation of this dwelling?

Noticing these things, I rode over a short causeway to the house where a servant in waiting took my horse. I entered the archway of the hall and an attendant then led me in silence through many dark and intricate passages in my progress to the studio of his master. The attendant now threw open a door and ushered me into the presence of his master.

The room in which I found myself was very large and lofty. The windows were long, narrow, and pointed. Dark draperies hung upon the walls and the furniture was comfortless, antique, and tattered. Many books and musical instruments lay scattered about, but failed to give any vitality to the scene. I felt that I breathed an atmosphere of sorrow. An air of deep and irredeemable gloom hung over and pervaded all.

Upon my entrance, a man rose from a sofa on which he had been reclining and greeted me.

Source: Adapted from Poe, E.A. (1938). The fall of the house of Usher. In *The complete tales and poems of Edgar Allan Poe* (pp. 231–245). New York: The Modern Library.

Accountable Miscues

Full Miscues: _____ × 1 = _____

Half Miscues: _____ × $\frac{1}{2}$ = _____

                           TOTAL   _____

COMPREHENSION CHECK

		Probed Recall	Free Recall

L 1. What is the setting of this story? Where does this story take place?   _____ _____

(in a dreary house)

L 2. What is the mood or feeling expressed by the author?   _____ _____

(gloomy) (sad)

I 3. How does the author get the reader to feel this way about the story?   _____ _____

(by using certain words and phrases, such as *insufferable gloom, decayed trees, vacant eye-like windows*)

I 4. Who is telling the story?   _____ _____

(the visitor)

L 5. Name one character in this story other than the visitor.   _____ _____

(master) (servant) (attendant)

C 6. Would you like to live in the house described in this story? Why?   _ _ _ _

(Accept any logical response, such as "No, because it sounds like a depressing place to live.")

Total Comprehension Errors _____

                                      (L & I)

PRIOR KNOWLEDGE

Have you ever read this story before?

_____Yes   _____ No

LEVEL OF INTEREST

How much did you like reading this story?

This story was:

horrible	fair	good	very good	terrific
(1)	(2)	(3)	(4)	(5)

LEVELS OF WORD RECOGNITION AND COMPREHENSION

Word Recognition MISCUES		*Comprehension* ERRORS
0	Independent Level	0
1,2,3		½
4,5,6		
7,8	Instructional Level	
9,10,11		1
12,13,14		
15,16		1½
17,18,19	Questionable Level	
20,21		2
22,23,24		
25		2½
	Frustration Level	

The Visitor (9)

CATEGORIES OF ACCOUNTABLE MISCUES IN WORD RECOGNITION

FULL MISCUES	NUMBER	HALF MISCUES	NUMBER
Nonword Substitutions		Whole Word Substitutions	
Whole Word Substitutions		Omissions	
Omissions		Insertions	
Insertions			
Reversals			
Repetitions			
Pronounced by Examiner			

CATEGORIES OF COMPREHENSION ERRORS

	FREE AND PROBED RECALL	
	Items Attempted (Free and Probed)	*Number of Errors*
Literal		
Interpretive		
Critical/Creative		

Story Retelling Form to Assess Sense of Story Structure and Comprehension

Student's Name: _____ Sex: _____ Age: _____ years _____ months

School: _____ School System: _____ Grade Placement: _____

Examiner: _____ Date of Administration: _____

Title of Story: _____ Form: _____

Based on (Check one): _____ Oral Comprehension _____ Silent Comprehension

_____ Listening Comprehension

DIRECTIONS: Score each item according to the directions given below. Add the results in the *second* column to obtain the Student's Score. Compare the Student's Score to the Highest Possible Score to determine the student's comprehension level for this passage.

If an item does not apply, enter "NA" and do not consider it in the scoring.

Setting

a. Begins story with an introduction (Score "1" if included in retelling) _____

b. Includes statement about time or place (1) _____

Character

a. Names main character (1) (Credit can be given if student says "girl," "boy," or "dog" in place of character's name.) _____

b. Number of other characters named (Credit plurals as "2," e.g., "friends" in place of the names of four characters.) _____

c. Actual number of other characters _____

d. Score for "other characters" (b/c) _____

Initiating Event

Refer's to main character's primary goal or problem to be solved (1) _____

Plot Episodes

(Credit can be given if the student understands the *gist* of the plot.)

a. Number of episodes recalled _____

b. Number of episodes in story _____

c. Score for "plot episodes" (a/b) _____

Resolution

a. Names problem solution/goal attainment (1) _____

b. Ends story (1) _____

Sequence

Retells story in structural order: setting, initiating event, plot episodes, resolution
(Score "2" for proper order, "1" for partial, "0" for no sequence)   _____

Theme

States central idea or moral of story (1)   _____

Highest Possible Score: _____   **Student's Score:** _____

Retelling Comprehension Score: _____

(Student's Score/Highest Possible Score)

Level of Comprehension: _____

Independent Level   90–100%
Instructional Level   75–89%
Questionable Level   50–74%
Frustration Level   Below 50%

Any prompting required? If yes, describe below.

Additional Comments:

Source: Adapted from Morrow, Lesley Mandel (1988). Retelling stories as a diagnostic tool. In *Reexamining reading diagnosis: New trends and procedures,* S. M. Glazer, L. W. Searfoss, and L. M. Gentile (Eds.). Newark, DE: International Reading Association, pp. 143–144. Reprinted with permission of Lesley M. Morrow and the International Reading Association. All rights reserved.

Quick List of Instructions for Administering the Dictated Story Assessment Strategy

(Refer to pages 44–55 in Section Two for more information about how to administer the Dictated Story Assessment Strategy.)

1. Assemble the following materials needed to implement this procedure:
   Pad of paper
   Sheet of carbon paper
   Set of photographs to stimulate discussion (pages 127, 129, 131, 133, 135, 137, 139, 141, 143, and 145)
   Photocopy of questions for photographs (pages 128, 130, 132, 134, 136, 138, 140, 142, 144, and 146)
   Dictate Story Assessment Strategy Record Form (pages 245–247)

2. Have the student select a photograph to talk about from the collection provided.

3. Use the photograph to stimulate discussion.

4. A suggested list of questions to prompt or guide the discussion about each photograph is provided on the reverse side of each photograph.

5. At the appropriate moment say:
   "Now, I want you to remember what we just talked about and tell me a story about this photograph. As you talk, I will write down your thoughts and ideas. If you wish, you may look at the photograph. Please begin."

6. The student should be encouraged to dictate no less than three nor more than six sentences. *Note:* Carbon paper can be used by the examiner to produce two copies of this story.

7. At the completion of the dictation ask, **What would be a good title for your story?** or, **Can you think of a good name for this story?** Although this question may be asked at the outset, it is preferable to have the entire story dictated before the title is requested. At that point in the activity students are better prepared to generate an appropriate title for the story.

8. Write the title, and below it enter a credit line (e.g., by Daniel Cohen).

9. Beginning with the title, read the story back to the student, pointing to or running your hand under each word as it is read.

10. Then, read the story again, but this time with the student.

11. Now, determine how much of the story the student can read back without teacher assistance.

12. As the student reads aloud from the original copy of the story, maintain a record of the student's performance on the second copy. If the student has difficulty, ask the pupil to read back only selected parts of the story. If there is still a problem, ask, **"Are there any words in the story that you can pronounce for me? Please read them."**

13. Place a check above each word pronounced correctly, and use the Marking System for Oral Reading Miscues (presented in Table 2.1 on page 22) to record miscues in word recognition. *Note:* If a student has difficulty reading a story on his or her own (cannot read more than 10 percent of the words in the text), consider assessing the student's print and word awareness. The directions for this diagnostic procedure are found on pages 49–50.

14. Check the student's recognition of words in isolation. Begin by selecting five to seven words from the story to present in scrambled order. List these words vertically on a sheet of paper, using carbon paper so that both teacher and student may keep a copy.

15. Point to the first word at the top of the page and have the student pronounce this word quickly (exposure time is less than 1 second).

16. If this word is pronounced correctly, place a + next to the word in the Flashed column on the record sheet.

17. Record the miscue according to the coding system described on pages 19–20 for the Graded Words in Context Test.

18. Move down the list of words at a steady pace.

19. When all words on a list have been exposed, return to the words that were missed and present them again, but this time with delayed exposure.

20. Place a + in the second column next to each word recognized.

21. If the student takes too much time with a word (about 10 seconds or when it becomes apparent that the word is unknown) or says that he or she does not know a word, write **DK** (don't know).

22. Record miscues by using the same coding system as before.

23. Record the percentage of words pronounced correctly in the flashed presentation test.

24. Have the student copy his or her story.

25. Record the results on the Dictated Story Assessment Strategy Record Form found on pages 245–247.

Dictated Story Assessment Strategy Record Form

(Student's test materials appear on pages 125–126.)

Student's Name: _____ Sex: _____ Age: _____ years _____ months

School: _____ School System: _____ Grade Placement: _____

Examiner: _____ Date of Administration: _____

Source of Stimulus: _____ Topic of Dictated Story: _____
(i.e., photograph, object, activity, etc.)

	FOR THE MOST PART	TO A CERTAIN DEGREE	NOT AT ALL	NOT APPLICABLE OR OBSERVABLE
(Place check on line in appropriate column.)				

I. QUALITY OF DICTATED STORY

		FOR THE MOST PART	TO A CERTAIN DEGREE	NOT AT ALL	NOT APPLICABLE OR OBSERVABLE
A.	Does the student present ideas with little prompting from the teacher?	_____	_____	_____	_____
B.	Does the story make sense?	_____	_____	_____	_____
C.	Are the ideas/events presented in a logical sequence?	_____	_____	_____	_____
D.	Does the student speak in complete sentences?	_____	_____	_____	_____
E.	Does the student use proper grammatical structures?	_____	_____	_____	_____

(*Note:* Make notation below if English is a second language or if the student is using a dialect of American English.)

		FOR THE MOST PART	TO A CERTAIN DEGREE	NOT AT ALL	NOT APPLICABLE OR OBSERVABLE
F.	Are ideas expressed with a variety of words?	_____	_____	_____	_____
G.	Does the student express ideas that show uniqueness and originality?	_____	_____	_____	_____
H.	Is the student able to give an appropriate title for the story?	_____	_____	_____	_____

Comments:

II. LANGUAGE FACILITY

A. Story Read by Student after Teacher Has Read Story Aloud

Check ONE that applies:

_____ 1. The student read back most of the story.

_____ 2. The student read back only selected parts of the story (i.e., sentences, parts of sentences).

_____ 3. The student read back only a few words and/or short phrases.

_____ 4. The student was unable to read back any part of the story.

	FOR THE MOST PART	TO A CERTAIN DEGREE	NOT AT ALL	NOT APPLICABLE OR OBSERVABLE
		(Place check on line in appropriate column.)		

B. Word Recognition

	FOR THE MOST PART	TO A CERTAIN DEGREE	NOT AT ALL	NOT APPLICABLE OR OBSERVABLE
1. Was the recognition of words automatic (fluent) throughout the reading?	_____	_____	_____	_____
2. Were miscues NOT disruptive to the meaning of the text?	_____	_____	_____	_____
3. Can the student recognize words from the story presented in isolation with flashed exposure?	_____	_____	_____	_____
4. Can the student recognize words from the story presented in isolation with delayed exposure?	_____	_____	_____	_____

Comments:

III. WRITING/COPYING SKILLS

	FOR THE MOST PART	TO A CERTAIN DEGREE	NOT AT ALL	NOT APPLICABLE OR OBSERVABLE
Is the student able to copy the story accurately?	_____	_____	_____	_____

Comments:

IV. PRINT AND WORD AWARENESS

Consider administering this part if

1. The student is unable to read back any part of the story.

2. The student can read back only a few words and/or phrases.

3. The student makes miscues that account for more than 10 percent of the words in the text.

	FOR THE MOST PART	TO A CERTAIN DEGREE	NOT AT ALL	NOT APPLICABLE OR OBSERVABLE
	(Place check on line in appropriate column.)			

A. Is the student able to

1. Identify the boundaries of written words?	_____	_____	_____	_____
2. Match words?	_____	_____	_____	_____
3. Match sentences?	_____	_____	_____	_____
4. Build a word from a model?	_____	_____	_____	_____
5. Supply a spoken word that begins with the same phoneme as a given printed word?	_____	_____	_____	_____

B. Does the student understand terms such as

1. Beginning?	_____	_____	_____	_____
2. End?	_____	_____	_____	_____
3. Same?	_____	_____	_____	_____
4. Different?	_____	_____	_____	_____
5. First?	_____	_____	_____	_____
6. Last?	_____	_____	_____	_____
7. Line?	_____	_____	_____	_____
8. Top?	_____	_____	_____	_____
9. Bottom?	_____	_____	_____	_____

C. Can the student name letters?
(Circle the letters identified.)

A a	G g	L l	Q q	V v
B b	H h	M m	R r	W w
C c	I i	N n	S s	X x
D d	J j	O o	T t	Y y
E e	K k	P p	U u	Z z
F f				

Comments:

Source: Part IV adapted from Agnew, A.T. (1982). Using children's dictated stories to assess code consciousness. In *The Reading Teacher, 35,* 450–454. Copyright by the International Reading Association. All rights reserved.

SIRI Synthesis of Information Rubric

Student's Name: _____ Sex: _____ Age: _____ years _____ months

School: _____ School System: _____ Grade Placement: _____

Examiner: _____ Date of Administration: _____

ESTIMATED READING LEVELS		
	GRADE LEVELS	
	Expository	*Narrative*
Independent		
Instructional*		
Frustration		
Listening		

*List as one grade level or range of two grade levels (e.g., 5–6).

▢ Shaded areas are used to record results of diagnostic options.

DIRECTIONS: Place an **x** at a point on each scale to rate the student on the items below. Use the following scale as a guide in making your decisions.

```
|---------|---------|---------|---------|
1         2         3         4         5
poor      fair      good      very      excellent
                              good
```

Refer to pages 84–86 for information on using this rubric.

KNOWLEDGE AND PERCEPTIONS OF READING

Knowledge of Reading

```
|---------|---------|---------|---------|
1         2         3         4         5
```
Lacks knowledge   Exhibits strong
of the nature   knowledge of
of reading   the nature
                                              of reading

Perceptions of Reading and Reading Ability

```
|---------|---------|---------|---------|
1         2         3         4         5
```
Has weak   Has strong
self-perceptions   self-perceptions

Comments:

READING INTERESTS

Narrative Text

```
|---------|---------|---------|---------|
1         2         3         4         5
```
Dislikes reading   Enjoys reading
narrative text   narrative text

Expository Text

```
|---------|---------|---------|---------|
1         2         3         4         5
```
Dislikes reading   Enjoys reading
expository text   expository text

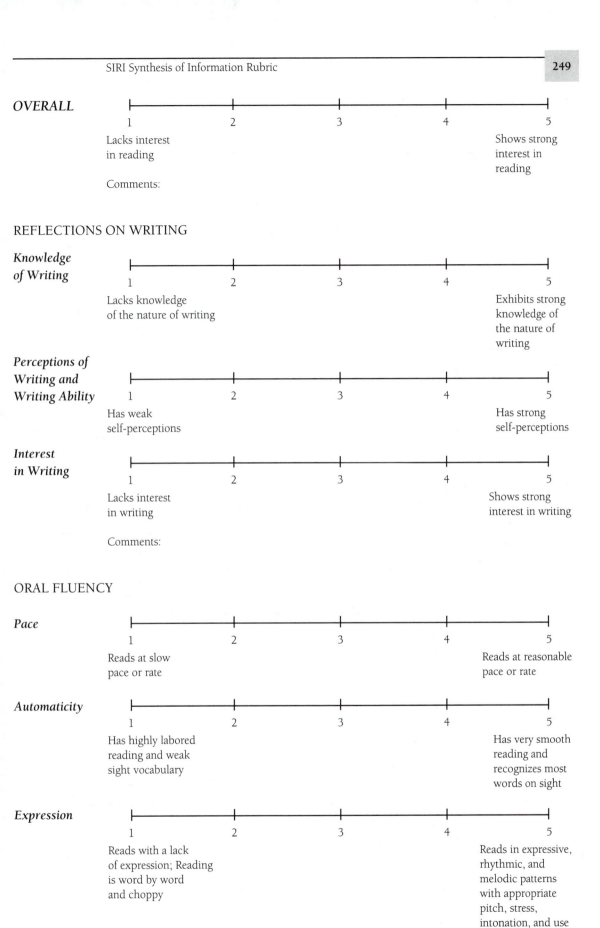

OVERALL

| 1 | 2 | 3 | 4 | 5 |

Lacks interest
in reading

Shows strong
interest in
reading

Comments:

REFLECTIONS ON WRITING

*Knowledge
of Writing*

| 1 | 2 | 3 | 4 | 5 |

Lacks knowledge
of the nature of writing

Exhibits strong
knowledge of
the nature of
writing

*Perceptions of
Writing and
Writing Ability*

| 1 | 2 | 3 | 4 | 5 |

Has weak
self-perceptions

Has strong
self-perceptions

*Interest
in Writing*

| 1 | 2 | 3 | 4 | 5 |

Lacks interest
in writing

Shows strong
interest in writing

Comments:

ORAL FLUENCY

Pace

| 1 | 2 | 3 | 4 | 5 |

Reads at slow
pace or rate

Reads at reasonable
pace or rate

Automaticity

| 1 | 2 | 3 | 4 | 5 |

Has highly labored
reading and weak
sight vocabulary

Has very smooth
reading and
recognizes most
words on sight

Expression

| 1 | 2 | 3 | 4 | 5 |

Reads with a lack
of expression; Reading
is word by word
and choppy

Reads in expressive,
rhythmic, and
melodic patterns
with appropriate
pitch, stress,
intonation, and use
of punctuation

OVERALL

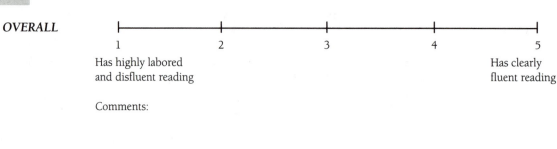

| 1 | 2 | 3 | 4 | 5 |

Has highly labored
and disfluent reading

Has clearly
fluent reading

Comments:

WORD RECOGNITION

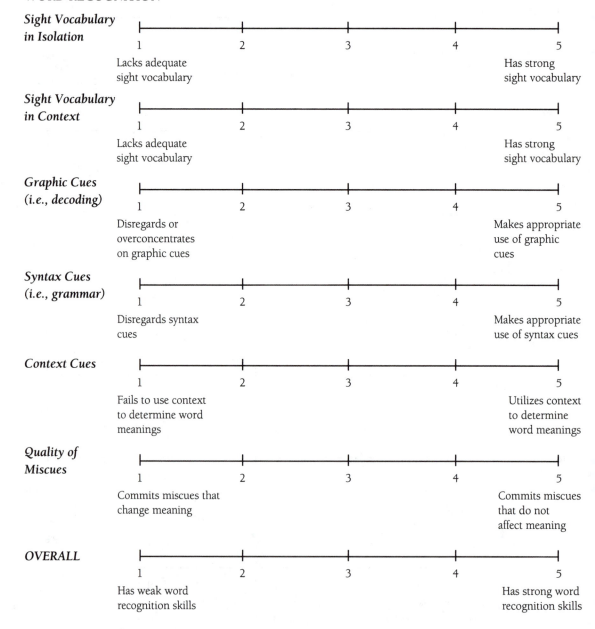

**Sight Vocabulary
in Isolation**

| 1 | 2 | 3 | 4 | 5 |

Lacks adequate
sight vocabulary

Has strong
sight vocabulary

**Sight Vocabulary
in Context**

| 1 | 2 | 3 | 4 | 5 |

Lacks adequate
sight vocabulary

Has strong
sight vocabulary

**Graphic Cues
(i.e., decoding)**

| 1 | 2 | 3 | 4 | 5 |

Disregards or
overconcentrates
on graphic cues

Makes appropriate
use of graphic
cues

**Syntax Cues
(i.e., grammar)**

| 1 | 2 | 3 | 4 | 5 |

Disregards syntax
cues

Makes appropriate
use of syntax cues

Context Cues

| 1 | 2 | 3 | 4 | 5 |

Fails to use context
to determine word
meanings

Utilizes context
to determine
word meanings

**Quality of
Miscues**

| 1 | 2 | 3 | 4 | 5 |

Commits miscues that
change meaning

Commits miscues
that do not
affect meaning

OVERALL

| 1 | 2 | 3 | 4 | 5 |

Has weak word
recognition skills

Has strong word
recognition skills

Comments:

COMPREHENSION

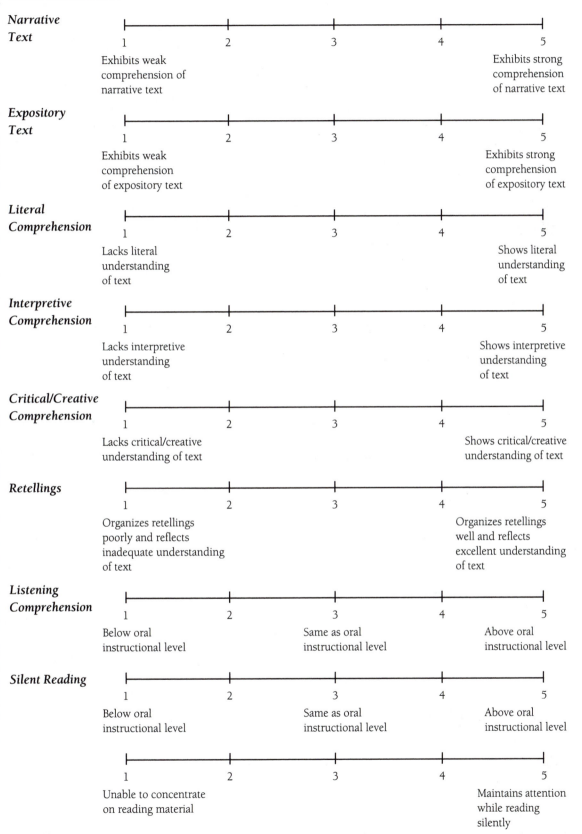

Narrative Text

| 1 | 2 | 3 | 4 | 5 |

Exhibits weak comprehension of narrative text

Exhibits strong comprehension of narrative text

Expository Text

| 1 | 2 | 3 | 4 | 5 |

Exhibits weak comprehension of expository text

Exhibits strong comprehension of expository text

Literal Comprehension

| 1 | 2 | 3 | 4 | 5 |

Lacks literal understanding of text

Shows literal understanding of text

Interpretive Comprehension

| 1 | 2 | 3 | 4 | 5 |

Lacks interpretive understanding of text

Shows interpretive understanding of text

Critical/Creative Comprehension

| 1 | 2 | 3 | 4 | 5 |

Lacks critical/creative understanding of text

Shows critical/creative understanding of text

Retellings

| 1 | 2 | 3 | 4 | 5 |

Organizes retellings poorly and reflects inadequate understanding of text

Organizes retellings well and reflects excellent understanding of text

Listening Comprehension

| 1 | 2 | 3 | 4 | 5 |

Below oral instructional level

Same as oral instructional level

Above oral instructional level

Silent Reading

| 1 | 2 | 3 | 4 | 5 |

Below oral instructional level

Same as oral instructional level

Above oral instructional level

| 1 | 2 | 3 | 4 | 5 |

Unable to concentrate on reading material

Maintains attention while reading silently

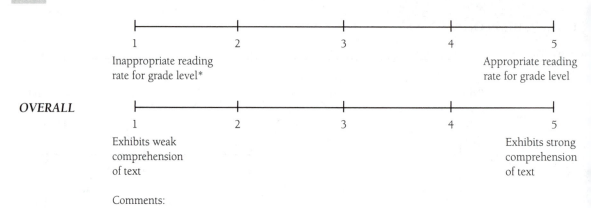

```
    |————————|————————|————————|————————|
    1        2        3        4        5
Inappropriate reading                    Appropriate reading
rate for grade level*                    rate for grade level
```

OVERALL

```
    |————————|————————|————————|————————|
    1        2        3        4        5
Exhibits weak                            Exhibits strong
comprehension                            comprehension
of text                                  of text
```

Comments:

BEHAVIORS EXHIBITED DURING TESTING

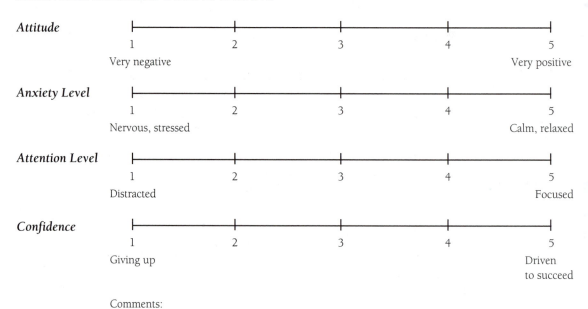

Attitude

```
    |————————|————————|————————|————————|
    1        2        3        4        5
Very negative                            Very positive
```

Anxiety Level

```
    |————————|————————|————————|————————|
    1        2        3        4        5
Nervous, stressed                        Calm, relaxed
```

Attention Level

```
    |————————|————————|————————|————————|
    1        2        3        4        5
Distracted                               Focused
```

Confidence

```
    |————————|————————|————————|————————|
    1        2        3        4        5
Giving up                                Driven
                                         to succeed
```

Comments:

SUMMARY OF RESULTS

1. What are student's apparent strengths?

2. What might be this student's major needs?

3. Is additional information needed? If yes, specify.

4. What program of instruction is recommended for this student?

---

*Determinations of reading rate should *not* be based on frustration-level material.

Diagnostic Options

Writing Reflections Interview Form   254

Quick List of Instructions for Administering the Graded Words
    in Isolation Test   257

Graded Words in Isolation Test: Form A   258

Graded Words in Isolation Test: Form B   263

Practice Passages   268

Graded Reading Passages Test: Form C—Expository   272

Graded Reading Passages Test: Form D—Narrative   290

Summary Sheet of Silent Reading Performance   308

Summary Sheet of Accountable Miscues   309

Summary Sheet for Recording and Analyzing Miscue   310

Summary Sheet for Categories of Comprehension Errors   312

Dictated Story Assessment Strategy Record Form
    for Follow-Up Session   313

The Stieglitz Assessment of Phonemic Awareness Record Form   315

Writing Reflections Interview Form

Student's Name: _____ Sex: _____ Age: _____ years _____ months

School: _____ School System: _____ Grade Placement: _____

Interviewer: _____ Date of Interview: _____

INTERVIEWER INSTRUCTIONS: During the interview, feel free to probe to elicit information about the student's knowledge of the writing process, perceptions of writing and his or her writing ability, and interest in writing. General probe questions such as, Can you tell me more about that? or, Anything else? may be used and, when asked, should be recorded on this form.

Throughout the interview, look for patterns of responses. This can serve as the basis for answering the summary questions listed at the end of this form.

STUDENT DIRECTIONS: Read the following directions to the student.

"I will be asking you some questions to find out what you think and feel about writing. There are no right or wrong answers. Just do the best you can to answer each question. As you are answering these questions, I will be taking some notes. This is to help me remember what you have said. Let's begin with this question."

Knowledge of Writing

1. What is writing? _____

_____

_____

2. Why do people write? _____

_____

_____

Perceptions of Writing and Writing Ability

3. What do you think a good writer needs to do to write well?_____

_____

_____

4. How does your teacher decide which pieces of writing are the good ones? _____

_____

_____

5. How did you learn to write? _____

_____

6. Do you ever rewrite (revise or edit) a piece of writing to make it better? If yes, describe what you do.

_____

_____

_____

7. Do you ever write at home just because you want to? _____

If you do, how often do you write at home just because you want to?

_____

_____

8. Do you like to have others read your writing? _____

Who? _____

9. What do you really *like* about your writing? _____

_____

_____

10. What would you like to improve about your writing? _____

_____

_____

Interest in Writing

11. What kind of writing do you like to do? _____

_____

_____

12. How do you decide what to write about? _____

_____

_____

13. In general, how do you feel about writing? _____

_____

_____

_____

SUMMARY

What does the student know about the nature of writing?

What are the student's perceptions of writing and his or her writing ability?

What are the student's writing interests?

How do the student's responses to questions on the Reading and Writing Reflections Interviews compare?

Additional comments:

Quick List of Instructions for Administering the Graded Words in Isolation Test

(Refer to pages 61–63 in Section Two for more information about how to administer the Graded Words in Isolation Test.)

1. Have a copy of the appropriate form to record the results of the Graded Words in Isolation Test (see pages 258–262 or 263–267).

2. Use the student's base-level score on the Graded Words in Context Test to determine the level at which to begin the Graded Words in Isolation Test.

3. Give the following directions to the student:
   "I want you to read some lists of words for me. Some of these words will be easy, and others may be more difficult. Try hard to read as many words as possible. I will be taking notes as you read the words on each list. This is to help me remember what you have read. Do you have any questions? Let's begin with this word."

4. Open the test booklet to the appropriate page.

5. Point to the first word at the top of the page and have the student pronounce this word quickly (exposure time is less than 1 second).

6. If this word is pronounced correctly, place a + next to the word in the Flashed column on the record sheet.

7. Record the miscue according to the coding system described on pages 19–20 for the Graded Words in Context Test.

8. Move down the list of words at a steady pace.

9. When all words on a list have been exposed, return to the words that were missed and present them again, but this time with delayed exposure.

10. Place a + in the second column next to each word recognized.

11. If the student takes too much time with a word (about 10 seconds or when it becomes apparent that the word is unknown) or says that he or she does not know a word, write in **DK** (don't know).

12. Record miscues by using the same coding system as before.

13. Record the percentage of words pronounced correctly in the flashed presentation test. Each correct response is worth 5 points on lists for grade 1 through grade 8. Each correct response is worth 10 points on preprimer- and primer-level lists.

14. Continue to administer this test until the base and ceiling levels are reached. (Use only the results of the flashed presentations to determine these levels.) The base level is the highest list at which the student is able to read every word correctly. The ceiling level is the list on which the student misses five or more words (a score of 75 percent or less) on a list.

15. Record the results on the Summary of Student Performance Sheet provided on page 179.

Graded Words in Isolation Test: Form A

(Student's test materials appear on pages 148–151.)

Preprimer

		Flashed	Delayed
1.	at	_____	_____
2.	in	_____	_____
3.	dog	_____	_____
4.	but	_____	_____
5.	red	_____	_____
6.	get	_____	_____
7.	like	_____	_____
8.	to	_____	_____
9.	ride	_____	_____
10.	want	_____	_____
		_____ %	

Primer

		Flashed	Delayed
1.	sit	_____	_____
2.	eat	_____	_____
3.	may	_____	_____
4.	take	_____	_____
5.	two	_____	_____
6.	saw	_____	_____
7.	away	_____	_____
8.	mother	_____	_____
9.	little	_____	_____
10.	found	_____	_____
		_____ %	

Grade 1

		Flashed	Delayed
1.	bus	_____	_____
2.	stay	_____	_____
3.	far	_____	_____
4.	hear	_____	_____
5.	again	_____	_____
6.	sister	_____	_____
7.	off	_____	_____
8.	town	_____	_____
9.	wish	_____	_____
10.	isn't	_____	_____
11.	give	_____	_____
12.	story	_____	_____
13.	than	_____	_____
14.	zoo	_____	_____
15.	long	_____	_____
16.	morning	_____	_____
17.	another	_____	_____
18.	hand	_____	_____
19.	right	_____	_____
20.	please	_____	_____
		_____ %	

Grade 2

		Flashed	Delayed
1.	low	_____	_____
2.	deer	_____	_____
3.	few	_____	_____
4.	afraid	_____	_____
5.	rest	_____	_____
6.	mile	_____	_____
7.	such	_____	_____
8.	I'd	_____	_____
9.	carry	_____	_____
10.	puppy	_____	_____
11.	owl	_____	_____
12.	seven	_____	_____
13.	quick	_____	_____
14.	mountain	_____	_____
15.	visit	_____	_____
16.	follow	_____	_____
17.	dragon	_____	_____
18.	anyone	_____	_____
19.	farmer	_____	_____
20.	evening	_____	_____
		_____ %	

Grade 3

		Flashed	Delayed
1.	crop	_____	_____
2.	force	_____	_____
3.	motor	_____	_____
4.	usual	_____	_____
5.	yesterday	_____	_____
6.	bother	_____	_____
7.	enjoy	_____	_____
8.	history	_____	_____
9.	nibble	_____	_____
10.	scratch	_____	_____
11.	parent	_____	_____
12.	television	_____	_____
13.	whisker	_____	_____
14.	treat	_____	_____
15.	accident	_____	_____
16.	dare	_____	_____
17.	understood	_____	_____
18.	notebook	_____	_____
19.	amaze	_____	_____
20.	familiar	_____	_____
		_____ %	

Grade 4

		Flashed	Delayed
1.	plot	_____	_____
2.	rhyme	_____	_____
3.	uproar	_____	_____
4.	bold	_____	_____
5.	fashion	_____	_____
6.	property	_____	_____
7.	aware	_____	_____
8.	cookbook	_____	_____
9.	hoarse	_____	_____
10.	represent	_____	_____
11.	slope	_____	_____
12.	excellent	_____	_____
13.	telegraph	_____	_____
14.	oyster	_____	_____
15.	fortunate	_____	_____
16.	subject	_____	_____
17.	taxi	_____	_____
18.	downhill	_____	_____
19.	increase	_____	_____
20.	thunderstorm	_____	_____
		_____ %	

Grade 5

		Flashed	Delayed
1.	conquer	_____	_____
2.	injure	_____	_____
3.	plantation	_____	_____
4.	wrist	_____	_____
5.	gratitude	_____	_____
6.	attract	_____	_____
7.	delightful	_____	_____
8.	furnish	_____	_____
9.	emerald	_____	_____
10.	manufacturer	_____	_____
11.	shrewd	_____	_____
12.	treatment	_____	_____
13.	obvious	_____	_____
14.	satisfactory	_____	_____
15.	assignment	_____	_____
16.	brightness	_____	_____
17.	dreary	_____	_____
18.	universe	_____	_____
19.	somersault	_____	_____
20.	prehistoric	_____	_____
		_____ %	

Grade 6

	Flashed	Delayed
1. minor	_____	_____
2. sympathy	_____	_____
3. evident	_____	_____
4. collision	_____	_____
5. igloo	_____	_____
6. minimum	_____	_____
7. politician	_____	_____
8. ordeal	_____	_____
9. yield	_____	_____
10. comprehend	_____	_____
11. frustrate	_____	_____
12. examination	_____	_____
13. legendary	_____	_____
14. unconscious	_____	_____
15. slouch	_____	_____
16. weakness	_____	_____
17. appreciation	_____	_____
18. quantity	_____	_____
19. wanderer	_____	_____
20. embarrassment	_____	_____
	_____ %	

Grade 7

	Flashed	Delayed
1. oasis	_____	_____
2. vicinity	_____	_____
3. confidential	_____	_____
4. identical	_____	_____
5. prominent	_____	_____
6. repetition	_____	_____
7. zoologist	_____	_____
8. authentic	_____	_____
9. disadvantage	_____	_____
10. hibernation	_____	_____
11. luxurious	_____	_____
12. unsuspecting	_____	_____
13. translation	_____	_____
14. breakthrough	_____	_____
15. evaluate	_____	_____
16. sophisticated	_____	_____
17. frequency	_____	_____
18. mayonnaise	_____	_____
19. resemblance	_____	_____
20. interpretation	_____	_____
	_____ %	

Grade 8

		Flashed	Delayed
1.	serial	_____	_____
2.	urgency	_____	_____
3.	beverage	_____	_____
4.	novelty	_____	_____
5.	assumption	_____	_____
6.	voluntarily	_____	_____
7.	transformation	_____	_____
8.	optimistic	_____	_____
9.	perishable	_____	_____
10.	convincingly	_____	_____
11.	qualification	_____	_____
12.	grievance	_____	_____
13.	exhilarating	_____	_____
14.	knowledgeable	_____	_____
15.	implication	_____	_____
16.	rehabilitation	_____	_____
17.	unaccustomed	_____	_____
18.	habitual	_____	_____
19.	phenomenal	_____	_____
20.	monotonous	_____	_____

_____ %

Graded Words in Isolation Test: Form B

(Student's test materials appear on pages 152–155.)

Preprimer		Flashed	Delayed
1.	no	_____	_____
2.	the	_____	_____
3.	he	_____	_____
4.	will	_____	_____
5.	have	_____	_____
6.	and	_____	_____
7.	with	_____	_____
8.	man	_____	_____
9.	from	_____	_____
10.	that	_____	_____
		_____ %	

Primer		Flashed	Delayed
1.	all	_____	_____
2.	has	_____	_____
3.	work	_____	_____
4.	put	_____	_____
5.	new	_____	_____
6.	call	_____	_____
7.	tree	_____	_____
8.	them	_____	_____
9.	green	_____	_____
10.	window	_____	_____
		_____ %	

Grade 1		Flashed	Delayed
1.	wet	_____	_____
2.	hop	_____	_____
3.	miss	_____	_____
4.	coat	_____	_____
5.	horse	_____	_____
6.	shoe	_____	_____
7.	which	_____	_____
8.	black	_____	_____
9.	food	_____	_____
10.	leg	_____	_____
11.	better	_____	_____
12.	kind	_____	_____
13.	table	_____	_____
14.	money	_____	_____
15.	dark	_____	_____
16.	guess	_____	_____
17.	never	_____	_____
18.	bark	_____	_____
19.	should	_____	_____
20.	birthday	_____	_____
		_____ %	

Grade 2

	Flashed	Delayed
1. set	_____	_____
2. pull	_____	_____
3. forest	_____	_____
4. job	_____	_____
5. meet	_____	_____
6. crow	_____	_____
7. eight	_____	_____
8. you'll	_____	_____
9. mail	_____	_____
10. hang	_____	_____
11. send	_____	_____
12. wheel	_____	_____
13. cowboy	_____	_____
14. scare	_____	_____
15. number	_____	_____
16. trap	_____	_____
17. kitchen	_____	_____
18. question	_____	_____
19. pass	_____	_____
20. unhappy	_____	_____

_____ %

Grade 3

	Flashed	Delayed
1. chop	_____	_____
2. expect	_____	_____
3. knife	_____	_____
4. visitor	_____	_____
5. lettuce	_____	_____
6. insist	_____	_____
7. fry	_____	_____
8. serious	_____	_____
9. husband	_____	_____
10. sugar	_____	_____
11. complain	_____	_____
12. refrigerator	_____	_____
13. alarm	_____	_____
14. tongue	_____	_____
15. kettle	_____	_____
16. princess	_____	_____
17. difference	_____	_____
18. obey	_____	_____
19. useful	_____	_____
20. immediate	_____	_____

_____ %

Grade 4

		Flashed	Delayed
1.	cane	_____	_____
2.	wisdom	_____	_____
3.	duty	_____	_____
4.	publish	_____	_____
5.	argue	_____	_____
6.	cautious	_____	_____
7.	mosquito	_____	_____
8.	habit	_____	_____
9.	bitter	_____	_____
10.	original	_____	_____
11.	uniform	_____	_____
12.	jealous	_____	_____
13.	valuable	_____	_____
14.	honest	_____	_____
15.	nation	_____	_____
16.	patience	_____	_____
17.	flake	_____	_____
18.	raincoat	_____	_____
19.	entertain	_____	_____
20.	suggestion	_____	_____
		_____ %	

Grade 5

		Flashed	Delayed
1.	shack	_____	_____
2.	baggage	_____	_____
3.	error	_____	_____
4.	cabinet	_____	_____
5.	legal	_____	_____
6.	weird	_____	_____
7.	series	_____	_____
8.	fumble	_____	_____
9.	accurate	_____	_____
10.	machinery	_____	_____
11.	operation	_____	_____
12.	dismiss	_____	_____
13.	eventual	_____	_____
14.	poisonous	_____	_____
15.	nuisance	_____	_____
16.	worthless	_____	_____
17.	landmark	_____	_____
18.	organize	_____	_____
19.	investigate	_____	_____
20.	conclusion	_____	_____
		_____ %	

Grade 6

		Flashed	Delayed
1.	infant	_____	_____
2.	nourish	_____	_____
3.	acrobat	_____	_____
4.	perfume	_____	_____
5.	monitor	_____	_____
6.	fatigue	_____	_____
7.	historian	_____	_____
8.	recommend	_____	_____
9.	boost	_____	_____
10.	garment	_____	_____
11.	differ	_____	_____
12.	technical	_____	_____
13.	candidate	_____	_____
14.	sympathize	_____	_____
15.	probable	_____	_____
16.	tragic	_____	_____
17.	occurrence	_____	_____
18.	violence	_____	_____
19.	elevate	_____	_____
20.	accomplishment	_____	_____

_____ %

Grade 7

		Flashed	Delayed
1.	omitted	_____	_____
2.	visibility	_____	_____
3.	conflict	_____	_____
4.	inhale	_____	_____
5.	privacy	_____	_____
6.	regardless	_____	_____
7.	questionable	_____	_____
8.	analyze	_____	_____
9.	disapproval	_____	_____
10.	humidity	_____	_____
11.	glamorous	_____	_____
12.	uncertainty	_____	_____
13.	leadership	_____	_____
14.	boulevard	_____	_____
15.	eliminated	_____	_____
16.	simultaneous	_____	_____
17.	fundamental	_____	_____
18.	margarine	_____	_____
19.	requirement	_____	_____
20.	inconvenience	_____	_____

_____ %

Grade 8

		Flashed	Delayed
1.	synthetic	_____	_____
2.	unworthy	_____	_____
3.	bankrupt	_____	_____
4.	xylophone	_____	_____
5.	authorized	_____	_____
6.	vulnerable	_____	_____
7.	testimonial	_____	_____
8.	optimism	_____	_____
9.	prohibited	_____	_____
10.	celebrity	_____	_____
11.	wealthiest	_____	_____
12.	ferocity	_____	_____
13.	excavation	_____	_____
14.	legislation	_____	_____
15.	immerse	_____	_____
16.	replacement	_____	_____
17.	accelerator	_____	_____
18.	humane	_____	_____
19.	pumpernickel	_____	_____
20.	miscellaneous	_____	_____

_____ %

Practice Passages

(Student's test materials appear on pages 156–157.)

N *The Fall Is Nice (1)*

INTRODUCTION: Please read this story about something children like to do.

The Fall Is Nice

It is fall. The leaves are falling. How fast they fall.

Let's catch all the leaves we can. There are red ones. There are brown ones. There are yellow ones. We like the red leaves the most.

Let's make a big pile right here. Then we can run and jump in them. It is fun to play in the leaves. We like fall.

Accountable Miscues

Full Miscues: ____ × 1 = ____

Half Miscues: ____ × $\frac{1}{2}$ = ____

TOTAL ____

COMPREHENSION CHECK

	Probed Recall	Free Recall

L 1. What season of the year is it?   ____ ____

(fall)

L 2. What is happening to the leaves in this story?   ____ ____

(They are falling.)

(They are being caught.)

(They are being jumped on.)

L 3. What color leaf do the children like the most?   ____ ____

(red)

L 4. Name two things the children like to do with the leaves.   ____ ____

(catch leaves)

(make a pile of leaves)

(jump in the leaves)

(run in the leaves)

I 5. Who is telling this story?   ____ ____

(some children)

(a group of people)

C 6. What might happen to the leaves after the children are finished playing with them?   ‒ ‒   ‒ ‒

(Accept any logical response, such as "They will be placed in bags and thrown away.")

Total Comprehension Errors   _____

(L & I)

PRIOR KNOWLEDGE

Have you ever read this story before?

_____Yes _____ No

LEVEL OF INTEREST

How much did you like reading this story?

This story was:

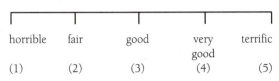

horrible	fair	good	very good	terrific
(1)	(2)	(3)	(4)	(5)

LEVELS OF WORD RECOGNITION AND COMPREHENSION

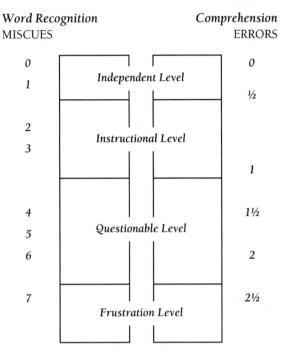

Word Recognition MISCUES		Comprehension ERRORS
0	Independent Level	0
1		½
2	Instructional Level	
3		1
4	Questionable Level	1½
5		
6		2
7	Frustration Level	2½

The First Paper Maker (3)

INTRODUCTION: Please read this article to learn something about an insect.

The First Paper Maker

Do you know who the first paper maker was? It was the wasp.

A wasp needs paper in order to build a nest. To make a nest, a wasp must fly from place to place until he has found the right kind of wood. He tears off little pieces with his mouth. He lays these pieces side by side, just as you may lay sticks.

At last, he gathers them in a little bundle, and flies with them to his nest. Then he begins to chew the wood. As he chews it, he wets it with a kind of gum that runs from his mouth. While the chewed wood is still soft and wet, the wasp spreads it out as thin flakes. The flakes soon dry and then they are paper. He uses this paper to build the cells of his nest. While this is good paper to build nests with, it is not good paper to write on.

Source: Story adapted from Baldwin, J. (1897). *School reading by grades: Third year* (pp. 45–47). New York: American Book Company.

Accountable Miscues

Full Miscues: _____ × 1 = _____

Half Miscues: _____ × $\frac{1}{2}$ = _____

TOTAL _____

COMPREHENSION CHECK

		Probed Recall	*Free Recall*
L 1.	Who was the first paper maker?	_____	_____
	(the wasp)		
L 2.	What does the wasp make paper out of?	_____	_____
	(wood)		
L 3.	What does the wasp do with the paper he makes?	_____	_____
	(uses it to build a nest)		
	(uses it to build the cells of a nest)		
L 4.	How does the wasp tear off little pieces from the wood he has found?	_____	_____
	(He uses his mouth to tear off little pieces.)		
I 5.	How does the wasp turn the wood he has gathered into paper?	_____	_____
	(any correct description of the process detailed in the article)		
C 6.	Why do you think the paper made by the wasp is not good paper to write on?	— —	— —
	(Accept any logical response, such as "The pieces are too small.")		

Total Comprehension Errors   _____

(L & I)

PRIOR KNOWLEDGE

How much did you know about how wasps make paper before reading this article?

I knew:

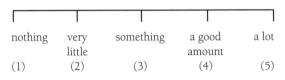

nothing	very little	something	a good amount	a lot
(1)	(2)	(3)	(4)	(5)

LEVEL OF INTEREST

How much did you like reading this article?

This article was:

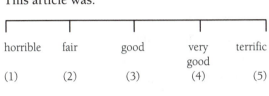

horrible	fair	good	very good	terrific
(1)	(2)	(3)	(4)	(5)

LEVELS OF WORD RECOGNITION AND COMPREHENSION

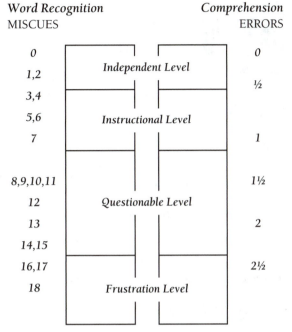

Word Recognition MISCUES		Comprehension ERRORS
0	Independent Level	0
1,2		½
3,4		
5,6	Instructional Level	
7		1
8,9,10,11		1½
12	Questionable Level	
13		2
14,15		
16,17		2½
18	Frustration Level	

Graded Reading Passages Test: Form C—Expository

(Student's test materials appear on pages 158–166.)

 Light (1)

INTRODUCTION: Please read this article about light.

Light

Where does light come from? You know it comes from the sun. It comes from the stars too. A fire makes light. A lamp makes light. What is the same about all these things? They are all hot.

Have you ever been in a place with no light at all? Most places have some light. Think of your room at night. Can you see a little bit when your lamp is out? If you can, there is some light getting in.

Without light, we could not see. We see things only when light falls on them.

Accountable Miscues

Full Miscues: _____ × 1 = _____

Half Miscues: _____ × $\frac{1}{2}$ = _____

TOTAL _____

COMPREHENSION CHECK

	Probed Recall	*Free Recall*

L 1. We know that light comes from the sun and from a lamp. Name one other place light comes from.   _____ _____

(fire) (stars)

L 2. What is the same about things that make light?   _____ _____

(They are all hot.)

(They all give off heat.)

L 3. What does this article tell you about a person's room at night?   _____ _____

(If you can see a little bit, there is some light getting in.)

L 4. What couldn't we do without light?   _____ _____

(see) (see things)

I 5. Fill in the missing word. The person who wrote this article wants you to think that light is very _____.   _____ _____

(important) (necessary)

C 6. Why would your teacher have you read an article such as this one? — — — —

(Accept any logical response, such as "To learn something.")

Total Comprehension Errors   _____

(L & I)

PRIOR KNOWLEDGE

How much did you know about the information on light before reading this article?

I knew:

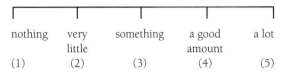

| nothing | very little | something | a good amount | a lot |
| (1) | (2) | (3) | (4) | (5) |

LEVEL OF INTEREST

How much did you like reading this article?

This article was:

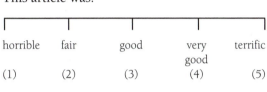

| horrible | fair | good | very good | terrific |
| (1) | (2) | (3) | (4) | (5) |

LEVELS OF WORD RECOGNITION AND COMPREHENSION

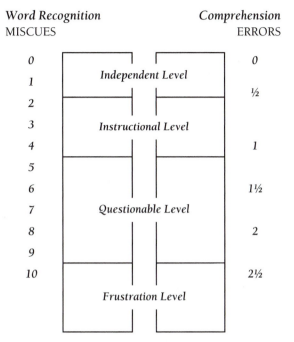

Word Recognition MISCUES

Comprehension ERRORS

0 — Independent Level — 0

1 — ½

2

3 — Instructional Level

4 — 1

5

6 — 1½

7 — Questionable Level

8 — 2

9

10 — 2½

Frustration Level

Light (1)
CATEGORIES OF ACCOUNTABLE MISCUES IN WORD RECOGNITION

FULL MISCUES	NUMBER	HALF MISCUES	NUMBER
Nonword Substitutions		Whole Word Substitutions	
Whole Word Substitutions		Omissions	
Omissions		Insertions	
Insertions			
Reversals			
Repetitions			
Pronounced by Examiner			

CATEGORIES OF COMPREHENSION ERRORS

	FREE AND PROBED RECALL	
	Items Attempted (Free and Probed)	*Number of Errors*
Literal		
Interpretive		
Critical/Creative		

Our Best Friends (2)

INTRODUCTION: Have you ever had a pet? Please read this article to learn about the first pets.

Our Best Friends

Many people have pets. Do you ever wonder how animals came to live with people?

Long ago, all animals were wild. People then hunted for food. They hunted many kinds of animals. They grew to like those that were smart, friendly, or useful. Horses were once food. So were rabbits and some birds. Today they are pets.

Wolves often followed hunters. They wanted some of the meat. Some were taken in to live with the hunters. Dogs come from the wolf family. They are the oldest pets.

Most pets come from families of wild animals that live in groups. One well known pet does not fit this picture. When you pet it, it makes a strange sound. This pet is the cat.

Accountable Miscues

Full Miscues: _____ × 1 = _____

Half Miscues: _____ × $\frac{1}{2}$ = _____

TOTAL _____

COMPREHENSION CHECK

Probed Recall   *Free Recall*

L 1. Long ago, what did people have to do?   ____ ____

(hunt for food)

(hunt many kinds of animals)

(kill animals for food)

L 2. Name a pet today that was used for food long ago.   ____ ____

(horses) (rabbits) (birds)

L 3. Which animal often followed the hunters of long ago?   ____ ____

(the wolf)

L 4. Most pets come from families of wild animals that live in groups. Name a pet that does not fit this picture.   ____ ____

(the cat)

I 5. Why do you think the hunters of long ago grew to like the wolf?   ____ ____

(The wolf was probably smart.)

(The wolf was probably friendly.)

(The wolf was probably useful.)

C 6. Based on what you have read, why did some animals never become pets?   ____ ____

(Accept any logical response, such as "People of long ago did not grow to like some animals" or "People of long ago did not find some animals to be smart, friendly, or useful.")

Total Comprehension Errors   _____

(L & I)

PRIOR KNOWLEDGE

How much did you know about how animals became pets long ago before reading this article?

I knew:

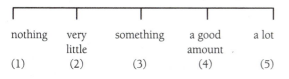

nothing	very little	something	a good amount	a lot
(1)	(2)	(3)	(4)	(5)

LEVEL OF INTEREST

How much did you like reading this article?

This article was:

horrible	fair	good	very good	terrific
(1)	(2)	(3)	(4)	(5)

LEVELS OF WORD RECOGNITION AND COMPREHENSION

Word Recognition
MISCUES

Comprehension
ERRORS

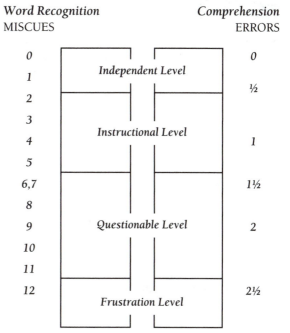

Our Best Friends (2)

CATEGORIES OF ACCOUNTABLE MISCUES IN WORD RECOGNITION

FULL MISCUES	NUMBER	HALF MISCUES	NUMBER
Nonword Substitutions		Whole Word Substitutions	
Whole Word Substitutions		Omissions	
Omissions		Insertions	
Insertions			
Reversals			
Repetitions			
Pronounced by Examiner			

CATEGORIES OF COMPREHENSION ERRORS

	FREE AND PROBED RECALL	
	Items Attempted (Free and Probed)	Number of Errors
Literal		
Interpretive		
Critical/Creative		

The Ant Lion (3)

INTRODUCTION: Please read this article to learn something about a lion that doesn't roar.

The Ant Lion

If you were an ant, you would not want to meet an ant lion. Ant lions feed on ants. They trap them in holes that they dig in dry, loose soil.

The ant lion is an insect. It digs its hole by walking backwards in a circle. As it walks, it pushes its tail into the soil. This moves the dirt up over its wide back. By jerking its head, the ant lion throws the soil off to the side. The ant lion walks in smaller and smaller circles. At last, it reaches the center of its cone-shaped hole. The ant lion then hides in the soil at the bottom.

An unlucky ant walking on the edge slides down the soft sides of the hole. The waiting ant lion traps the ant in its jaws. The juices from the ant's body then become the ant lion's meal.

Accountable Miscues

Full Miscues: _____ × 1 = _____

Half Miscues: _____ × $\frac{1}{2}$ = _____

TOTAL _____

COMPREHENSION CHECK

	Probed Recall	Free Recall

L 1. What do ant lions like to eat?   _____ _____

(ants)

L 2. What is an ant lion?   _____ _____

(an insect) (a bug)

L 3. What is the shape of the hole dug by the ant lion?   _____ _____

(cone-shaped)

I 4. How does the ant lion trap its meal?   _____ _____

(any correct description of how the ant lion captures its prey)

L 5. What does the ant lion do with the ant's body?   _____ _____

(The juices from the ant's body become the ant lion's meal.)

C 6. What would happen to the ant lion if the soil became dry and hard?   _ _ _ _

(It couldn't dig holes to capture its prey and would probably die.)

Note: If pupil responds, "It couldn't dig holes," probe with, "Then what would happen?"

Total Comprehension Errors _____

(L & I)

PRIOR KNOWLEDGE

How much did you know about ant lions before reading this article?

I knew:

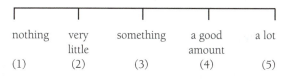

nothing	very little	something	a good amount	a lot
(1)	(2)	(3)	(4)	(5)

LEVEL OF INTEREST

How much did you like reading this article?

This article was:

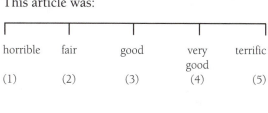

horrible	fair	good	very good	terrific
(1)	(2)	(3)	(4)	(5)

LEVELS OF WORD RECOGNITION AND COMPREHENSION

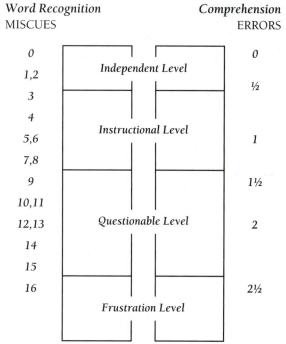

Word Recognition
MISCUES

Comprehension
ERRORS

Word Recognition MISCUES	Level	Comprehension ERRORS
0	Independent Level	0
1,2		½
3		
4	Instructional Level	
5,6		1
7,8		
9		1½
10,11		
12,13	Questionable Level	2
14		
15		
16	Frustration Level	2½

The Ant Lion (3)

CATEGORIES OF ACCOUNTABLE MISCUES IN WORD RECOGNITION

FULL MISCUES	NUMBER	HALF MISCUES	NUMBER
Nonword Substitutions		Whole Word Substitutions	
Whole Word Substitutions		Omissions	
Omissions		Insertions	
Insertions			
Reversals			
Repetitions			
Pronounced by Examiner			

CATEGORIES OF COMPREHENSION ERRORS

	FREE AND PROBED RECALL	
	Items Attempted (Free and Probed)	Number of Errors
Literal		
Interpretive		
Critical/Creative		

Pop Goes the Kernel (4)

INTRODUCTION: Please read this article to learn something about a favorite snack food.

Pop Goes the Kernel

You put a handful of kernels in. You plug in the popper. As they heat up, the kernels start to explode. Before you know it, that little pile of kernels has become a big bowl of popcorn.

What makes popcorn pop? The answer to that question has to do with what a kernel is made of and how it is put together.

The tough yellowish shell of a kernel covers a starchy inside. The secret to the popping, though, is the water. The tightly packed center of the kernel is moist. As the water heats up, it pushes against the walls of the kernel. Pressure builds up until, POP, the walls burst. The starchy center puffs out into bubbles that form the soft white part of the popcorn.

Popcorn fills about forty times more space than the unpopped kernels do, but it weighs less. Can you guess why? It's because something is missing.

Accountable Miscues

Full Miscues: ____ × 1 = ____

Half Miscues: ____ × $\frac{1}{2}$ = ____

TOTAL ____

COMPREHENSION CHECK

	Probed Recall	Free Recall

L 1. These will start to explode when heated. What are they? ____ ____

(kernels)

L 2. What does the tough yellowish shell of the kernel cover? ____ ____

(a starchy inside)

L 3. What is the secret to the popping? ____ ____

(the water)

L 4. What happens to the water when it is heated up? ____ ____

(As the water heats up, it pushes against the walls of the kernel. Pressure builds up until, POP, the walls burst.)

I 5. Why does popcorn weigh less than the unpopped kernels? ____ ____

(It is missing the water.)

(The water evaporates inside the kernel.)

C 6. What would probably happen to a kernel that was dry instead of moist in the center? ─ ─ ─ ─

(It wouldn't pop.)

Total Comprehension Errors _____

(L & I)

PRIOR KNOWLEDGE

How much did you know about what makes corn kernels pop before reading this article?

I knew:

nothing | very little | something | a good amount | a lot
(1) | (2) | (3) | (4) | (5)

LEVEL OF INTEREST

How much did you like reading this article?

This article was:

horrible | fair | good | very good | terrific
(1) | (2) | (3) | (4) | (5)

LEVELS OF WORD RECOGNITION AND COMPREHENSION

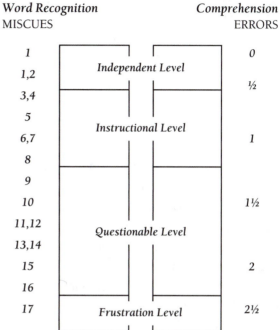

Word Recognition
MISCUES

Comprehension
ERRORS

1
1,2   *Independent Level*   0
3,4   ½
5
6,7   *Instructional Level*   1
8
9
10   1½
11,12
13,14   *Questionable Level*
15   2
16
17   *Frustration Level*   2½

Pop Goes the Kernel (4)

CATEGORIES OF ACCOUNTABLE MISCUES IN WORD RECOGNITION

FULL MISCUES	NUMBER	HALF MISCUES	NUMBER
Nonword Substitutions		Whole Word Substitutions	
Whole Word Substitutions		Omissions	
Omissions		Insertions	
Insertions			
Reversals			
Repetitions			
Pronounced by Examiner			

CATEGORIES OF COMPREHENSION ERRORS

	FREE AND PROBED RECALL	
	Items Attempted (Free and Probed)	*Number of Errors*
Literal		
Interpretive		
Critical/Creative		

The Spirit to Win (5)

INTRODUCTION: This article is a true story about a woman named Wilma Rudolph. Please read this article to find out what made her famous.

The Spirit to Win

When, at the age of four, Wilma Rudolph lost the ability to walk, she could not have dreamed that she would one day be the fastest woman runner in the world. But that is just what happened.

Wilma was born in Clarksville, Tennessee. When she was four years old, she was struck by polio. This crippling disease left Wilma's left leg paralyzed.

With constant exercise, Wilma's muscles regained some of their strength. After two years, Wilma was able to take a step or two. Every day, she pushed herself to go farther. When she was eight, she could walk with the aid of a leg brace. Wilma was not satisfied with that, though. She kept working. At eleven, she could walk without the brace. At thirteen, she joined the school basketball team. By fifteen, she was a star player and a member of the track team.

At sixteen, she ran in the Olympics and won a bronze medal. Four years later, in the 1960 Olympics, she won three gold medals. She was then voted the top amateur athlete in the United States. Wilma Rudolph's spirit and determination made her a winner in every way.

Accountable Miscues

Full Miscues: _____ × 1 = _____

Half Miscues: _____ × $\frac{1}{2}$ = _____

TOTAL _____

COMPREHENSION CHECK

		Probed Recall	Free Recall

L 1. What happened to Wilma Rudolph at the age of four? _____ _____

(She lost the ability to walk.)

(She became paralyzed.)

(She was struck by polio.)

L 2. What did Wilma do in order to regain some of the strength in her legs? _____ _____

(She exercised a lot.)

L 3. Which school team did Wilma join at the age of thirteen? _____ _____

(the basketball team)

L 4. Wilma was an athlete in which Olympic sport? _____ _____

(track)

(running)

I 5. In 1960, how did Wilma Rudolph compare to the rest of the runners in the world? _____ _____

(She proved that she was one of the fastest woman runners in the world.)

C 6. What can we all learn from someone like Wilma Rudolph? _ _ _ _

(Accept any logical response, such as "If you don't give up and you keep trying, you can accomplish what you want.")

Total Comprehension Errors _____

(L & I)

PRIOR KNOWLEDGE

How much did you know about Wilma Rudolph before reading this article?

I knew:

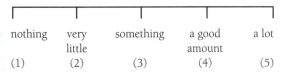

nothing	very little	something	a good amount	a lot
(1)	(2)	(3)	(4)	(5)

LEVEL OF INTEREST

How much did you like reading this article?

This article was:

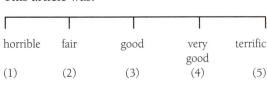

horrible	fair	good	very good	terrific
(1)	(2)	(3)	(4)	(5)

LEVELS OF WORD RECOGNITION AND COMPREHENSION

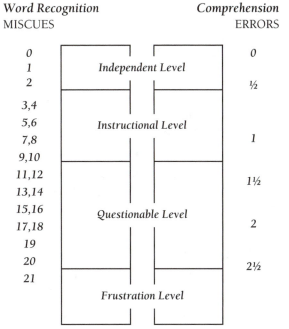

Word Recognition
MISCUES

Comprehension
ERRORS

MISCUES	Level	ERRORS
0, 1, 2	Independent Level	0, ½
3,4 5,6 7,8 9,10	Instructional Level	1
11,12 13,14 15,16 17,18	Questionable Level	1½, 2
19 20 21	Frustration Level	2½

The Spirit to Win (5)

CATEGORIES OF ACCOUNTABLE MISCUES IN WORD RECOGNITION

FULL MISCUES	NUMBER	HALF MISCUES	NUMBER
Nonword Substitutions		Whole Word Substitutions	
Whole Word Substitutions		Omissions	
Omissions		Insertions	
Insertions			
Reversals			
Repetitions			
Pronounced by Examiner			

CATEGORIES OF COMPREHENSION ERRORS

	FREE AND PROBED RECALL	
	Items Attempted (Free and Probed)	*Number of Errors*
Literal		
Interpretive		
Critical/Creative		

Time Zones (6)

INTRODUCTION: Please read the following article to learn something about time zones.

Time Zones

When it is noon in New York, it is nine o'clock in Los Angeles. We know this because time zones divide the globe into neat time slots. But time zones are not natural elements. How and why did they come about?

Time zones developed from a railroad scheduling nightmare in the mid-1800s. At that time, people set their clocks by the sun. When the sun appeared to be directly overhead, they would set their clocks to noon. But what looked like overhead to one person did not to another. Also, because of the earth's rotation, the sun was overhead at different times in different places. So no one agreed on the time. This caused real problems for people attempting to catch trains and for people attempting to schedule them. The railroads pushed for some kind of standard time system.

Finally, a decision was made to divide the earth into twenty-four hour time zones, to match the twenty-four hours in a day. The width in each time zone was made equal to the distance the sun travels in one hour. Within each zone, the time would be the same.

The United States switched from sun time to official time on November 18, 1883. In some places on that day, noon came twice!

Accountable Miscues

Full Miscues: _____ × 1 = _____

Half Miscues: _____ × $\frac{1}{2}$ = _____

TOTAL _____

COMPREHENSION CHECK

		Probed Recall	Free Recall

L 1. How did people in the mid-1800s use the sun to set their clocks? _____ _____

(When the sun appeared to be directly overhead, people would set their clocks to noon.)

L 2. In the mid-1800s, why did no one agree on the time? _____ _____

(What looked like overhead to one person did not to another.)

(Because of the earth's rotation, the sun was overhead at different times in different places.)

L 3. Why did the railroads push for some kind of standard time system? _____ _____

(because of scheduling nightmares)

L 4. Today, the earth is divided into how many time zones? _____ _____

(24)

I 5. At noontime, why doesn't the sun appear to be directly overhead to everyone who lives in the same time zone? _____ _____

(Because the sun is directly overhead only in the middle of a time zone.)

C 6. The switch was made from a sun time system to a standard time system in 1883. Why didn't this happen 200 years earlier—let's say in 1683? _ _ _ _

(Accept any logical response, such as "The reasons for needing a standard time system probably didn't exist in 1683.")

Total Comprehension Errors _____

(L & I)

PRIOR KNOWLEDGE

How much did you know about the start of time zones before reading this article?

I knew:

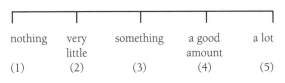

nothing	very little	something	a good amount	a lot
(1)	(2)	(3)	(4)	(5)

LEVEL OF INTEREST

How much did you like reading this article?

This article was:

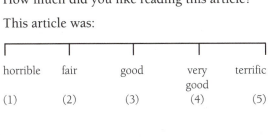

horrible	fair	good	very good	terrific
(1)	(2)	(3)	(4)	(5)

LEVELS OF WORD RECOGNITION AND COMPREHENSION

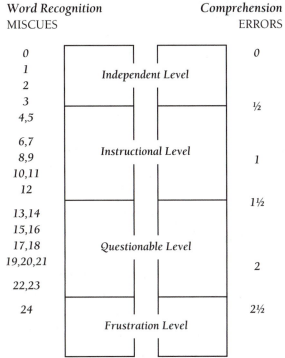

Word Recognition
MISCUES

Comprehension
ERRORS

MISCUES	Level	ERRORS
0, 1, 2, 3	Independent Level	0
4,5		½
6,7, 8,9, 10,11, 12	Instructional Level	1
13,14, 15,16		1½
17,18, 19,20,21	Questionable Level	
22,23		2
24	Frustration Level	2½

Time Zones (6)

CATEGORIES OF ACCOUNTABLE MISCUES IN WORD RECOGNITION

FULL MISCUES	NUMBER	HALF MISCUES	NUMBER
Nonword Substitutions		Whole Word Substitutions	
Whole Word Substitutions		Omissions	
Omissions		Insertions	
Insertions			
Reversals			
Repetitions			
Pronounced by Examiner			

CATEGORIES OF COMPREHENSION ERRORS

	FREE AND PROBED RECALL	
	Items Attempted (Free and Probed)	*Number of Errors*
Literal		
Interpretive		
Critical/Creative		

The Game of Frisbee (7)

INTRODUCTION: Please read this article to learn something about a popular game.

The Game of Frisbee

On beaches, in parks, across backyards, people toss these plastic disks to one another. Playing Frisbee is as common now as playing catch. But until the 1960s, it was unheard of. Where did the Frisbee come from?

Well, its name comes from the Frisbee Pie Company. Frisbee Pies, which were made in Connecticut, were sold in metal pie plates with the company name stamped into them. In the early part of the century, some college students who liked the pies found that the plates were also enjoyable. They flipped the empty tins to one another in an outdoor game very much like you-know-what.

In 1948, a man named Fred Morrison, who had at one time had fun tossing pie pans, created a plastic flying saucer that could be played with in the same way. Plastic was a new product at the time. It made a much safer toy than the hard metal tins, and it could be molded into shapes that flew better. Morrison called his original flying saucers Pluto Platters.

He started out selling them on street corners. Then he got together with a new toy company named Wham-O. Wham-O improved the design of the disks. They also changed the name to Frisbee and sponsored Frisbee tournaments all over the country to promote Frisbee as a sport. The game caught on fast, and it looks as though it's here to stay.

Accountable Miscues

Full Miscues: ____ ×   1   = ____

Half Miscues: ____ × $\frac{1}{2}$ = ____

TOTAL   ____

COMPREHENSION CHECK

	Probed Recall	Free Recall

L 1. Where did the name Frisbee come from?   ____ ____

(It was originally the name of a pie company.)

L 2. College students in the early part of this century played a game like Frisbee. What did they flip to one another?   ____ ____

(empty metal pie plates/tins)

L 3. What did Fred Morrison call his original flying saucers?   ____ ____

(Pluto Platters)

I 4. What did Fred Morrison do to improve the design of the pie plates?   ____ ____

(He used plastic to make them safer.)

(He molded them into shapes that flew better.)

I 5. Why do you think the Wham-O Company sponsored Frisbee tournaments all over the country?   ____ ____

(to increase sales of the product)

(to increase the popularity of the product)

Note: If student responds, "To promote Frisbee as a sport," ask, "Why do you think the Wham-O Company wanted to promote Frisbee as a sport?"

C 6. What might have happened to the Frisbee if plastic had not been invented?   __ __ __ __

(Accept any logical response, such as "It wouldn't have caught on as well.")

Total Comprehension Errors   _____

(L & I)

PRIOR KNOWLEDGE

How much did you know about the history of the game of Frisbee before reading this article?

I knew:

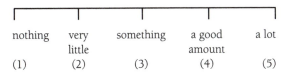

nothing	very little	something	a good amount	a lot
(1)	(2)	(3)	(4)	(5)

LEVEL OF INTEREST

How much did you like reading this article?

This article was:

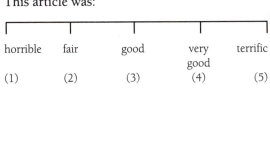

horrible	fair	good	very good	terrific
(1)	(2)	(3)	(4)	(5)

LEVELS OF WORD RECOGNITION AND COMPREHENSION

Word Recognition MISCUES		*Comprehension* ERRORS
0		0
1	Independent Level	
2		
3		½
4,5		
6,7		
8	Instructional Level	1
9		
10,11		
12,13		
14		
15,16		1½
17,18		
	Questionable Level	
19,20		2
21,22		
23,24		
25		2½
	Frustration Level	

The Game of Frisbee (7)

CATEGORIES OF ACCOUNTABLE MISCUES IN WORD RECOGNITION

FULL MISCUES	NUMBER	HALF MISCUES	NUMBER
Nonword Substitutions		Whole Word Substitutions	
Whole Word Substitutions		Omissions	
Omissions		Insertions	
Insertions			
Reversals			
Repetitions			
Pronounced by Examiner			

CATEGORIES OF COMPREHENSION ERRORS

	FREE AND PROBED RECALL	
	Items Attempted (Free and Probed)	*Number of Errors*
Literal		
Interpretive		
Critical/Creative		

To Buy or Not to Buy (8)

INTRODUCTION: Please read this article to learn something about the arrangement of items in a store.

To Buy or Not to Buy

As a consumer, or buyer, you have been in a tremendous number of stores in your life. Have you ever given a thought to how those stores are arranged?

Carefully considered choices are made about where to display each type of merchandise. Where should the basic items go? How can you be made to notice items that you may not be looking for, and how can you be persuaded to make an unplanned purchase? These are questions that a store planner must answer.

Think about the stores that most people go into frequently: drugstores and supermarkets. Where are the basic items such as prescriptions, dairy products, produce, and meat situated? They are usually toward the back, forcing you to pass by numerous other products that may catch your eye.

There is even a whole category of products that are displayed where you are most likely to notice them: at the checkout counter. They are referred to as impulse items. The thinking is that when you spot one of these inexpensive items, you will decide you want it. Some common impulse items are magazines, candy, and batteries.

In a technique called scrambled merchandising, stores sometimes offer the same item in several places. For example, batteries might be placed in the hardware section as well as near the register. Seasons, too, affect the placement of merchandise. In summer, picnic supplies might stand in the busy front section of the store, while in November and December, holiday decorations occupy that space. So, when you walk into a drugstore next summer, remember that it is no accident that the sunglasses are right up in front.

Accountable Miscues

Full Miscues: ____ × 1 = ____

Half Miscues: ____ × $\frac{1}{2}$ = ____

TOTAL ____

COMPREHENSION CHECK

Probed Recall   Free Recall

L 1. What is a question that a store planner must answer? ____ ____

(Where should the basic items go?)

(How can you be made to notice items that you may not be looking for?)

(How can you be persuaded to make an unplanned purchase?)

L 2. Why are the basic items found in a supermarket usually placed toward the back? ____ ____

(to force you to pass by numerous other products that may catch your eye)

L 3. What is scrambled merchandising? ____ ____

(when stores offer the same item in several places)

I 4. Why must the arrangement of items in a store be carefully planned? ____ ____

(to increase sales)

I 5. Why is the information presented in this article important to consumers? ____ ____

(to teach consumers about the "tricks of the trade" in order to cut down on the number of unnecessary purchases)

C 6. You have been hired as a store planner for a supermarket. Name an item you would display in the front section of the store in winter. Why would you place this item there? __ __ __ __

(Accept any logical response, such as ice melter and antifreeze, because these are items needed in the winter season.)

Total Comprehension Errors _____

(L & I)

PRIOR KNOWLEDGE

How much did you know about the arrangement of items in a store before reading this article?

I knew:

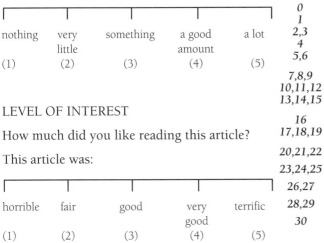

nothing	very little	something	a good amount	a lot
(1)	(2)	(3)	(4)	(5)

LEVEL OF INTEREST

How much did you like reading this article?

This article was:

horrible	fair	good	very good	terrific
(1)	(2)	(3)	(4)	(5)

LEVELS OF WORD RECOGNITION AND COMPREHENSION

Word Recognition MISCUES

Comprehension ERRORS

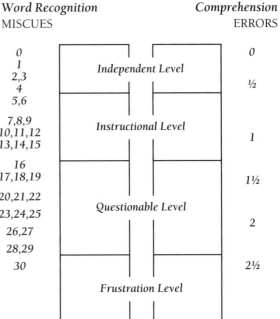

To Buy or Not to Buy (8)

CATEGORIES OF ACCOUNTABLE MISCUES IN WORD RECOGNITION

FULL MISCUES	NUMBER	HALF MISCUES	NUMBER
Nonword Substitutions		Whole Word Substitutions	
Whole Word Substitutions		Omissions	
Omissions		Insertions	
Insertions			
Reversals			
Repetitions			
Pronounced by Examiner			

CATEGORIES OF COMPREHENSION ERRORS

	FREE AND PROBED RECALL	
	Items Attempted (Free and Probed)	*Number of Errors*
Literal		
Interpretive		
Critical/Creative		

The Pencil—A Lasting Impression (9)

INTRODUCTION: Please read this article to learn something about a common object—the pencil.

The Pencil—A Lasting Impression

Lincoln wrote part of the Gettysburg Address with one, and one of these instruments can draw a line thirty-five miles long. The device we call the pencil has had a long and glorious evolution dating back to the 1500s.

It took a hurricane to uncover the world's first mineral deposit of graphite, and thus make possible the invention of the pencil. After the storm, farmers found black material underneath an uprooted tree. These farmers found it useful to mark their sheep. Playwrights were happy to find a less messy method than feather pen and ink to record their stories. The first pencils were eventually wrapped in rope or encased in metal until the Germans invented a way to enclose the graphite in wood, the method we still use today.

For a long time, scientists thought the material they were writing with was actually lead, because of its similar appearance. However, in the late eighteenth century they discovered that the "lead" was actually a form of carbon. So, as a result of this discovery, scientists graciously renamed the material "graphite" from the Greek word meaning "to write."

Today's manufacturers mark their pencils with numbers ranging from one to four to identify the hardness of the graphite the pencil contains. This advancement was made possible by a Frenchman who developed a process of mixing graphite with clay to vary the texture.

Soon afterward, another breakthrough was made, without which pencils may have been written out of our history. When the known mineral deposits of graphite were beginning to diminish, an American discovered a way to manufacture graphite using coke.

However, most writers would agree that we are all most indebted to an American by the name of Hyman Lipman, who patented his idea of attaching erasers to pencils in 1858, five years before Lincoln authored the Gettysburg Address.

Accountable Miscues

Full Miscues: _____ × 1 = _____

Half Miscues: _____ × $\frac{1}{2}$ = _____

TOTAL _____

COMPREHENSION CHECK

		Probed Recall	Free Recall
L 1.	How did a hurricane play an important role in the evolution of the pencil?	____	____

(As a result of this storm, the world's first mineral deposit of graphite was uncovered.)

| L 2. | What did farmers of long ago use graphite for? | ____ | ____ |

(to mark their sheep)

| L 3. | What is mixed with the graphite to vary the texture of the pencil? | ____ | ____ |

(clay)

| I 4. | We know that an American discovered a way to manufacture graphite out of coke. Why was this an important discovery? | ____ | ____ |

(Without this discovery, we may have run out of the graphite needed to make pencils.)

| I 5. | Why is a graphite pencil usually known as a lead pencil? | ____ | ____ |

(Until the eighteenth century it was believed that the material used to make pencils was lead, and it was really graphite.)

| C 6. | What is your opinion of the contribution made by Hyman Lipman to the evolution of the pencil? | _ _ | _ _ |

(Accept any logical response, such as "I feel that it was a clever idea to attach an eraser to a pencil. Otherwise, we would always need to carry an eraser.")

Total Comprehension Errors _____

(L & I)

PRIOR KNOWLEDGE

How much did you know about the invention and evolution of the pencil before reading this article?

I knew:

nothing	very little	something	a good amount	a lot
(1)	(2)	(3)	(4)	(5)

LEVEL OF INTEREST

How much did you like reading this article?

This article was:

horrible	fair	good	very good	terrific
(1)	(2)	(3)	(4)	(5)

LEVELS OF WORD RECOGNITION AND COMPREHENSION

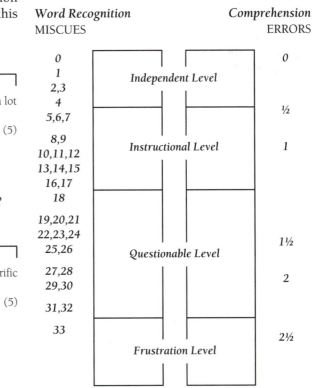

Word Recognition MISCUES / *Comprehension* ERRORS

MISCUES	Level	ERRORS
0, 1, 2,3	Independent Level	0
4		½
5,6,7		
8,9, 10,11,12, 13,14,15, 16,17	Instructional Level	1
18		
19,20,21, 22,23,24, 25,26	Questionable Level	1½
27,28, 29,30		2
31,32		
33	Frustration Level	2½

The Pencil—A Lasting Impression (9)

CATEGORIES OF ACCOUNTABLE MISCUES IN WORD RECOGNITION

FULL MISCUES	NUMBER	HALF MISCUES	NUMBER
Nonword Substitutions		Whole Word Substitutions	
Whole Word Substitutions		Omissions	
Omissions		Insertions	
Insertions			
Reversals			
Repetitions			
Pronounced by Examiner			

CATEGORIES OF COMPREHENSION ERRORS

	FREE AND PROBED RECALL	
	Items Attempted (Free and Probed)	*Number of Errors*
Literal		
Interpretive		
Critical/Creative		

Graded Reading Passages Test: Form D—Narrative

(Student's test materials appear on pages 167–175.)

N *A Day by the Lake (1)*

INTRODUCTION: Please read this story to find out what a girl likes to do.

A Day by the Lake

Pat stood by the lake. A soft wind blew.

Across the grass, ducks swam near the shore.

There were big ducks and baby ducks.

Two stood on the grass near Pat. Pat

opened a paper bag. She put her hand in

it. It came out full of bits of bread. She

dropped some bread around her on the

ground. She threw some on the water. The

ducks swam to it.

They quacked and ate the bread. Pat

laughed and threw some more bread.

Accountable Miscues

Full Miscues: ____ × 1 = ____

Half Miscues: ____ × $\frac{1}{2}$ = ____

TOTAL ____

COMPREHENSION CHECK

		Probed Recall	Free Recall

L 1. Who was standing by the lake?   ____ ____

(Pat)

L 2. What did Pat see?   ____ ____

(ducks)

(big ducks)

(baby ducks)

L 3. What did Pat take out of the paper bag?   ____ ____

(bread)

(bits of bread)

L 4. Where did Pat throw some of the bread?   ____ ____

(on the water)

I 5. Was Pat having a good time? How do you know?   ____ ____

(Yes. She laughed.)

(She kept on feeding the ducks.)

C 6. Could this story have happened? What makes you think so?   __ __   __ __

(Accept any logical response, such as "because the events sounded real.")

Total Comprehension Errors _____

(L & I)

PRIOR KNOWLEDGE

Have you ever read this story before?

_____Yes _____ No

LEVEL OF INTEREST

How much did you like reading this story?

This story was:

horrible	fair	good	very good	terrific
(1)	(2)	(3)	(4)	(5)

LEVELS OF WORD RECOGNITION AND COMPREHENSION

Word Recognition
MISCUES

Comprehension
ERRORS

Word Recognition Miscues	Level	Comprehension Errors
0	Independent Level	0
1		½
2	Instructional Level	
3		1
4		
5		1½
6	Questionable Level	
7		2
8		
9		
10	Frustration Level	2½

A Day by the Lake (1)

CATEGORIES OF ACCOUNTABLE MISCUES IN WORD RECOGNITION

FULL MISCUES	NUMBER	HALF MISCUES	NUMBER
Nonword Substitutions		Whole Word Substitutions	
Whole Word Substitutions		Omissions	
Omissions		Insertions	
Insertions			
Reversals			
Repetitions			
Pronounced by Examiner			

CATEGORIES OF COMPREHENSION ERRORS

	FREE AND PROBED RECALL	
	Items Attempted (Free and Probed)	*Number of Errors*
Literal		
Interpretive		
Critical/Creative		

The Lesson (2)

INTRODUCTION: Please read this story about a father who tries to teach his children a lesson.

The Lesson

There were once some children who were always fighting. Their father tried to get them to stop. They would not listen. They could not get along together. Finally, the father asked his children to do something to teach them a lesson. The father asked, "Bring me a bunch of sticks."

The children did as they were told. One child held out the bunch of sticks. The father said, "Try to break the bunch of sticks." The child tried. He could not break the bunch of sticks. Each child took a turn. No one could break the bunch of sticks. The father then handed one stick to each child. "Now try to break your stick," said the man.

Each child easily broke a stick in two. The father then said, "Take a lesson from the sticks, my children. Only together are they not able to be broken."

Accountable Miscues

Full Miscues: _____ × 1 = _____

Half Miscues: _____ × $\frac{1}{2}$ = _____

TOTAL   _____

COMPREHENSION CHECK

	Probed Recall	Free Recall

L 1. What were the children in the story always doing?   _____ _____

(fighting)

L 2. What did the father ask his children to bring to him?   _____ _____

(a bunch of sticks)

L 3. What did the father ask each child to do with the bunch of sticks?   _____ _____

(to break each bunch)

L 4. What could each child easily break into two pieces?   _____ _____

(one stick)

I 5. Why did the father want to teach his children a lesson?   _____ _____

(He didn't want them to fight anymore.)

C 6. What can we learn from this story?   _ _   _ _

(Accept any logical response, such as "People are stronger if they are united.")

Total Comprehension Errors   _____

(L & I)

PRIOR KNOWLEDGE

Have you ever read this story before?

_____Yes _____ No

LEVEL OF INTEREST

How much did you like reading this story?

This story was:

horrible	fair	good	very good	terrific
(1)	(2)	(3)	(4)	(5)

LEVELS OF WORD RECOGNITION AND COMPREHENSION

Word Recognition MISCUES		Comprehension ERRORS
0	Independent Level	0
1		
2		½
3		
4	Instructional Level	
5		
6		1
7,8		
9		1½
10		
11	Questionable Level	
12,13		2
14		
15		
16		2½
	Frustration Level	

The Lesson (2)

CATEGORIES OF ACCOUNTABLE MISCUES IN WORD RECOGNITION

FULL MISCUES	NUMBER	HALF MISCUES	NUMBER
Nonword Substitutions		Whole Word Substitutions	
Whole Word Substitutions		Omissions	
Omissions		Insertions	
Insertions			
Reversals			
Repetitions			
Pronounced by Examiner			

CATEGORIES OF COMPREHENSION ERRORS

	FREE AND PROBED RECALL	
	Items Attempted (Free and Probed)	Number of Errors
Literal		
Interpretive		
Critical/Creative		

The Blind Woman (3)

INTRODUCTION: Please read this story about a woman who could not see.

The Blind Woman

A woman who had become blind called a doctor. She promised that if he could cure her, she would reward him well. If he failed, he would get nothing. The doctor agreed.

He went often to the woman's apartment. He would pretend to treat her eyes. But he would also steal furniture and other objects. Little by little, he took all her belongings. Finally, he used his skill to cure her and asked for his money.

Every time he asked for his payment, the woman made up a reason for not paying him. Eventually he took her to court. The woman said to the judge, "I did promise to pay the doctor if he gave me back my sight. However, how can I be cured? If I truly could see, wouldn't I see furniture and other belongings in my house?"

Accountable Miscues

Full Miscues: _____ × 1 = _____

Half Miscues: _____ × $\frac{1}{2}$ = _____

TOTAL _____

COMPREHENSION CHECK

		Probed Recall	Free Recall
L 1.	Who did the woman ask for help? (a doctor)	____	____
L 2.	What promise did the woman make to the doctor? (to pay him well only if he cured her)	____	____
L 3.	What did the doctor do while in the woman's apartment? (took furniture) (took all her belongings)	____	____
L 4.	Why did the doctor take the woman to court? (because he wanted his payment)	____	____
I 5.	Why didn't the woman want to pay the doctor for curing her blindness? (She felt he didn't deserve to be paid because he was a thief.)	____	____
C 6.	What would you do if you were the judge in this case? (Accept any logical response, such as "I would place the doctor in jail for being dishonest.")	_ _	_ _

Total Comprehension Errors   _____

(L & I)

PRIOR KNOWLEDGE

Have you ever read this story before?

_____Yes _____ No

LEVEL OF INTEREST

How much did you like reading this story?

This story was:

horrible	fair	good	very good	terrific
(1)	(2)	(3)	(4)	(5)

LEVELS OF WORD RECOGNITION
AND COMPREHENSION

Word Recognition
MISCUES

Comprehension
ERRORS

Word Recognition MISCUES	Level	Comprehension ERRORS
0		0
1,2	Independent Level	
3		½
4,5		
6	Instructional Level	1
7		
8,9		1½
10		
11,12	Questionable Level	2
13,14		
15		2½
	Frustration Level	

The Blind Woman (3)

CATEGORIES OF ACCOUNTABLE MISCUES IN WORD RECOGNITION

FULL MISCUES	NUMBER	HALF MISCUES	NUMBER
Nonword Substitutions		Whole Word Substitutions	
Whole Word Substitutions		Omissions	
Omissions		Insertions	
Insertions			
Reversals			
Repetitions			
Pronounced by Examiner			

CATEGORIES OF COMPREHENSION ERRORS

	FREE AND PROBED RECALL	
	Items Attempted (Free and Probed)	*Number of Errors*
Literal		
Interpretive		
Critical/Creative		

The Promise (4)

INTRODUCTION: This story is about two girls walking together. Please read to find out what happens to them.

The Promise

Long ago, in a distant land beside the sea, people often spotted mermaids. The mermaids had fantastic treasures. Sometimes the mermaids would swim to shore. They would spread their treasures around them on the sand. If anyone came near, however, they would jump back in the sea.

One day, two little girls walking on a beach spied a mermaid. To their surprise, she did not swim away when she saw them. Instead, she smiled and called them over. She gave each a bundle of treasure. "Do not open them until you get home," she warned. The girls promised not to. Then off they went, happy and excited.

One girl soon grew impatient. When she was out of sight of the mermaid, she decided to open her gift. To her disappointment, she found only ashes and dust.

The other girl kept her promise. She did not look inside until she got home. In her bundle she found gold, silver, and sparkling jewels. Her family was delighted, and they never forgot their good fortune.

Accountable Miscues

Full Miscues: ____   ×   1   =   ____

Half Miscues: ____   × $\frac{1}{2}$ =   ____

TOTAL   ____

COMPREHENSION CHECK

		Probed Recall	Free Recall

L 1. Where does this story take place?   ____ ____

(by the sea)

(on a beach)

L 2. Who did the little girls see?   ____ ____

(a mermaid)

L 3. What did the mermaid give to each girl?   ____ ____

(a bundle of treasure)

L 4. What was the promise both girls made to the mermaid?   ____ ____

(not to open their bundles of treasure until they got home)

I 5. How did the girl who opened up the first bundle of treasure feel?   ____ ____

(sad)

(upset)

(disappointed)

C 6. What is the lesson we can learn from this story?   _ _   _ _

(Accept any logical response, such as "If you keep your promise, many good things will come your way" or "Listen to people and heed their warnings.")

Total Comprehension Errors   _____

(L & I)

PRIOR KNOWLEDGE

Have you ever read this story before?

_____Yes _____ No

LEVEL OF INTEREST

How much did you like reading this story?

This story was:

horrible	fair	good	very good	terrific
(1)	(2)	(3)	(4)	(5)

LEVELS OF WORD RECOGNITION
AND COMPREHENSION

Word Recognition MISCUES		*Comprehension* ERRORS
0	Independent Level	0
1,2		½
3,4		
5,6	Instructional Level	
7		1
8,9		
10,11		1½
12		
13,14	Questionable Level	2
15,16		
17,18		
19		2½
	Frustration Level	

The Promise (4)

CATEGORIES OF ACCOUNTABLE MISCUES IN WORD RECOGNITION

FULL MISCUES	NUMBER	HALF MISCUES	NUMBER
Nonword Substitutions		Whole Word Substitutions	
Whole Word Substitutions		Omissions	
Omissions		Insertions	
Insertions			
Reversals			
Repetitions			
Pronounced by Examiner			

CATEGORIES OF COMPREHENSION ERRORS

	FREE AND PROBED RECALL	
	Items Attempted (Free and Probed)	*Number of Errors*
Literal		
Interpretive		
Critical/Creative		

A Surprise for Miss Stern (5)

INTRODUCTION: Please read this story about a boy and his teacher.

A Surprise for Miss Stern

Ricky Glen loved the outdoors. He always carried with him as much of his favorite environment as he could.

Last Tuesday, a shining early spring day, he carried a bit too much of it into Miss Stern's classroom. As usual, Miss Stern had Ricky leave his nature collection on her desk during class. That day it included a stick with a light brown papery ball attached to it. It was that strange ball that caused the trouble.

All was fine until one o'clock, when Miss Stern said, "Now take out your math books." Perhaps it was the warm sun shining onto the desk that started the whole thing. Whatever it was, that ball began to wiggle and shake. Twenty amazed pairs of eyes stared as hundreds of tiny green specks jumped from it. They hopped around on Miss Stern's desk. They even hopped on Miss Stern. Bolting for the door, she yelled, "Ricky! What is the meaning of this!"

"They're baby grasshoppers, Miss Stern!"

The words, "Get rid of those tiny insects, Ricky!" faded down the hallway with Miss Stern.

Ricky scooped the babies from Miss Stern's desk, the flower pots, the floor, and the windowsills. He gathered them all up in a box and carried them outside—all, that is, except the ones that rode out in Miss Stern's hair.

Accountable Miscues

Full Miscues: ____ × 1 = ____

Half Miscues: ____ × $\frac{1}{2}$ = ____

                                        TOTAL ____

COMPREHENSION CHECK

	Probed Recall	Free Recall

L 1. What did Ricky Glen love to do?   ____   ____

(play outdoors)

(collect things from nature)

(learn from nature)

L 2. What did Ricky leave on Miss Stern's desk?   ____   ____

(his nature collection)

(a stick with a light brown papery ball attached to it)

(a strange ball)

L 3. What happened to the brown ball on Miss Stern's desk?   ____   ____

(It started to wiggle, shake.)

(Hundreds of tiny green specks jumped from it.)

(It got warm and the eggs hatched out of it.)

L 4. What were the tiny green specks that jumped from the brown ball?   ____   ____

(grasshoppers)

(tiny insects)

I 5. Why is the title of this story "A Surprise for Miss Stern"?   ____   ____

(Miss Stern didn't expect to see grasshoppers hatching on her desk.)

(Miss Stern didn't expect to have grasshoppers in her hair.)

C 6. What do you think happened the next day in Miss Stern's class?   _ _   _ _

(Accept any logical response, such as "Ricky might be punished and told not to bring his nature collection to class again.")

Total Comprehension Errors   _____

                                        (L & I)

PRIOR KNOWLEDGE

Have you ever read this story before?

_____ Yes _____ No

LEVEL OF INTEREST

How much did you like reading this story?

This story was:

horrible	fair	good	very good	terrific
(1)	(2)	(3)	(4)	(5)

LEVELS OF WORD RECOGNITION
AND COMPREHENSION

Word Recognition
MISCUES

Comprehension
ERRORS

Word Recognition MISCUES	Level	Comprehension ERRORS
0	*Independent Level*	0
1,2,3		½
4,5		
6,7		
8,9	*Instructional Level*	1
10		
11,12		
13,14		1½
15,16		
17,18	*Questionable Level*	2
19,20		
21,22,23		
24		2½
	Frustration Level	

A Surprise for Miss Stern (5)

CATEGORIES OF ACCOUNTABLE MISCUES IN WORD RECOGNITION

FULL MISCUES	NUMBER	HALF MISCUES	NUMBER
Nonword Substitutions		Whole Word Substitutions	
Whole Word Substitutions		Omissions	
Omissions		Insertions	
Insertions			
Reversals			
Repetitions			
Pronounced by Examiner			

CATEGORIES OF COMPREHENSION ERRORS

	FREE AND PROBED RECALL	
	Items Attempted (Free and Probed)	*Number of Errors*
Literal		
Interpretive		
Critical/Creative		

The Strange Day (6)

INTRODUCTION: Jane will remember this day for a long time. Please read this story to find out what happens to her.

The Strange Day

On that crisp Monday morning in late October, Jane's alarm sounded at seven, as usual. Jane pulled herself out of bed and proceeded to get ready for school. It was as ordinary a morning as a morning can be. Jane showered, ate breakfast, got dressed, patted the cat good-bye, and headed out the door. That's when things began to look a bit out of the ordinary.

Why was it so quiet? Usually the sidewalks were dotted with kids going to school, but today Jane emerged as the sole pedestrian. Even cars were scarce.

By the time she reached the school, Jane was feeling decidedly uneasy. There, she encountered the strangest thing of all. Not a soul was in sight, and the school doors were locked tight. What was going on? Her senses reeling, Jane leaned her head against the locked door.

A minute later, Jane nearly jumped out of her skin when a deep voice boomed, "What are you doing here so early?" Spinning around, she found herself facing Mr. Cheston, the school janitor. Her heart hammering, Jane screeched, "Where is everyone?" Mr. Cheston leaned closer and said in a low voice, "You forgot to set your clock back, didn't you?"

As his words penetrated, Jane went limp and echoed, "Clock?" "That's right," laughed Mr. Cheston heartily. "Daylight saving time is over. You're an hour ahead of the rest of us!"

Accountable Miscues

Full Miscues: ____ × 1 = ____

Half Miscues: ____ × $\frac{1}{2}$ = ____

TOTAL ____

COMPREHENSION CHECK

Probed Recall   Free Recall

L 1. In what month does this story take place?   ____ ____

(October)

L 2. How did Jane react to Mr. Cheston's deep, booming voice?   ____ ____

(She nearly jumped out of her skin.)

(She was startled.)

(She was surprised.)

L 3. What had Jane forgotten to do?   ____ ____

(set her clock back)

L 4. Describe one "out of the ordinary" event experienced by Jane in this story.   ____ ____

(She was the only one on the street.)

(There weren't many cars outside.)

(There weren't any other students outside of the school building.)

(The doors to the school were locked.)

I 5. How do you think Jane felt at the end of the story?   ____ ____

(foolish)

(embarrassed)

C 6. Could this story have happened? What makes you think so?   _ _ _ _

(Accept any logical response, such as "Yes, because someone could have forgotten to set his or her clock back.")

Total Comprehension Errors   _____

(L & I)

PRIOR KNOWLEDGE

Have you ever read this story before?

_____Yes _____ No

LEVEL OF INTEREST

How much did you like reading this story?

This story was:

horrible	fair	good	very good	terrific
(1)	(2)	(3)	(4)	(5)

LEVELS OF WORD RECOGNITION AND COMPREHENSION

Word Recognition MISCUES			*Comprehension* ERRORS
0		Independent Level	0
1,2,3			½
4,5			
6,7		Instructional Level	
8,9			1
10,11,12			
13,14			1½
15,16			
17,18		Questionable Level	2
19,20,21			
22,23,24			
25			2½
		Frustration Level	

The Strange Day (6)

CATEGORIES OF ACCOUNTABLE MISCUES IN WORD RECOGNITION

FULL MISCUES	NUMBER	HALF MISCUES	NUMBER
Nonword Substitutions		Whole Word Substitutions	
Whole Word Substitutions		Omissions	
Omissions		Insertions	
Insertions			
Reversals			
Repetitions			
Pronounced by Examiner			

CATEGORIES OF COMPREHENSION ERRORS

	FREE AND PROBED RECALL	
	Items Attempted (Free and Probed)	*Number of Errors*
Literal		
Interpretive		
Critical/Creative		

Up, Up, and Away (7)

INTRODUCTION: Please read this story about two people having a good time at an amusement park.

Up, Up, and Away

Though the sun had set long ago, the heavy air stuck to my skin like a damp cloth. The July sky blazed with stars so bright they rivaled the gaudy reds, greens, and yellows that turned night on the ground into a weird artificial day. Shouts, laughter, music, screams of terror and delight, dings, rings, and hums filled the air.

Transported by the exotic scent of popcorn and cotton candy, Jeff and I wrestled our way through the crowd to my favorite ride. We climbed aboard and the attendant banged the safety bar into place. The seat swung back and forth as the big wheel began to turn, carrying us back and up, up, a hundred feet into the night sky.

As we climbed, the noise fell away and the scene below us grew and grew, till it looked like a picture in a book, complete and removed from us. The wheel paused, with Jeff and me swinging madly at the top, and I inhaled the dreamy scene mingled with the cool, fresh air of the higher altitudes. Suddenly we dropped back to earth. My heart and stomach leaped to my throat, and I shouted in spite of myself. There isn't a better way to spend a summer night.

Accountable Miscues

Full Miscues: _____ × 1 = _____

Half Miscues: _____ × $\frac{1}{2}$ = _____

TOTAL _____

COMPREHENSION CHECK

		Probed Recall	Free Recall
L 1.	When does this story take place? (on a summer night) (in July)	____	____
I 2.	Who is telling this story? (the author)	____	____
L 3.	Name two sounds that filled the air. (shouts, laughter, music, screams of terror, etc.)	____	____
I 4.	Why is the title of this story "Up, Up, and Away"? (This story is about the author's experience riding a Ferris wheel at an amusement park.)	____	____
L 5.	When did the wheel pause? (when it reached the top)	____	____
C 6.	In this story the author said, "My heart and stomach leaped to my throat, and I shouted in spite of myself." Can you think of a time when you felt this way? Describe it. (Accept any logical response, such as "I felt this way when I rode on a roller coaster" or "I felt this way when I was watching a scary movie and someone tapped me on the shoulder.")	_ _	_ _

Total Comprehension Errors _____

(L & I)

PRIOR KNOWLEDGE

Have you ever read this story before?

_____Yes _____ No

LEVEL OF INTEREST

How much did you like reading this story?

This story was:

horrible	fair	good	very good	terrific
(1)	(2)	(3)	(4)	(5)

LEVELS OF WORD RECOGNITION AND COMPREHENSION

Word Recognition MISCUES		*Comprehension* ERRORS
0		0
1,2	Independent Level	
3		½
4,5		
6,7	Instructional Level	
8,9		1
10,11		
12,13		1½
14,15		
16,17	Questionable Level	
18,19		2
20,21,22		
23		2½
	Frustration Level	

Up, Up, and Away (7)

CATEGORIES OF ACCOUNTABLE MISCUES IN WORD RECOGNITION

FULL MISCUES	NUMBER	HALF MISCUES	NUMBER
Nonword Substitutions		Whole Word Substitutions	
Whole Word Substitutions		Omissions	
Omissions		Insertions	
Insertions			
Reversals			
Repetitions			
Pronounced by Examiner			

CATEGORIES OF COMPREHENSION ERRORS

	FREE AND PROBED RECALL	
	Items Attempted (Free and Probed)	*Number of Errors*
Literal		
Interpretive		
Critical/Creative		

Stage Fright (8)

INTRODUCTION: Please read this story about a student's experience as an actor.

Stage Fright

Civic duty, volunteerism, getting involved—whatever you call it, one of these noble descriptive phrases motivated my brief but memorable venture into the world of acting.

It all began innocently. My school's drama club was to present an original play about the Roman Empire. It seemed the entire student body was participating; so who was I to resist the lure of stardom?

So the process ensued—auditions, rehearsals, and finally, the night of the fated fiasco itself. I was to serve as the narrator, introducing the cast and events to the audience. A rather innocuous role I assumed. How was I to know an overzealous cleaning man had unwittingly "staged" a surprise for my first and only "stage left"?

When the time approached for my debut, I realized my breathing had quickened and my stomach had become queasy. Stage fright had set in. But worst of all, a frog-sized lump was lodged in my throat. How was I to narrate anything?

Not to worry. As I took my first step toward the limelight, my knees locked and my feet slid out from under. With all the grace of an elephant, I made my entrance and exit almost simultaneously, sliding on my toga across the overwaxed stage. A sprained ankle relieved me of my duties as narrator. And so ended my glorious career as an entertainer— although I did receive a standing ovation as the cast carried me out on a stretcher for the final curtain call. Mom would have been proud—if she'd stayed.

Accountable Miscues

Full Miscues: _____ × 1 = _____

Half Miscues: _____ × $\frac{1}{2}$ = _____

TOTAL _____

COMPREHENSION CHECK

		Probed Recall	Free Recall
L 1.	What motivated the person in this story to enter the world of acting? (civic duty) (volunteerism) (getting involved) (the lure of stardom)	_____	_____
L 2.	What role did this person have in the play? (narrator)	_____	_____
L 3.	What did the cleaning man do to the stage? (He overwaxed it.)	_____	_____
I 4.	Why did the audience give the narrator a standing ovation? (probably to make him feel better about what had happened)	_____	_____
I 5.	What word could be used to describe how the mother felt? (embarrassed)	_____	_____
C 6.	Describe a situation when you felt a frog-sized lump was lodged in your throat. (Accept any logical response, such as "When I had to give an oral report in a history class.") *Note:* If student responds, "When I was on stage," ask, "Have you ever felt this way doing something else? Tell me about it."	_ _	_ _

Total Comprehension Errors _____

(L & I)

PRIOR KNOWLEDGE

Have you ever read this story before?

_____Yes _____ No

LEVEL OF INTEREST

How much did you like reading this story?

This story was:

horrible	fair	good	very good	terrific
(1)	(2)	(3)	(4)	(5)

LEVELS OF WORD RECOGNITION AND COMPREHENSION

Word Recognition
MISCUES

Comprehension
ERRORS

Word Recognition Miscues	Level	Comprehension Errors
0		0
1,2	*Independent Level*	
3		½
4,5		
6,7,8	*Instructional Level*	
9,10,11		1
12,13,14		
15,16		1½
17,18,19	*Questionable Level*	
20,21,22		2
23,24		
25,26		
27		2½
	Frustration Level	

Stage Fright (8)

CATEGORIES OF ACCOUNTABLE MISCUES IN WORD RECOGNITION

FULL MISCUES	NUMBER	HALF MISCUES	NUMBER
Nonword Substitutions		Whole Word Substitutions	
Whole Word Substitutions		Omissions	
Omissions		Insertions	
Insertions			
Reversals			
Repetitions			
Pronounced by Examiner			

CATEGORIES OF COMPREHENSION ERRORS

	FREE AND PROBED RECALL	
	Items Attempted (Free and Probed)	*Number of Errors*
Literal		
Interpretive		
Critical/Creative		

The White Trail (9)

INTRODUCTION: Many times the author of a story describes an important event or scene. The following passage was taken from a longer story. Please read this passage to see whether you can imagine what is happening.

The White Trail

The sleds were singing their eternal lament to the creaking of the harnesses and the tinkling bells of the leaders, but the men and dogs were tired and made no sound. The trail was heavy with new-fallen snow, and they had traveled far, and the runners, burdened with quarters of frozen moose, clung to the unpacked surface and resisted with a stubbornness almost human. Darkness was coming on, but there was no camp in the vicinity that evening. The snow fell gently through the still air, not in flakes, but in tiny frost crystals. It was very warm—barely ten degrees below zero—and the men did not mind.

The dogs had become fatigued early in the afternoon, but they now began to show new vigor. Among the intelligent ones there was a certain restlessness—an impatience, a sniffling of snouts and raising of ears, and these became irritated with their more sluggish brothers, urging them on with numerous sly nips on their hindquarters. Those, thus scolded, perked up and assisted in spreading the excitement. At last, the leader of the foremost sled uttered a short whine of satisfaction, crouching lower in the snow and throwing himself against the collar. The rest followed suit. There was a tightening of muscles in the harness; the sleds leaped forward, and the men clung to the gee-poles, violently accelerating their pace to escape going under the runners. The weariness of the day fell from them, and they whooped encouragement to the dogs. The animals responded with joyous yelps. They were swinging through the gathering darkness at a rattling gallop.

Source: Story adapted from London, J. (1982). An odyssey of the north. In *Jack London: Novels and stories* (pp. 333–364). New York: Literary Classics of the United States.

Accountable Miscues

Full Miscues: ____ × 1 = ____

Half Miscues: ____ × $\frac{1}{2}$ = ____

TOTAL   ____

COMPREHENSION CHECK

	Probed Recall	Free Recall

I 1. What is this story about?

(men and their dogsled teams attempting to overcome the difficulties of a harsh environment)

____   ____

L 2. At the beginning of this story, how did the men and their dogs feel?

(tired)

____   ____

L 3. The scene described in this story takes place during what time of day?

(twilight)

(near darkness)

____   ____

L 4. What did the men think of the below-zero temperature?

(They did not mind it.)

(It didn't bother them.)

____   ____

I 5. What is the mood of the dogs at the end of the story?

(upbeat)

(The dogs were excited.)

____   ____

C 6. If you could choose to be a character in this story, animal or human, which one would it be? Explain why.

(Accept any logical response, such as "I would like to be the driver of a sled. I would enjoy doing this because it would be a real challenge.")

__ __   __ __

Total Comprehension Errors _____

(L & I)

PRIOR KNOWLEDGE

Have you ever read this story before?

_____Yes _____ No

LEVEL OF INTEREST

How much did you like reading this story?

This story was:

horrible	fair	good	very good	terrific
(1)	(2)	(3)	(4)	(5)

LEVELS OF WORD RECOGNITION AND COMPREHENSION

Word Recognition MISCUES		Comprehension ERRORS
0		0
1,2,3	Independent Level	½
4,5,6		
7,8		
	Instructional Level	
9,10,11		1
12,13,14		
15,16		1½
17,18,19		
20,21	Questionable Level	2
22,23,24		
25,26,27		
28		2½
	Frustration Level	

The White Trail (9)

CATEGORIES OF ACCOUNTABLE MISCUES IN WORD RECOGNITION

FULL MISCUES	NUMBER	HALF MISCUES	NUMBER
Nonword Substitutions		Whole Word Substitutions	
Whole Word Substitutions		Omissions	
Omissions		Insertions	
Insertions			
Reversals			
Repetitions			
Pronounced by Examiner			

CATEGORIES OF COMPREHENSION ERRORS

	FREE AND PROBED RECALL	
	Items Attempted (Free and Probed)	Number of Errors
Literal		
Interpretive		
Critical/Creative		

Summary Sheet of Silent Reading Performance

GRADED READING PASSAGES TEST SILENT READING				
EXPOSITORY				
Grade Level	Silent Comp.	Prior Knowledge (1–5)	Interest (1–5)	Words per Minute
1				
2				
3				
4				
5				
6				
7				
8				
9				
NARRATIVE				
Grade Level	Silent Comp.	Prior Knowledge (Y–N)	Interest (1–5)	Words per Minute
1				
2				
3				
4				
5				
6				
7				
8				
9				

ESTIMATED SILENT READING LEVELS		
	GRADE LEVELS	
	Expository	*Narrative*
Independent		
Instructional*		
Frustration		

*List as one grade level or range of two grade levels (e.g., 5–6).

Comments

Summary Sheet of Accountable Miscues

NUMBER OF ACCOUNTABLE MISCUES IN WORD RECOGNITION

	EXPOSITORY		NARRATIVE	
	Number	% of Total*	Number	% of Total*
Full Miscues				
Half Miscues				
TOTAL		100.0		100.0

*Round off to nearest tenth of a percent (e.g., 87.38 = 87.4, 24.35 = 24.4).

CATEGORIES OF ACCOUNTABLE MISCUES IN WORD RECOGNITION

FULL MISCUES	NUMBER		HALF MISCUES	NUMBER	
	Expos	Narr		Expos	Narr
Nonword Substitutions			Whole Word Substitutions		
Whole Word Substitutions			Omissions		
Omissions			Insertions		
Insertions					
Reversals					
Repetitions					
Pronounced by Examiner					

Summary Sheet for Recording and Analyzing Miscues

Form of Graded Reading Passages Test

Grade Level of Passage	Estimated Reading Level (Independent, Instructional, Frustration)	Miscue Numbers (e.g., 1–7)
_____	_____	_____
_____	_____	_____
_____	_____	_____

			PART A Is the meaning changed by the miscue?			PART B Is the miscue graphically similar to the text?		
Miscue Number	Reader's Miscue	Text	No Change	Partial Change	Complete Change	Begin-ning	Middle	End
1								
2								
3								
4								
5								
6								
7								
8								
9								
10								
11								
12								
13								
14								
15								
16								
17								

			PART A			PART B		
			Is the meaning changed by the miscue?			*Is the miscue graphically similar to the text?*		
Miscue Number	Reader's Miscue	Text	No Change	Partial Change	Complete Change	Begin-ning	Middle	End
18								
19								
20								
21								
22								
23								
24								
25								
	Number of Miscues Checked							
	Number of Miscues Listed					XXX	XXX	XXX
	Number of Miscues Analyzed		XXX	XXX	XXX			
	Percent*							

*Percent for Part A = Number of Miscues Checked ÷ Number of Miscues Listed

Percent for Part B = Number of Miscues Checked ÷ Number of Miscues Analyzed

(Round off to nearest tenth of a percent [e.g., 87.38 = 87.4 or 76.65 = 76.7].)

Summary Sheet for Categories of Comprehension Errors

	EXPOSITORY		
	Free and Probed Recall		
	Items Attempted (Free & Probed)	**Number of Errors**	**% of Errors* (Col. 2/Col. 1)**
Literal			
Interpretive			
Critical/Creative			

	NARRATIVE		
	Free and Probed Recall		
	Items Attempted (Free & Probed)	**Number of Errors**	**% of Errors* (Col. 2/Col. 1)**
Literal			
Interpretive			
Critical/Creative			

*Round off to nearest tenth of a percent.

Dictated Story Assessment Strategy Record Form for Follow-Up Session

Name: _____ Date: _____

I. LANGUAGE FACILITY

   A.   Story Read by Student without Teacher Assistance

      Check ONE that applies:

      _____ 1. The student read back most of the story on his or her own.

      _____ 2. The student read back only selected parts of the story (i.e., sentences, parts of sentences).

      _____ 3. The student read back only a few words and/or short phrases.

      _____ 4. The student was unable to read back any part of the story.

   B.   Story Read by Student after Teacher Has Read Story Aloud

      Check ONE that applies:

      _____ 1. The student read back most of the story on his or her own.

      _____ 2. The student read back only selected parts of the story (i.e., sentences, parts of sentences).

      _____ 3. The student read back only a few words and/or short phrases.

      _____ 4. The student was unable to read back any part of the story.

   C.   Word Recognition

      Based on (check one):

      _____ Story read without teacher assistance

      _____ Story read with teacher assistance

	FOR THE MOST PART	TO A CERTAIN DEGREE	NOT AT ALL	NOT APPLICABLE OR OBSERVABLE
(Place check on line in appropriate column.)				
1. Was the recognition of words automatic (fluent) throughout the reading?	_____	_____	_____	_____
2. Were miscues NOT disruptive to the meaning of the text?	_____	_____	_____	_____
3. Can the student recognize words from the story presented in isolation with flashed exposure?	_____	_____	_____	_____
4. Can the student recognize words from the story presented in isolation with delayed exposure?	_____	_____	_____	_____

Comments:

II. LISTENING COMPREHENSION LEVEL

Form of Graded Reading Passages Test: _____

ASSESSMENT OF LISTENING COMPREHENSION

Grade Level	Listening Comp. %	Prior Knowledge Y–N or 1–5	Interest 1–5
1			
2			
3			
4			
5			
6			
7			
8			
9			

Student's Listening Comprehension Level: _____

III. COMPARISON OF RESULTS

Compare the results of the two Dictated Story Assessment Strategy sessions. Were there any differences? Please explain below.

The Stieglitz Assessment of Phonemic Awareness (SAPhA) Record Form

Student's Name: _____ Sex: _____ Age: _____ years _____ months

School: _____ School System: _____ Grade Placement: _____

Examiner: _____ Date of Test: _____

CONTENT	SUMMARY OF INDIVIDUAL SCORE	MEAN SCORE*
Part 1. Rhyming Words	_____/20	15/20
Comments:		
Part 2. Blending Speech Sounds into Words	_____/30	20/30
Comments:		
Part 3. Isolating Speech	_____/15	9/15
Comments:		
Part 4. Complete Segmentation of Phonemes	_____/22	12/22
Comments:		

Student's Level of Reading Acquisition
(Refer to page 72 for description of levels.)

_____ Emergent   _____ Transitional   _____ Beginning   _____ Above Beginning Level

Additional comments:

*Correct responses of kindergarten children performing task (Yupp, 1988).

PART 1: RHYMING WORDS

Purpose of Task

To recognize whether pairs of words rhyme

Level of Task

Simplest

EXAMINER INSTRUCTIONS: Place a **+** sign on the line next to each word pair when a correct response is given and a **−** sign for an incorrect response. If necessary, a word pair can be repeated once. Stop testing after three consecutive errors.

STUDENT DIRECTIONS: Read the following passage to the student.

"I am going to play a word game with you. Do you know what a rhyming word is? [Provide description below if child's response in unsatisfactory.]

"Rhymes are words that sound the same at the end. For example, the words *top, hop, mop,* **and** *stop* **rhyme because they sound the same at the end. All these words end with the sound /op/. But the words** *coat* **and** *fire* **do not rhyme because they do not sound the same at the end.**

"I am going to say two words and I want you to tell me if they rhyme. Let's try a few for practice. Listen carefully.

     "Do *cat* **and** *mat* **rhyme?**

     "Do *eye* **and** *nail* **rhyme?**

[If necessary, provide student with additional examples.] **"Now let's try these.** [Begin with item 1.]"

| PRACTICE: | A. cat | mat | _____ |
| | B. eye | nail | _____ |

1.	fun	sun	_____	11.	walk	talk	_____
2.	pet	box	_____	12.	coat	cone	_____
3.	comb	car	_____	13.	write	pipe	_____
4.	toy	boy	_____	14.	long	song	_____
5.	rat	run	_____	15.	wall	will	_____
6.	bug	rug	_____	16.	tap	tip	_____
7.	go	do	_____	17.	blue	glue	_____
8.	hit	hot	_____	18.	hook	look	_____
9.	beet	seat	_____	19.	train	rain	_____
10.	sing	ring	_____	20.	sock	pot	_____

Score _____/20 **correct responses**

PART 2: BLENDING SPEECH SOUNDS INTO WORDS

Purpose of Task

To listen to speech sounds and then blend these sounds into words

Level of Task

Easy

EXAMINER INSTRUCTIONS: Segment each word according to how it is presented on the record sheet. Pronounce each segment without making it too obvious what the word is. Emphasize the sounds and not the letters in each word.

Place a + sign on the line next to each word identified correctly. If an incorrect answer is given, record the student's actual response on this line. For example, if the examiner says /c/–/u/–/p/ and the student's response is *cap*, record the student's incorrect response on this line. Write **DK** (don't know) when it becomes apparent that the word is unknown or the student says that he or she does not know the word.

If necessary, the segmentation of a word can be repeated once. Stop testing after three consecutive errors.

STUDENT DIRECTIONS: Read the following passage to the student.

"**Let's play another word game.**

"**I will say words in a secret language. Your job is to guess the word I am saying. I will break the word into parts. When you say the parts together, you will know what the secret word is. For example, if I say these sounds /m/–/e/, I am saying the word** *me*. **Or, if I say, /p/–/e/–/n/, I am saying the word** *pen*.

"**Let's try a few for practice. Tell what word we would have if these sounds were put together. Listen carefully.**

"**If I say /i/–/t/, what word am I saying?**

"**If I say /m/–/eet/, what word am I saying?**

"**If I say /t/–/a/–/n/, what word am I saying?**

[If necessary, provide student with additional examples.] "**Now let's try these. [Begin with item 1.]**"

PRACTICE: A. i–t   _____

B. m–eet   _____

C. c–a–n   _____

1. b–e	_____	11. h–am	_____	21. n–a–p	_____
2. i–f	_____	12. r–ed	_____	22. c–a–ke	_____
3. s–o	_____	13. p–ill	_____	23. b–oi–l	_____
4. u–p	_____	14. f–un	_____	24. sh–ou–t	_____
5. w–ay	_____	15. s–oup	_____	25. t–ee–th	_____
6. t–o	_____	16. ch–air	_____	26. f–a–s–t	_____
7. h–igh	_____	17. m–ost	_____	27. s–w–i–m	_____
8. a–te	_____	18. k–ind	_____	28. r–i–ch	_____
9. e–gg	_____	19. t–ent	_____	29. b–l–a–ck	_____
10. sh–e	_____	20. y–ard	_____	30. j–u–m–p	_____

Score _____/30 correct responses

PART 3: ISOLATING SPEECH SOUNDS

Purpose of Task

To isolate speech sounds in the beginning, middle, and end positions of words

Level of Task

Higher Level

EXAMINER INSTRUCTIONS: Place a **+** sign on the line next to each word when the sound is correctly identified. If an incorrect answer is given, record the student's actual response on this line. For example, if the examiner asks for the final sound in the word *net* and the student says /d/, record the student's incorrect response on this line. Write **DK** (don't know) when it becomes apparent that the sound is unknown or the student says that he or she does not know the sound.

   If necessary, a word can be repeated once. Stop testing after three consecutive errors.

STUDENT DIRECTIONS: Read the following passage to the student.

"I am going to say some words. I want you to say the sound found at the beginning of the word, in the middle of the word, or at the end of the word. For example, if I say the word *bat*, and ask for the sound at the beginning of the word, the answer is /b/. Or if I say the word *sip*, and ask for the sound in the middle of the word, the answer is /i/. Finally, if I say the word *pail*, and ask for the sound at the end of the word, the answer is /l/.

   "Let's try a few for practice. Listen carefully.

   "What is the sound at the beginning of this word? *hen*

   "What is the sound in the middle of this word? *boat*

   "What is the sound at the end of this word? *rug*

[If necessary, provide student with additional examples.] **"Now let's try these. [Begin with item 1.]"**

PRACTICE: A. **m**an   _____

            B. boat   _____

            C. rug   _____

Beginning		Middle		End	
1. sun	_____	6. pail	_____	11. net	_____
2. dog	_____	7. bed	_____	12. lip	_____
3. team	_____	8. kite	_____	13. car	_____
4. jar	_____	9. gum	_____	14. track	_____
5. ship	_____	10. moon	_____	15. fish	_____

Score   _____/15 correct responses

PART 4: COMPLETE SEGMENTATION OF PHONEMES

Purpose of Task

To segment the sounds of words, each two or three phonemes in length

Level of Task

More Difficult

EXAMINER INSTRUCTIONS: Place a **+** sign on the line next to each word when the word is segmented correctly. If an incorrect answer is given, record the student's actual response on this line. For example, if the student segments the word *with* as /w/–/i/–**/d/**, record the student's incorrect response on this line. Write **DK** (don't know) when the student does not attempt to segment a word.

If necessary, a word can be repeated once. Also, the examiner may use an object such as a pen or pencil to demonstrate the separate sounds in a word. For example, in the practice word *wig*, the examiner should tap the pencil as each of the three sounds is made. Then, at the discretion of the examiner, the student could do the same with this object as he or she attempts to segment the words in this part. Stop testing after three consecutive errors.

STUDENT DIRECTIONS: Read the following passage to the student.

"Now we're going to play a different word game. I am going to say a word and I want you to break the word apart. You are going to tell me each sound in the word in the order that you hear them. For example, if I say the word *to*, you should say /t/–/o/. Or, if I say the word *old*, you should say /o/–/l/–/d/. [The examiner should emphasize the sounds and not the letters in each word.]
     "Let's begin with these for practice.

     "What sounds do you hear in the word *so*?

     "What sounds do you hear in the word *at*?

     "What sounds do you hear in the word *wig*?

[If necessary, provide student with additional examples.] **"Now let's try these.** [Begin with item 1.]"

PRACTICE: A. so   _____

              B. at   _____

              C. wig   _____

1. see	_____	9. they	_____	16 mop	_____
2. day	_____	10. pain	_____	17. let	_____
3. if	_____	11. five	_____	18. good	_____
4. my	_____	12. joke	_____	19. stay	_____
5. no	_____	13. hill	_____	20. cheap	_____
6. add	_____	14. can	_____	21. them	_____
7. boy	_____	15. heat	_____	22. wash	_____
8. zoo	_____				

Score _____ /22 correct responses

Refer to pages 70–77 for additional information on how to administer and score the SAPhA.

The Development
of the SIRI

*T*he Stieglitz Informal Reading Inventory was developed in several stages. The following discussion outlines the planning of the SIRI, the writing and editing of the various components, and the field testing of this instrument.

The development of the SIRI started with a review of the current literature on reading assessment and an examination of commercially prepared informal reading inventories. Information from these sources was used to create a preliminary design for the SIRI. This preliminary design was then shared with and reviewed by experts in the field. A modified design was created based on the input of these experts.

During the next phase of development, Form A of the Graded Words in Context Test, Forms A and B of the Graded Reading Passages Test, and the Dictated Story Assessment Strategy were written and field tested. The following components of the SIRI were constructed in the second phase of test development: Form B of the Graded Words in Context Test, Forms A and B of the Graded Words in Isolation Test, Forms C and D of the Graded Reading Passages Test, and the Practice Passages.

Refinements and improvements were made in the various components of the SIRI throughout the test development process and the use of this instrument during the past 10 years. These adjustments were based on the advice of classroom teachers, reading specialists, and college faculty. Refinements in this third edition of the SIRI include: (1) directions for using the SIRI that are more user-friendly, (2) procedures for interviewing students to discover what they know and how they feel about reading and writing, (3) an instrument that can be used to assess an emergent reader's phonemic awareness skills, (4) new photographs to be used with the Dictated Story Assessment Strategy, and (5) a rubric designed to help the diagnostician synthesize information from the various components of the SIRI and draw conclusions about a student's reading strengths and weaknesses.

A more detailed description of how this inventory was constructed is presented below.

Constructing the Word List Tests

Two sources of vocabulary were used for the selection of target words in Forms A and B of the Graded Words in Context Test: *Basic Reading Vocabularies* (Harris & Jacobson, 1982) and *A Cluster Approach to Elementary Vocabulary Instruction* (Marzano & Marzano, 1988).

The first source presents a core list of words for grade levels preprimer through grade 8 found in eight basal reading series. The second source contains 7,230 words found in elementary school textbooks. These words are organized into sixty-one instructional clusters (e.g., clothing, occupations, chemicals). A recommended grade level for introducing each word is provided. The range in levels is from kindergarten through grade 6.

Target words for the Graded Words in Context Test were randomly selected from these vocabulary lists. Both lists were used in the selection of words to guarantee that each word chosen was on the appropriate level. For example, words appearing at the preprimer and primer levels of the Harris and Jacobson list were included only if they also appeared as kindergarten words on the Marzano and Marzano list. The three exceptions are *get, found,* and *window.* These words are not designated as kindergarten words on the Marzano and Marzano list. For target words chosen for inclusion on the grade 1 through grade 6 sentence sets, there is agreement from both sources. *Basic Reading Vocabularies* was the sole source of words chosen for the seventh- and eighth-grade-level sentence sets because the Marzano and Marzano text does not include words above the sixth-grade level.

Words surrounding a target word in a sentence were chosen only if they were below the grade level of the target word based on the Harris and Jacobson list. The exception, of course, were words surrounding target words in the preprimer sentence set where all words selected are on the preprimer level.

The results of the pilot test were used to make minor changes in the items of the Graded Words in Context Test. Some words were replaced and a few sentences were rewritten. An analysis of the results of ninety administrations of the Graded Reading Passages Test (expository and narrative forms) revealed the usefulness of Form A of the Graded Words in Context Test as an instrument for predicting the starting level on the passages test. The correct starting point or independent level was identified in 46.7 percent of the cases. The correct starting point was underestimated by one grade level in 26.7 percent of the cases and by two grade levels in 6.7 percent of the cases. Finally, the correct starting point was overestimated by one grade level in 14.3 percent of the cases and by two grade levels in 5.6 percent of the cases.

Teachers have the option of administering a Graded Words in Isolation Test. All words chosen for this test are the same as those included on matching forms of the Graded Words in Context Test.

Designing the Dictated Story Assessment Strategy

The design of a strategy for using dictated stories to assess the reading performance of emergent and initial readers started with a review of the literature. Information from several sources was used to create a preliminary design. This preliminary design was then shared with experts in the field. A modified design was created based on the input of these experts. The next step was to gather a collection of interesting photographs to be used as a vehicle for the creation of individually dictated stories. Photographs were obtained from the *Providence Journal-Bulletin,* Allyn and Bacon, and professional and amateur photographers. Ten photographs were eventually chosen for inclusion in the SIRI. Classroom teachers, reading specialists, and students in a master's-level reading course participated in the field test of this strategy with fourteen students in kindergarten through grade 2. Refinements and improvements were made in the Dictated Story Assessment Strategy, and the form was used to record the results throughout the test development process. These adjustments were based on the advice of educators who pilot tested the strategy.

Constructing the Graded Reading Passages Test

The next step was to construct Forms A and B of the Graded Reading Passages Test. Six of the expository selections were written by this author, two were taken from a popular children's magazine, and one was adapted from an article in a newspaper. For the narrative selections, one was written by this author, one was taken from a children's literary magazine, one was written by a professional writer, and six were adapted from other sources. The passages for grade 1 through grade 3 were checked for readability with the *Spache Readability Formula* (Spache, 1974) and the passages for grade 4 through grade 9 were checked with the *Fry Readability Graph* (Fry, 1977). A computer program was used to complete the calculations for the Spache (Minnesota Educational Computing Consortium, 1982), whereas calculations for the Fry were completed manually. Readability estimates for each passage are summarized in Tables 1.1 and 1.2.

Once the passages were written, sets of questions to assess comprehension were prepared for each selection, and forms were developed to record the results. Preliminary field testing of the SIRI was then conducted with nineteen students from schools in Providence and Pawtucket, Rhode Island, and Attleboro, Massachusetts. Soon after this trial administration of the SIRI, a professional editor was hired to review the content and the clarity of the selections in the Graded Reading Passages Test. The results of the field test and the comments of the editor were used to revise Forms A and B of the passages test. Some selections were found to be unsuitable, and they were replaced with new material. Other selections were rewritten to improve the presentation of content. Changes were also made in the Comprehension Check for each selection. Forms A and B of the Graded Reading Passages Test were then ready for field testing with a larger population of students.

Forms C and D of the Graded Reading Passages Test were modeled after Forms A and B of this test. They were designed to be used as alternate or parallel forms in the Graded Reading Passages Test. Professional writers were hired to write the selections (nine expository passages for Form C and nine narrative passages for Form D) according to precise specifications. Once the passages were written and tested for readability, sets of questions were prepared by this author to assess comprehension. A preliminary field test of Forms C and D was then conducted with eighteen students from elementary schools in Providence, Rhode Island, and Cumberland, Rhode Island. The results of this field test were used to make minor revisions in the selections and questions to check comprehension.

A total of thirty-one educators was involved in the pilot testing of Forms A and B of the Graded Reading Passages Test. This population consisted of reading specialists, classroom teachers, and students in an advanced-level graduate course in the Master of Education in Reading program at Rhode Island College. A total of seventy-five students in grade 1 through grade 9 were tested. Another group of twelve reading specialists and classroom teachers was involved in the pilot testing of Forms C and D. This group administered the SIRI to a population of forty-eight students in grade 1 through grade 12. Prior to giving this test, field testers attended a training session and were given a set of directions for administering the SIRI.

For a test to be useful, the examiner must have confidence in the results. Therefore, steps were taken to validate the passages designed to assess students' reading performance. The process of validating the passages consisted of (1) examining the validity of the graded passages as an instrument for estimating a reader's instructional level, (2) determining whether parallel forms of the expository and narrative passages tests produce equivalent results, (3) determining reader familiarity with the content of the passages, (4) examining reader interest in the content of the passages, and (5) determining whether higher-order questions were more difficult for students to answer than lower-order questions.

Estimating Instructional Levels

A study was conducted to examine the validity of the Graded Reading Passages Test as an instrument for correctly estimating a student's instructional reading level. Prior to administering the Graded Reading Passages Test, examiners were asked to estimate each student's instructional level in reading and to enter this information on the record form. This judgment was based on a student's level of performance in the classroom or special reading class, and such information was provided to the examiner by either the student's classroom teacher or a reading specialist. In a few cases, the examiner was the source of this information. Because the pilot testing of this instrument was completed toward the end rather than the beginning of the school year, teachers were in a better position to provide more accurate estimates of their students' instructional levels.

The next step was to administer different forms of the Graded Reading Passages Test to students participating in the study. The test results were used to determine each student's instructional level. The composite inventory results from administering Forms A, B, C, and D were then compared to teacher perceptions of students' instructional levels.

Given a total of 240 valid administrations of all forms of the Graded Reading Passages Test, more than half the students were given identical placements (56.3 percent), 28.3 percent were placed one grade level higher or lower, 10.8 percent were placed two grade levels higher or lower, and 4.6 percent were placed three grade levels higher or lower. A nonparametric test of correlation indicated that this comparison was significant beyond the .001 level. This means that there is a strong correlation between teachers' estimate of students' instructional level and students' instructional level as determined by the results of the SIRI.

Because an examiner is given the option of using an expository or narrative form of the SIRI to estimate a student's instructional level, it was important to determine whether either form of the test would reveal similar results. An analysis of the data collected from seventy-three valid administrations of Forms A and B revealed that estimates of instructional level were the same in most cases regardless of which prose type was used. In 68.5 percent of the comparisons, there was not any difference. There was a discrepancy of one grade level higher or lower in 26.0 percent of the cases, two grade levels higher or lower in 4.1 percent of the cases, and three grade levels higher or lower in 1.4 percent of the cases. A nonparametric test of correlation demonstrated that these comparisons were significant beyond the .05 level. It could therefore be concluded that either an expository or narrative form of the SIRI could be used to estimate a student's overall instructional level. However, it is recommended that teachers not rely solely on the results of a single administration of the SIRI for all placement decisions. Both expository and narrative forms should be administered to determine how well students can interact with the two prose types.

Determining Alternate Form Reliability

A study was conducted to determine whether parallel forms of the expository and narrative passages tests produce equivalent results. Forms A and C were administered to twenty students in grades 3 through 11. The instructional level results of the two administrations were compared to determine the degree of discrepancy in the figures. The results showed that most students were given identical placements (80.0 percent) regardless of the form used. There was a discrepancy of one grade level higher or lower in 20.0 percent of the cases. A nonparametric test of correlation revealed that this comparison was significant beyond the .01 level.

The same kind of comparison was made with the two narrative forms. Forms B and D were administered to twenty-eight students in grades 1 through 12. Here, too, the results showed that most students were given identical placements (85.7 percent). The remaining students were placed one level higher or lower (14.3 percent). A nonparametric test of correlation indicated that these comparisons were significant beyond the .001 level. The results of these two comparisons show good alternate form reliability between Forms A and C and Forms B and D of the Graded Reading Passages Test.

Examining Reader Familiarity

Data were also collected to determine students' self-perceptions of familiarity with the content of each passage. A Prior Knowledge scale was used to indicate the familiarity level of each expository passage. After each passage was read, students were asked to respond to items on a 5-point scale. A rating of 1 or 2 indicated that a student's perceived level of knowledge was low; a rating of 4 or 5 showed a student's perceived level of knowledge was high. Because the goal was to assemble a collection of passages with unfamiliar content, an average rating of below 3 was desired. The results presented in Table 6.1 showed that all the passages in Form A were less than familiar to the students.

For the narrative selections, students were asked whether each story was familiar to them. The results showed that students were, for the most part, unfamiliar with the stories included in the SIRI (see Table 6.2). Familiarity data for passages in Forms C and D are not available due to the low number of cases. In all likelihood,

TABLE 6.1   *Level of Student Familiarity with Expository Passages in Form A*

GRADE LEVEL OF PASSAGE	NUMBER OF STUDENTS RESPONDING	AVERAGE LEVEL OF FAMILIARITY*
1	21	2.7
2	35	2.1
3	51	2.0
4	55	2.6
5	49	1.2
6	46	2.3
7	38	1.9
8	21	1.8
9	19	1.9

*Based on students responding to descriptors on a 5-point scale where 1 = low level of familiarity and 5 = high level of familiarity.

TABLE 6.2   *Level of Student Familiarity with Narrative Passages in Form B*

GRADE LEVEL OF PASSAGE	NUMBER OF STUDENTS RESPONDING	PERCENTAGE OF STUDENTS FAMILIAR WITH PASSAGE*	PERCENTAGE OF STUDENTS UNFAMILIAR WITH PASSAGE*
1	18	11.1	88.9
2	31	0.0	100.0
3	48	10.4	89.6
4	48	0.0	100.0
5	44	0.0	100.0
6	45	2.2	97.8
7	42	0.0	100.0
8	21	0.0	100.0
9	19	0.0	100.0

*Based on Yes or No response to question about having read story before.

the results would be similar to the data reported for Forms A and B because careful attempts were made in the development of the SIRI to match the content of Forms A and C, and B and D.

Determining Reader Interest

Another important factor to consider in the design of an informal reading inventory is the student's level of interest in the topic of a passage. A 5-point scale similar to the one for assessing prior knowledge of expository text was used to determine students' level of interest in each passage. A rating of 1 or 2 indicated that the student tended to dislike the selection; a rating of 4 or 5 showed that the student tended to enjoy the selection. An average rating of above 3 was desired. The results presented in Table 6.3 showed that most of the expository selections met this criterion. The exception was the passage for the grade 8 article. The results presented in Table 6.4

TABLE 6.3   *Level of Student Interest in Expository Passages in Form A*

GRADE LEVEL OF PASSAGE	NUMBER OF STUDENTS RESPONDING	AVERAGE LEVEL OF INTEREST*
1	22	3.6
2	35	3.7
3	50	3.2
4	55	3.6
5	48	3.4
6	46	3.2
7	38	3.3
8	20	2.7
9	19	3.1

*Based on students responding to descriptors on a 5-point scale where 1 = low level of interest and 5 = high level of interest.

TABLE 6.4   *Level of Student Interest in Narrative Passages in Form B*

GRADE LEVEL OF PASSAGE	NUMBER OF STUDENTS RESPONDING	AVERAGE LEVEL OF INTEREST*
1	18	4.2
2	31	3.6
3	48	3.4
4	48	3.2
5	45	3.2
6	46	3.8
7	41	2.7
8	21	3.1
9	19	2.5

*Based on students responding to descriptors on a 5-point scale where 1 = low level of interest and 5 = high level of interest.

showed that all but two of the passages used in Form B met the criterion for inter-est. The selections that students rated lower were descriptive passages at the higher levels (grade 7 and grade 9). Such passages lack the story line usually found in nar-rative prose. As a result, some readers may have found this type of discourse to be difficult or less interesting. Data on reading interests for Forms C and D are not re-ported because of the low number of cases. However, as stated in the discussion of reader familiarity with passages, the results would probably be similar to the data re-ported for Forms A and B because careful attempts were made in the development of the SIRI to match the content of parallel forms.

Examining Levels of Comprehension

The Comprehension Check for each passage included examples of literal-, interpretive-, and critical/creative-level questions. Data from the administrations of Forms A and B were collected and reviewed to determine whether the higher-order questions were more difficult for students to answer than lower-order questions. Questions above the literal level were placed in the higher-order category. For the expository passages in Form A, students responded incorrectly to 21.5 percent of the literal questions, 29.4 percent of the interpretive questions, and 29.6 percent of the critical/creative questions. For the narrative passages in Form B, the students re-sponded incorrectly to 14.3 percent of the literal questions, 32.6 percent of the in-terpretive questions, and 39.6 percent of the critical/creative questions. These data seem to show that higher-order questions were, as expected, more difficult for stu-dents to answer than lower-order questions.

References

Adams, M. J., & Huggins, A. W. F. (1985). The growth of children's sight vocabulary: A quick test with educational and theoretical implications. *Reading Research Quarterly, 20,* 262–281.

Agnew, A. T. (1982). Using children's dictated stories to assess code consciousness. *The Reading Teacher, 35,* 450–453.

Argyle, S. B. (1989). Miscue analysis for classroom use. *Reading Horizons, 29,* 93–102.

Beldin, H. O. (1970). Informal reading testing: Historical review and review of the research. In William K. Durr (Ed.), *Reading difficulties diagnosis, correction, and remediation,* (pp. 67–84). Newark, DE: International Reading Association.

Brozo, W. G. (1990). Learning how at-risk readers learn best: A case for interactive assessment. *Journal of Reading, 33,* 522–527.

Caldwell, J. (1985). A new look at the old informal reading inventory. *The Reading Teacher, 39,* 168–173.

Collins, M. D., & Cheek, E. H. Jr. (1999). *Assessing and guiding reading instruction.* New York: McGraw-Hill.

Dixon, C. N., & Nessel, D. (1983). *Language experience approach to reading (and writing), LEA for ESL.* Hayward, CA: Alemany Press.

Duffelmeyer, F. A., Robinson, S. S., & Squier, S. E. (1989). Vocabulary questions on informal reading inventories. *The Reading Teacher, 43,* 142–148.

Ekwall, E. E. (1986). *Ekwall reading inventory* (2nd ed.). Boston: Allyn and Bacon.

Ekwall, E. E., & Shanker, J. L. (1988). *Diagnosis and remediation of the disabled reader* (3rd ed.). Boston: Allyn and Bacon.

Flood, J., & Lapp, D. (1989). Reporting reading progress: A comparison portfolio for parents. *The Reading Teacher, 42,* 508–514.

Fry, E. (1977). Fry's readability graph: Clarifications, validity and extension to level 17. *Journal of Reading, 21,* 242–252.

Gillet, J. W., & Temple, C. (1994). *Understanding reading problems* (4th ed.). New York: HarperCollins College Publishers.

Goodman, K. S. (1965). A linguistic study of cues and miscues in reading. *Elementary English, 42,* 639–643.

Hall, D. P., & Cunningham, P. M. (1988). Context as a polysyllable decoding strategy. *Reading Improvement, 25,* 261–264.

Harris, A. J., & Jacobson, M. D. (1982). *Basic reading vocabularies.* New York: Macmillan.

Harris, A. J., & Sipay, E. R. (1990). *How to increase reading ability: A guide to developmental and remedial methods* (9th ed.). New York: Longman.

Harris, T. L., & Hodges, R. E. (Eds.) (1995). *The literacy dictionary: The vocabulary of reading and writing.* Newark, DE: International Reading Association.

Henk, W. A., & Melnick, S. A. (1995). The Reader Self-Perception Scale (RSPS): A new tool for measuring how children feel about themselves as readers. *The Reading Teacher, 48,* 470–482.

Henk, W. A. (1987). Reading assessments of the future: Toward precision diagnosis. *The Reading Teacher, 40,* 860–870.

International Reading Association. (August/September 2000). Moving beyond the debate: IRA endorses new NEA report. *Reading Today, 18,* 1, 9.

International Reading Association. (June/July 2000). National Reading Panel report: Work praised, but distortion fears persist. *Reading Today, 17,* 1, 4.

International Reading Association. (June/July 1998). IRA Board issues position statement on phonemic awareness. *Reading Today, 15,* 1, 3.

Johns, J. L. (1997). *Basic reading inventory: Pre-primer through grade twelve and early literacy assessments* (7th ed.). Dubuque, IA: Kendall/Hunt.

Johns, J. L. (1991). Emmett A. Betts on informal reading inventories. *Journal of Reading, 34,* 492–493.

Johnson, M. S., Kress, R. A., & Pikulski, J. J. (1987). *Informal reading inventories* (2nd ed.). Newark, DE: International Reading Association.

Kear, D. J., Coffman, G. A., McKenna, M. C., & Ambrosio, A. L. (2000). Measuring attitude toward writing: A new tool for teachers. *The Reading Teacher, 54,* 10–22.

Leslie, L., & Jett-Simpson, M. (1997). *Authentic literacy assessment: An ecological approach.* New York: Longman.

Lipson, M. Y., & Wixson, K. K. (1997). Assessment and instruction of reading and writing disability: An interactive approach (2nd ed.). New York: Longman.

Marzano, R. J., & Marzano, J. S. (1988). *A cluster approach to elementary vocabulary instruction.* Newark, DE: International Reading Association.

McKenna, M. C., & Kear, D. J. (1995/1996). Garfield revisited: Continued permission to use the ERAS. *The Reading Teacher, 49,* 332.

McKenna, M. C., & Kear, D. J. (1990). Measuring attitude toward reading: A new tool for teachers. *The Reading Teacher, 43,* 626–639.

McKenna, M. C. (1983). Informal reading inventories: A review of the issues. *The Reading Teacher, 36,* 670–679.

Morrow, L. M. (1988). Retelling stories as a diagnostic tool. In S. M. Glazer, L. W. Searfoss, & L. M. Gentile (Eds.), *Reexamining reading diagnosis: New trends and procedures* (pp. 128–149). Newark, DE: International Reading Association.

Nelson, O. G., & Linek, W. M. (1999). *Practical classroom applications of language experience: Looking back, looking forward.* Boston: Allyn and Bacon.

Nessel, D. D., & Jones, M. B. (1981). *Language experience approach to teaching: A handbook for teachers.* New York: Teachers College Press.

New Standards Primary Literacy Committee. (1999). *Reading grade by grade and writing: Primary literacy standards for kindergarten through third grade.* Washington, DC: National Center on Education and the Economy, Pittsburgh, PA: University of Pittsburgh.

Nicholson, T., Lillas, C., & Rzoska, A. M. (1988). Have we been misled by miscues? *The Reading Teacher, 42,* 6–10.

Phinney, M. Y. (1988). *Reading with the troubled reader.* Portsmouth, NH: Heinemann.

Pikulski, J. J. (1990). Assessment: Informal reading inventories. *The Reading Teacher, 43,* 514–516.

Reading/Language in Secondary Schools Committee. (1990). Portfolios illuminate the path for dynamic interactive readers. *Journal of Reading, 33,* 644–647.

Richards, M. (2000). Be a good detective: Solve the case of oral reading fluency. *The Reading Teacher, 53,* 534–539.

Rogers, S. F., Merlin, S., Brittain, M. M., Palmatier, R. A., & Terrell, P. (1983). A research view of clinic practicums in reading education. *Reading World, 23,* 134–146.

School utilities: Volume 2 [Computer software]. (1982). St. Paul, MN: Minnesota Educational Computer Consortium.

Shu, H., Anderson, R. C., & Zhang, H. (1995). Incidental learning of word meanings while reading: A Chinese and American cross-cultural study. *Reading Research Quarterly, 30,* 76–95.

Spache, G. D. (1974). *Good reading for poor readers* (9th ed.). Champaign, IL: Garrard.

Stahl, S. A., & Pickle, M. J. (1996). A model for assessment and targeted instruction for children with reading problems. In Lillian R. Putnam (Ed.), *How to become a better reading teacher: Strategies for assessment and intervention,* (pp. 141–155). Columbus, OH: Merrill.

Stieglitz, E. L. (1980). Assessment for individualization. In Diane Lapp (Ed.), *Making reading possible through effective classroom management* (pp. 80–115). Newark, DE: International Reading Association.

Strickland, D. S., & Morrow, L. M. (1990). The daily journal: Using language experience strategies in an emergent literacy curriculum. *The Reading Teacher, 43,* 422–423.

Tompkins, G. E. (2001). *Literacy for the 21st century: A balanced approach* (2nd ed.). Upper Saddle River, NJ: Prentice-Hall.

van den Bosch, K., van Bon, W., & Schreuder, R. (1995). Poor readers' decoding skills: Effects of training with limited exposure duration. *Reading Research Quarterly, 30,* 110–125.

Walker, B. J. (2000). *Diagnostic teaching of reading* (4th ed.). Upper Saddle River, NJ: Merrill.

Wilson, R. M., & Cleland, C. J. (1989). *Diagnostic and remedial reading for classroom and clinic* (6th ed.). Columbus, OH: Merrill.

Wixson, K. K., Bosky, A. B., Yochum, M. N., & Alvermann, D. E. (1984). An interview for assessing students' perceptions of classroom reading tasks. *The Reading Teacher, 37,* 346–352.

Yopp, H. K. (1995). A test for assessing phonemic awareness in young children. *The Reading Teacher, 49,* 20–29.

Yopp, H. K. (1988). The validity and reliability of phonemic awareness tests. *Reading Research Quarterly, 23,* 159–157.

Yopp, H. K., & Yopp. R. H. (2000). Supporting phonemic awareness development in the classroom. *The Reading Teacher, 54,* 130–143.